The Yachtsman's Pilot
# The Isle of Mull and adjacent coasts

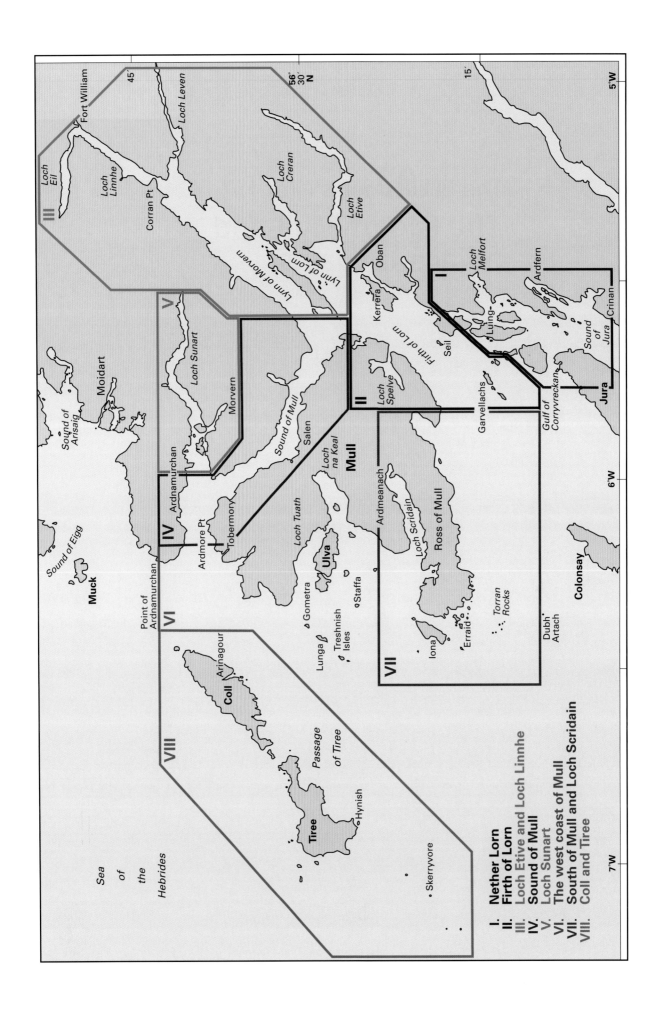

Fort William

Loch Eil

Loch Leven

III

Loch Linnhe

Corran Pt

45'

56°
30' N

Loch Creran

Loch Etive

15'

5°W

Lynn of Morvern

Lynn of Lorn

Oban

Kerrera

Loch Melfort

Ardfern

Sound of Arisaig

Moidart

Loch Sunart

Morvern

V

Firth of Lorn

Seil

Luing-

Sound of Jura

Crinan

I

Sound of Eigg

Ardnamurchan

IV

Sound of Mull

Salen

Loch Spelve

II

Garvellachs

Gulf of Corryvreckan

Jura

6°W

Muck

Point of Ardnamurchan

Ardmore Pt

Tobermory

Loch Tuath

Ulva

Staffa

Gometra

VI

Loch na Keal

Mull

Ardmeanach

Loch Scridain

Ross of Mull

Iona

Erraid

Torran Rocks

Dubh
Artach

Colonsay

VII

Lunga

Treshnish
Isles

Coll

Arinagour

VIII

Passage

of Tiree

Hynish

Tiree

Sea

of

the

Hebrides

Skerryvore

7°W

I.   Nether Lorn
II.  Firth of Lorn
III. Loch Etive and Loch Linnhe
IV.  Sound of Mull
V.   Loch Sunart
VI.  The west coast of Mull
VII. South of Mull and Loch Scridain
VIII. Coll and Tiree

# The Yachtsman's Pilot
# The Isle of Mull
## and adjacent coasts

MARTIN LAWRENCE

Imray Laurie Norie & Wilson

Published by
Imray Laurie Norie & Wilson Ltd
Wych House St Ives
Cambridgeshire PE27 5BT England
☎ +44(0)1480 462114
Fax +44(0)1480 496109
Email ilnw@imray.com
www.imray.com
2008

Martin Lawrence has asserted his right to be identified as the author of this
work in accordance with the Copyright, Designs and Patents Act 1988.

1st edition 1999
2nd edition 2004
3rd edition 2008

ISBN 987 184623 081 3

British Library Cataloguing in Publication Data.
A catalogue record for this book is available from the British Library.

All photographs by the author unless otherwise credited.

PLANS
The plans in this guide are not to be used for navigation. They are
designed to support the text and should at all times be used with
navigational charts.
The plans and tidal information have been reproduced with the
permission of the Hydrographic Office of the United Kingdom (Licence
No. HO151/951101/01) and the controller of Her Britannic Majesty's
Stationery Office.

CAUTION
Every effort has been made to ensure the accuracy of this book. It
contains selected information and thus is not definitive and does not
include all known information on the subject in hand; this is particularly
relevant to the plans, which should not be used for navigation. The author
believes that its selection is a useful aid to prudent navigation, but the
safety of a vessel depends ultimately on the judgement of the navigator,
who should assess all information, published or unpublished.

CORRECTIONS
The editors would be glad to receive any corrections, information or
suggestions which readers may consider would improve the book, as new
impressions will be required from time to time. Letters should be
addressed to the Editor, *The Yachtsman's Pilot to the Isle of Mull*, care of
the publishers. The more precise the information the better, but even
partial or doubtful information is helpful, if it is made clear what the
doubts are.

CORRECTIONAL SUPPLEMENTS
This pilot book will be amended at intervals by the issue of correctional
supplements. These are published on the internet at our web site
www.imray.com and may be downloaded free of charge. Printed copies
are also available on request from the publishers at the above address.

The last input of technical information was March 2008.

Printed in Singapore by Star Standard Industries.

# Contents

# Preface

'Several subsequent visits have not caused me to modify to any extent my original feeling that for a sailing yacht the waters of the West Coast of Scotland offer an indifferent cruising ground... I cannot acquire any enthusiasm for the locality, nor understand the enthusiasm of those who, year by year, take their pleasure and renew their health in its sounds and lochs.'

Those words were written in the early years of the twentieth century by a distinguished cruising yachtsman, Henry Reynolds, who had undertaken, and apparently enjoyed, several cruises on the west coast of Scotland. Perhaps they were written after he had wrecked his yacht on the shore of Jura, running up the Sound in heavy weather in the dark, a circumstance which might put anyone off a particular cruising ground.

Some discerning people who sailed for pleasure had turned to the Highland coasts since the middle of the 19th century, when increased affluence and leisure (for some), combined with improved transport, inspired individual yachtsmen to explore the country which Dr Johnson in 1773 described as being less well known to his countrymen than darkest Africa. At the same time a team of Admiralty surveyors, mostly under the command of Captain Henry Otter, were surveying the west coast of Scotland in such meticulous detail that many of the present-day charts are still largely based on those surveys. A sophisticated network of steamer services linked the islands and the lochs of the west coast to the new railways, making the area accessible for the first time.

A few amateur sailors wrote of their experiences, among the first of them being William Power from Kingstown, who wrote (and illustrated) the *Log of the Olivia* in the 1860s, from which one may learn today some useful information. Fortunately a facsimile edition was published a few years ago[1].

Among other literary favourites is *The Log of the Blue Dragon*, by C. C. Lynam, an Oxford schoolmaster, who sailed down the Thames and round the south and west coast of England and Wales in a 25′ clinker-built yawl, in 1892. Over the next ten years he left the *Blue Dragon* in Scotland, and came back to sail on the west coast during every school holiday – even Christmas and New Year – often single-handed. The remains of the *Blue Dragon* still exist and are awaiting reconstruction.

The first man to compile sailing directions specifically for yachts was Frank Cowper, who wrote a series of five volumes entitled *Sailing Tours*, one of which included the whole of the coast of Scotland, at the end of the 19th century. He sailed around all the coast of Britain, sometimes single-

handed or with a boy, in a 20-ton converted working boat, and in France he was arrested as a spy. Lynam was so dismissive of his efforts that Cowper found it necessary to sue him for libel, as a result of which he was awarded one farthing in damages.

When *Yachting Monthly* was founded in 1906, one of its regular contributors was Robert Groves, who sailed his Albert Strange-designed yawl, *Sheila*, (again, about 25′ and often single-handed) around the West Coast and wrote articles beautifully illustrated with his own drawings as well as plans providing greater detail than contemporary (or even subsequent) charts.

Other books came (and went), some including pilotage information, and some as general background. The most recent, and very much curently in print is Hamish Haswell Smith's *The Scottish Islands*, which provides a wealth of information about every island around the coast of Scotland, and highly to be recommended.

The members of the Clyde Cruising Club, which was founded in 1909, began accumulating local knowledge, initially published in the club Journal and, after interruption by the first world war, eventually gathered together into the first edition of *Sailing Directions* in 1923. These were succeeded by new editions until the 1970s when the Hydrographic Office of the Navy adopted metric units for its charts, and a fresh start was made with sketch plans on which the depths were shown in metres to match the official charts.

An article by Michael Gilkes in the *Royal Cruising Club Journal*, led me to the archives of the Hydrographic Office, which was willing to make available the original surveys by Captain Otter and his successors, which are so clearly drawn, and generally so accurate, that they could form the basis for plans at greater detail than any later publication. At the same time large-scale aerial photos by the RAF were found to provide intricate detail in areas where the clean sandy bottom showed clearly all the rocks and dangers.

In turn this inspired me, when the opportunity arose, to take my own aerial photos of specific subjects, but these have been frequently constrained by the desirability of low spring tides, a need for clear weather ands availability of aircraft and pilot. Imrays' proposal to publish pilots for the West Coast provided an opportunity to make use of this photography.

---

[1]. Published by Graham Laird, 4 The Hilders, Farm Lane, Ashtead KT2 1LS

Some photos have been taken from hilltops and some, to illustrate clearing marks or specific features, from sea level. Inevitably these have not always been taken under ideal circumstances, but the coverage is regularly being extended and improved.

The first volume in this series of *Yachtsman's Pilots to the Coasts of Scotland*, entitled *Crinan to Canna*, was published in 1987, followed by two others, which subsequently grew to a total of five. This book is effectively the sixth edition of *Crinan to Canna*, retitled to emphasise a change in coverage.

### Acknowledgements

Most of the plans in this book are based on British Admiralty charts with the permission of the Hydrographer of the Navy and the sanction of HM Stationery Office.

No publication of this sort can ever be a lone effort, and I have always been indebted to contributions from others, in particular Mike Bolton, the former honorary secretary of WHAM (for which see the *Introduction*), the late Hilary King, Kathy Murgatroyd, John Shepherd, Norman and Gillian Smith, Ian Wallace of BorroBoats and many others who have provided information in the past or patiently answered questions, without which the content would be less complete. I would also ask readers to let me know, through the publishers, of anything which even *appears* not to correspond with their experience. Relevant information is passed to the Hydrographic Office of the Admiralty, who appreciate any contribution from all mariners, including yachtsmen.

Drawings of views of approaches to anchorages, etc. were made by Harriet Lawrence, and the text was greatly improved by editorial input from Jean Lawrence. Clare Georgy and colleagues at Imrays have patiently made sense of my manuscript.

I would particularly like to thank Nigel Gardner, without whose support and encouragement this series of pilots would never have been written or published.

*Martin Lawrence*
*Perth*
*May 2008*

'Scotch smacks', as engraved here by E.W. Cooke in 1828, were
the workhorses of the coastal trade before the days of steam,
and among other goods carried slates from Easdale for the roofs
of Edinburgh and Dundee, by way of the Pentland Firth, before
the Forth and Clyde Canal was opened.

# Introduction

'This narrow strait' (the Sailing Directions said),
'Is full of rocks, and difficult to enter;
Whirlpools are common here at every tide;
There are uncharted reefs on every side
And currents (twenty knots) along the centre.'
'Come,' said the Skipper, 'we will go in there.'
(We went in there.)
'There is no sand' (the Sailing Directions said),
'The anchorage is thoroughly unsafe.
There is no shelter from the frequent squalls,
Save on the west, among the overfalls.
Boats should go on to Loch MacInchmaquaif.'
'Come,' said the Skipper, 'we will anchor here.'
(We anchored here.)
*From The Log of the Blue Dragon (1903)*

This Pilot is intended to provide as much information as possible about anchorages and passages where a moderate-sized yacht may go under suitable conditions. It is not confined to those considered suitable for all conditions. It is the skipper's responsibility to take into account all information available, from Pilots, charts and tidal information, and to judge whether current and forecast conditions are appropriate for the anchorage or passage intended.

As described in the Preface, illustrations have been taken from many sources, such as traditional engraved views on 19th-century charts, as well as the old charts themselves where they are at a larger scale or provide better detail than those currently published.

Photos were taken mainly at low spring tides to reveal as many hazards as possible. However if coverage isn't as comprehensive and some of the photos not as clear as might be, this is because it takes many years to visit each place at a specific time of day and month, whether by sea, land or air – with no guarantee that conditions will be suitable for photography when one gets there.

Inevitably a book of this kind is flavoured by the author's outlook and experience; it may be of interest to know that for much of the time I was preparing these books I had a steel ketch of traditional character and perhaps take a slightly more light-hearted view of rock-dodging than would the owner of a less robust vessel. Our subsequent boat *Thomasina* was a Bowman 36 centreboard yawl of traditional style, which can creep into shallower water than boats of deeper draft. Neither of these is so handy as more modern cruiser-racers, and any place into which they can find their way should present little difficulty to a modern yacht of moderate size.

These directions can be no more than the sum of my own observations together with a summary of all that I have read, and gleaned from charts and air photos, and from the observations of others. There could well be hazards which I have missed by luck rather than good management, and in spite of all the efforts of the editorial team at Imray, Laurie, Norie & Wilson there may be simple errors which have been overlooked – even the supplements to the Admiralty pilot contain the occasional instruction 'for E read W'. Scepticism and checking against all other information available is the safest course to adopt – with any directions. Again, if you find information which you think is inaccurate, or changes which have occurred since the publication of this volume, I should be very grateful if you would let me know, through the publishers.

The upper limit of size for which this Pilot caters is a draught of two metres, and it includes information specifically for shoal-draught boats – centreboarders, trailer-sailers, twin-keel boats and multihulls, and of course motor cruisers, who tend to be forgotten by writers of 'sailing directions' who usually have sailing boats. Many West Coast anchorages have areas only accessible to shoal-draught boats, particularly those which can dry out fairly upright. In most other parts of Britain, indeed in most other parts of Europe, having a shoal-draught boat is the best way to avoid the crowds, and this is increasingly becoming the case on the west coast of Scotland which has traditionally been considered a deep-water area.

However, while the smallest boats, even cruising dinghies, may be at home in much of the area described in this pilot, they must be soundly equipped and competently handled by experienced crews. Except within some very sheltered lochs and sounds, and bearing in mind the need to keep well away from the entrance where there may be strong tides, the West Coast is no place for anyone who is unable to deal with adverse conditions which may arise unexpectedly. A good way to gain experience on the West Coast is to take a berth on one of the skippered charter yachts or instructional courses which are available.

## Charts

All published charts whether on paper or electronic medium, derive from the Hydrographic Office (UKHO), and it is the user's responsibility to ensure that the information is the most recent available. Some of these charts are based on very old (sometimes 150 years old) surveys, and current Admiralty charts carry a Source Data Diagram which indicates how recent the survey information on which each part of the chart is based. This may include commercial surveys where relevant.

The principal published chart information is the Admiralty Chart, although its publishers, UKHO, are at present set up as an Agency, whose principal purpose is to make money for its shareholders (the government). It is sometimes felt that providing a useful service for the end-user, which includes yachtsmen, is a secondary consideration.

A list of published charts and maps is included in the Appendix, at the back of this book.

Imrays publish a comprehensive series of charts at a scale of around 1:150,000, printed on waterproof material, and folded, as well as an A2-size folio of 1:50,000 charts in an acetate wallet, specifically drawn to provide the most useful information for small-craft navigators. Both series contain inset plans at a larger scale where the information is most relevant.

Both Imrays and UKHO publish amendments and corrections through the internet, and the navigator must ensure that he has the current amendments.

UKHO publish some charts in 'Small Craft' editions, on thinner paper, folded, at a more modest price than regular charts. They have also begun to publish A2-size folios, one of which covers the area from Kintyre to Ardnamurchan, consisting of extracts from regular charts.

UKHO are in the process of changing the horizontal datum on which their charts are based, although in most cases the difference is almost insignificant, it may be critical when close to rocks, particularly at night or in bad visibility.

Some areas are not well served by nautical charts at a sufficiently large scale to be useful, but in these areas charts can be supplemented by Ordnance Survey maps, especially those at 1:25,000. In the area of this Pilot the OS map of Coll and Tiree is particularly useful.

In addition to paper charts, several forms of electronic chart or plotters are available. These may be facsimiles of paper charts, such as those published by UKHO or jointly by UKHO and RYA, as well as those published by Imrays. These are usually in the form of a CD, readable on a laptop computer, and containing all necessary software. It is not possible to correct these charts. Some may be in a proprietary format and not inter-operable with any others, usually used with dedicated chart plotters. It has been found, in some cases that these electronic charts do not contain all the information available to the nominal date of publication.

It has been observed, in yachts navigating through narrow but deep passages, that the plotter sometimes shows the yacht passing over dry land at the side of the channel. Electronic plotters are not a substitute for paper charts and all, even the UKHO's own plotter, clearly state this limitation. It should also be noted that it is possible to enlarge the image beyond its original size, but the accuracy of the detail is not increased accordingly.

Imray chart 2800 folio and C65, whose boundaries correspond closely with the scope of this pilot, is ideal as an overall chart of the area.

Ordnance Survey maps at 1:50,000 or 1:25,000 make up for the lack of topographical detail on current charts (see Appendix I).

Equipment should be as robust and reliable as for a yacht going a similar distance offshore anywhere in the English Channel or the North Sea.

You should have at least two anchors, of the sizes recommended by anchor manufacturers or independent reference books, rather than those supplied as standard by boat manufacturers, which are often on the light side.

Chain, rather than rope, will prevent a yacht roving around in gusts, but if you do use rope it will help to have a weight ('angel', 'Chum') which can be let down to the seabed on a traveller.

So many yachts are now kept in marinas and only sail to a harbour that anchoring is no longer an everyday operation, but on the west coast it is essential that the crew is thoroughly familiar with anchor handling. It is no use relying on visitors' moorings being available; where they do exist they are quite likely to be already occupied.

Chartering Plenty of boats are available, both for bareboat and skippered charters, and also instructional cruises. Many of the operators are members of the Association of Scottish Yacht Charterers (ASYC), Arduaine Farmhouse, Arduaine, Argyll PA34 4XQ ☎/Fax +44 (0) 1852 200258 Mobile +44 (0) 7787 303562 Email info@asyc.co.uk. Most operators, including some owners of individual yachts, also advertise in yachting magazines.

## Travel

Transport Public transport in the area is probably better than it has been at any time during the last 30 years. There are rail and bus services to Oban, Fort William and Corpach, Arisaig and Mallaig. If a crew change has to be made on Mull, there are frequent ferry crossings, some of which are met by buses to Tobermory and to the Ross of Mull.

Timetables for:
Citylink bus services to major destinations in the Highlands ☎ 0990 505050.
Scotrail services to Oban and Fort William ☎ 0345 484950.

With the exception of Tiree no part of this area has a regular air service although a non-scheduled seaplane service has been established to Oban and Tobermory.

There are good roads to Crinan and Oban and to Loch Leven, continuing to Fort William, but in between they are tortuous in places.

Most marinas have good launching facilities for trailed boats

Some anchorages are only accessible to shallow draft boats

## Trailed boats

A comprehensive guide to launching places for trailed boats throughout the UK can be had for £10.95, including postage, from Boatlaunch, 42 Half Moon Lane, London, SE24 9HU, or www.boatlaunch.co.uk/Good_Launch_Guide.html

Probably the most convenient launching place is at Creran Moorings in Loch Creran. There are also slips at Ardfern Yacht Centre (Loch Craignish), Craobh Yacht Haven (Loch Shuna), Airds Bay (Loch Etive), Dunstaffnage Yacht Haven, Ballachulish old ferry (Loch Leven), and Salen (Loch Sunart). Several yacht centres have mobile hoists.

Check by phone before arriving with the operators, listed under the relevant area in each chapter. Charges may be made for use of a slip and for car parking.

## Passage making

Most passages covered by this volume are within sounds or lochs or along a shore entailing only short hops across open sea, so that navigation is, in the main, a matter of pilotage by eye and satisfying yourself that what you see corresponds to the chart. It is useful to pick out from the chart transits such as tangents of islands, or beacons in line with headlands to give you position lines from time to time. Check by compass bearings as well, starting from something unmistakable such as, for instance, the south tangent of Mull, so as to avoid wrongly identifying a whole group of islands.

Traditional clearing marks for avoiding unmarked dangers, based on transits of natural features, are often much easier to use than compass bearings particularly where there are cross tides. Bearings are given in the text as a check on identification.

**At night** most of the main passages are fairly well lit, at least for a passage under power or with a fair wind, but they aren't up to the standard of Scandinavian countries as there isn't enough traffic to justify more lights. A few anchorages or passages are very well lit for local commercial users. At least during June and July there is little need to sail at night unless you are making a longer passage, beyond the limits of this book.

**Radiobeacons** Except for an aero beacon at Connel (call sign *CNL*, range 15M, frequency 404kHz) there are no radiobeacons in the area covered by this book.

**Submarines** Information about movement of submerged submarines is broadcast by Clyde Coastguard after the inshore weather forecasts below. Sea areas are referred to by code names, shown on the plan on page 156.

**Weather forecasts** A new schedule for forecasts, broadcast by the Coastguard on VHF was introduced in 2007, as follows:

HMCG will broadcast forecasts three hourly, that is eight times a day and will complete most transmissions around the coast within one hour. Four broadcasts will provide new forecasts and four will be repeats.

Two of the new forecasts will include gale warnings, the shipping forecast and inshore waters forecast and outlook, as well as navigation warnings and the three day fisherman's forecast when applicable.

The other two new forecasts will include inshore waters forecasts, a repeat of the previous 24 hour outlook and any gale warnings or strong wind warnings. Mariners will thus have new inshore waters forecasts every six hours.

The repeats are for the benefit of mariners who missed the new forecast made three hours previously and will consist of the inshore waters forecasts and gale warnings and any new strong wind warnings.

The full broadcasts will be based on 0710 and 1910 start times so as to catch navigators at the beginning of the sailing day or night passage. All broadcasts will be in local time to avoid confusion between UTC and BST.

Warnings for all forecasts will be transmitted on VHF Ch 16, indicating the forecast on VHF Ch 23, 84 or 86 (perhaps 10), which will remain unchanged. Aerials will be combined for the warnings to avoid apparent repetition.

Warnings will be brief: 'All stations – this is Clyde Coastguard – for a weather information broadcast listen to Ch 83' – but made slowly. The forecast broadcasts will be made clearly and at dictation speed.

Information is also available at www.metoffice.gov.uk/weather/marine/guide/ Frank Singleton's Weather Site www.franksingleton.clara.net/ is the most useful overall guide to weather services available.

## Tides

Within the area covered by Chapter I the tidal range is less than two metres but in several passages in that area tides run at up to eight knots. Elsewhere the range is up to four metres.

Tidal streams are strong wherever the movement of a large body of water is constricted by narrows and there are often overfalls at the seaward end of narrow passages, particularly with wind against tide.

Overfalls also occur off many headlands, and eddies are formed, usually down-tide of a promontory or islet or even a submerged reef, but sometimes in a bay up-tide of the obstruction. There are also usually overfalls wherever two tidal streams meet such as, for example, the ebb streams from the Sound of Mull and from Loch Linnhe. These eddies and overfalls are too common to be mentioned individually.

Tidal streams The flood tide generally runs north and west, but in the mouth of the Firth of Lorn it runs northeast. In the Dorus Mor the streams turn up to 2½ hours before HW and LW Oban, but in the Sound of Mull they turn about an hour after HW and LW Oban. This means that at least nine hours of fair tide can be carried going north although of course at the expense of the return passage.

See also the paragraphs on Tides under each relevant area. For tide tables and almanacs see Appendix I.

## Anchorages

This heading covers not only natural anchorages but also moorings and berths alongside pontoons or quays. Many places are only suitable for a short daytime visit in settled conditions and the inclusion of an anchorage is no indication that it is suitable for all conditions. The skipper must decide whether to use an anchorage at all, and for how long, in the light of conditions at the time and all the information available. Even the most apparently sheltered place will sometimes have the crew standing anchor watches throughout the night.

Within some anchorages there are often several suitable places to lie depending on conditions and it is not always practicable to describe them all, nor to mark each one on the plans. In any case, an anchorage suitable for a shoal-draught boat six metres long may be inaccessible to a 15-metre yacht with a draught of two metres, and a berth which would give shelter for the larger yacht might be uncomfortably exposed for the smaller.

Where visitors' moorings are provided it is the crew's responsibility to find out whether payment is due, and to whom – and to pay it. Some people have avoided paying in the past by claiming that they weren't asked for it, although many providers of moorings cannot afford the expense of employing staff to collect payments.

A few very general observations may be helpful. Steep high ground to windward is unlikely to provide good shelter; in fresh winds there may be turbulent gusts on its lee side, or the wind may be deflected to blow from a completely different direction. After a hot windless day there may be a strong katabatic wind down the slope, usually in the early morning – such conditions are by no means unknown in Scotland. Trees to windward will absorb a lot of wind and provide good shelter.

Rivers, burns and streams generally carry down debris, often leaving a shallow or drying bank of stones, sand or silt, over which the unwary may swing – frequently in the middle of the night.

Within any anchorage the quality of the bottom may vary greatly. Mud is common, (usually where there is little current) but its density may not be consistent and there are likely to be patches of rock, boulders and stones; also clay which tends to break out suddenly. Sand is also common, but sometimes it is so hard that an anchor, particularly a light one, will not dig in. Weed of all kinds appears to be on the increase, but it does vary from year to year.

Midges constitute a legendary hazard in woodland or undergrowth and may make life miserable for those unprepared. An effective insect repellent should be applied before going ashore.

Ticks are increasingly acknowledged as a hazard as carriers of Lyme's Disease. If a tick is found on one's body it should be removed in one piece at the earliest possible opportunity. The application of methylated spirit (or neat whisky) may be effective, although some medical authorities

Fog is not common, but may be an occasional hazard

disapprove of this method. Clegs (horseflies) have an irritating bite, but are not otherwise harmful.

**Man-made obstructions** Fish farms are increasing at an alarming rate, usually outwith the most popular places, but attempts are sometimes made to establish them in recognised anchorages as well.

Permission to establish any permanent fixture on the seabed, such as mooring, has to be obtained from the Crown Estates Commissioners who own the rights to the seabed, and also the Department of Transport (Marine Directorate), who consult the RYA (Scotland), who in turn refer to the Clyde Cruising Club and the West Highlands Anchorages and Moorings Association (WHAM), which represents the interests of both yachtsmen and fishermen; the comments are then passed back up the chain and may or may not be taken into account.

The Crown Estates Moorings Officer is P. J. Korbel ☎ 01880 820552.

Increasingly, moorings for yachts and fishing and other workboats, as well as fish farms, are being laid within established anchorages, preventing or restricting their use. The number of inshore fishing boats operating from some parts of the coast of Argyll has doubled in a few years. Preservation of anchorages is one of the main functions of West Highlands Anchorage and Mooring Association (WHAM) who wish to hear about any apparently unauthorised obstruction; the honorary secretary of WHAM is David Vass, 33 Ochlochy Park, Dunblane, FK15 0DX.

**Lighthouse installations** Lighthouses and light beacons, often at remote locations, may have jetties, steps, or landing places, which are no longer maintained, and should not be used, owing to the risk of damage and injury.

**Visitors' moorings** These may be seen as a convenience, necessity or obstruction depending on your point of view. Some are provided by local hotels free of charge to yachts whose crews patronise their establishments.

Visitors' moorings have been provided by the former Highlands and Islands Development Board, and its successor Highlands and Islands Enterprise, in several places to bring more business to local traders. They may be laid in the most suitable area for anchoring, and are arranged (as they have to be) to suit the largest boats likely to use them. The effect is to reduce the number of visiting boats which can use an anchorage. Visitors' moorings have large blue buoys, usually with no pick-up, and a rope has to be fed through a ring on top of the buoy. If your bow is so high that the buoy is out of reach and you cannot pass your rope through the ring, the best way to secure to one of these moorings is to lead a rope from the bow to the lowest point amidships, pick up the buoy there and take the end of the rope back to the bow. Beware of chafe at the ring and use chain if necessary. The practice of rafting-up is not now encouraged.

For the latest information go to http://homepages.rya-online.net/whisca/moorings.htm

Dunstaffnage and Ben Cruachan

**Marinas and yacht centres** are being established, sometimes obliterating the natural anchorages which are after all the main attraction of the west coast. A berth or mooring will usually be found for a visiting yacht; the charges vary widely and cost-conscious skippers will do well to enquire first.

A publication entitled *Welcome Anchorages* describes some establishments which cater for visiting yachts.

**Piers and jetties,** even in the most remote anchorages these should be treated in the same way as private moorings. Some are used by fishermen or workboats which may not treat an unattended yacht with as much delicacy as the owner would wish. Some piers are derelict and dangerous.

**Eating ashore** The prospect of eating and drinking ashore is still improving; hotels, restaurants and pubs are mentioned in the text, although not usually by name and without specific recommendations as management and standards may change rapidly.

**Access to land** New access rights relating to open country in Scotland came into effect in February 2005. The Access Code, published by SNH defining the terms and obligations governing access is available from tourist offices, etc. and may be downloaded from the internet at www.outdooraccess-scotland.com

## Communications

**Telephone** Much, but by no means all, of the west coast is covered by mobile phone networks, and public telephones are still essential. These are referred to where known.

**VHF radiotelephones** The mountainous nature of this coast puts some areas out of range of the coastguard.

Most yacht centres have VHF R/T, but they may not be continuously manned.

**Place names** Admiralty charts and sailing directions follow the Ordnance Survey convention of printing academic renderings of Gaelic names, with a variety of accents as they would appear in a Gaelic dictionary. Some of these are quite unpronounceable other than by Gaelic speakers (and, I believe, sometimes unrecognisable even to them). Both authorities sometimes use anglicised versions, or translations of Gaelic words, apparently quite arbitrarily; for example you may come across 'Old Woman Rock' among a patch of Gaelic names on a chart, or alternatively a Gaelic name alongside its equivalent anglicisation. The early surveyors often made up their own names, based on natural features, their own translations of the Gaelic, or events or personalities connected with the survey, and these names were used on earlier charts, although they have not often survived in common use.

Place names need to be communicated verbally, for example between the navigator, helmsman and lookout, so I have used the popular form of a name where there is one, as well as the name which appears on current charts. The spelling of these names matches that on the Admiralty charts, less any accents. You may find some discrepancies, but I hope they will not be so great as to cause confusion. Spelling of some names, e.g. *Lorn*, and *Ardinamir*, have been amended on recent editions of charts, and the amended spellings have been adopted here. See Appendix II.

## mSACs

The following note about marine Special Areas of Conservation has been provided by WHAM and Scottish Natural Heritage (www.snh.org.uk). There are currently four mSACs within the area covered by this volume.

Those who engage in boating and recreational diving on the west coast benefit from the many small harbours and anchorages and the unspoiled environment, and it is in everyone's interest that this environment is protected so that future generations can continue to enjoy it.

Under the European Habitats Directive the UK Government has agreed to identify a network of protected marine areas around our coasts to safeguard important species and their habitats. Around seventy sites have been identified around the UK and of these around two dozen are on the west coast of Scotland. For some of these sites, management committees have been established, including representatives from all local interest groups. Scottish Natural Heritage produces excellent leaflets giving details of the special features of the mSACs. In addition on land adjacent to some sites areas of Special Scientific Interest (SSSIs) are being designated.

There is no intention to try to restrict access to mSAC or to SSSIs; indeed that would be counter-productive as the aim is to make everyone aware of the special features of the sites so that they can be appreciated by visitors. In a few cases and by mutual agreement some types of fishing are being discouraged because of damage which may be caused to sea life on the bottom; in future in a few mSAC boat owners may be encouraged to anchor only in recognised anchorages for the same reason; an anchor and chain can cause considerable damage as it sweeps the bottom due to the action of tide and wind.

So as you travel the west coast keep in mind the wealth of wild life hidden below our seas; keep in mind the areas which have been identified as mSACs and give thought to any potential damage that your presence may cause to the environment.

## Emergencies

Serious and immediate emergencies (including medical ones) are usually best referred to the coastguard. If you don't have VHF R/T but are able to get ashore (for example, if a crew member is ill), phone the coastguard or police. For less serious problems, such as a mechanical breakdown out of range of a boatyard, mechanics experienced at least with tractor or fishing boat engines will often be found locally.

**Coastguard** The Marine Rescue Co-ordination Centre (MRCC) is Clyde Coastguard ☎ 01475 786955. Maritime Safety Information is broadcast by repeaters throughout the area on various VHF channnels after an initial announcement on Ch 16 at 0020 UT and every four hours thereafter. There is an auxiliary coastguard at Tobermory ☎ 01688 302200.

**Lifeboats** are stationed, within the limits of this volume, only at Oban and Tobermory; outside the immediate area there are lifeboats at Port Askaig (Islay), Mallaig, Portree (Skye) and Castle Bay (Barra).

## Notes on plans and pilotage directions

Generally the conventions used on Admiralty charts have been followed so that this pilot may be used in conjunction with them. Please see key on page 8.

Details of anchorages and passages are included which may be suitable only for restricted conditions,

**Bearings** are from seaward and refer to true north. A few of the plans are not orientated with north at the top in order to make the best use of the space available, but reference to the north point on the plan will make this clear.

**Distances** are given in nautical miles and cables (tenth of nautical mile); distances of less than ¼ cable may be expressed in metres.

**Depths and heights** are given in metres to correspond with the current Admiralty charts. Depths are related to the current chart datum which is generally the lowest level to which the surface of the sea is expected to fall owing to astronomical causes. If high barometric pressure and/or strong offshore winds coincide with a low spring tide the water may fall below this level, in which case there will be less depth than shown on the chart, or sketch plan. Heights of drying rocks, and heights below bridges on current charts are quoted in relation to HAT (Highest Astronomical Tide), and may vary slightly from figures previously quoted, and those on older charts.

**Tides** Heights of tides are represented by five figures; these are: Mean High Water Springs, Mean High Water Neaps, Mean Tide Level, Mean Low Water Neaps, Mean Low Water Springs. The word Mean is important because (for example) Low Water Springs in any particular fortnight may be substantially higher or lower than the mean. If you have tide tables which give heights of tides at Oban you will be able to relate the tide on any particular day to the mean figures there (4·0, 2·9, 2·4, 1·8, 0·7) and judge whether the rise and fall is greater or less than the mean.

The difference between times of tides at Oban and at Dover may vary by as much as 40 minutes, so that tide tables for Oban will give more accurate results than those for Dover. In addition to Admiralty tide tables and commercial almanacs, pocket tide tables for Oban are supplied by local chandlers, boatyards and marinas, and also by Glasgow chandlers.

**Plans** of anchorages and passages in this pilot are often drawn at a larger scale than those on current charts, and the information in them is compiled from many sources. These include the Admiralty's original surveys; air photographs mostly of RAF origin; observations by other yachtsmen; and my own surveys, both from the air and by sea, as well as from the land. Many of them are based directly on British Admiralty charts, with the permission of the Hydrographer of the Navy.

**Photographs** and views from sea level are used to illustrate transits and clearing marks, or to help identify landmarks, while air and hilltop photos often show more detail than can be included in the plans. Transits are in some cases more clearly illustrated when the marks used are not actually aligned; where this is done the marks are indicated by pointers.

**KEY TO SYMBOLS ON PLANS**

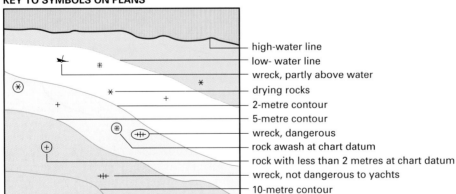

- high-water line
- low- water line
- wreck, partly above water
- drying rocks
- 2-metre contour
- 5-metre contour
- wreck, dangerous
- rock awash at chart datum
- rock with less than 2 metres at chart datum
- wreck, not dangerous to yachts
- 10-metre contour

All depths and heights are in metres

# I. Nether Lorn

Most yachts visiting the west coast will pass through these waters unless they go to the west of Jura, and Admiralty chart *2326* (available in 'Small Craft' folded format) at a scale of 1:25,000 is essential. There are probably more islands and passages in the area covered by this chart than in any equivalent area off the British mainland. Tidal streams in passages covered by chart *2326* are as strong as most around Britain; there are few artificial marks, and plenty of hidden dangers. However most of the passages are completely sheltered from the open sea and the hazards are easily avoided with care.

Several yacht centres of varying degrees of sophistication have grown up in this area in the last twenty five years and hundreds of yachts are now berthed in these waters. Inshore of a line between Ardnoe, the south point of Loch Crinan, and the south end of Luing the land is relatively pastoral, but the islands west of this line are bleak and rugged and almost uninhabited. The character of the tidal streams differs on either side of the same line; to the east the tides present few problems, but to the west they need close attention.

The chapter begins with the various channels which link the Sound of Jura (and the Crinan Canal) with the Firth of Lorn by the west of Luing, followed by the lochs on the East of Luing, and ends with Cuan Sound which joins Lochs Shuna and Melfort to the Firth of Lorn.

### Tides

The tidal range inside Jura and the islands northward is little more than two metres at springs but to the west of Jura it is more than three, so that the whole volume of water in the Sound of Jura has to pour out through a few narrow channels on the flood and back again on the ebb; each of these channels has tidal streams at springs of six to eight knots. It is therefore essential to work the tides unless you have a really hefty engine.

## The Sound of Luing

56°12′N 5°40′W

The main passage, the Sound of Luing, is straightforward enough but eddies and overfalls make it necessary to keep a very close watch on the course at all times but probably most of all under

A windy day in the Dorus Mor

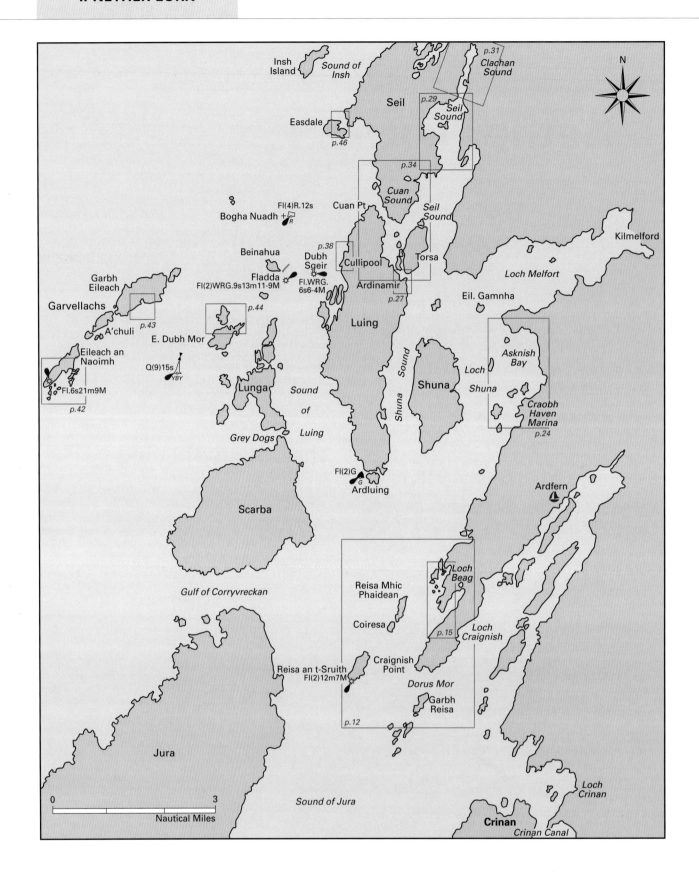

N

Insh Island
Sound of Insh

Seil

Clachan Sound
*p.31*

*p.29*

Seil Sound

Easdale
*p.46*

*p.34*

Cuan Sound

Seil Sound

Cuan Pt

Fl(4)R.12s

Bogha Nuadh ✛
R

Kilmelford

Loch Melfort

Beinahua

Dubh Sgeir
*p.38*

Eil. Gamnha

Garbh Eileach

Fladda
Fl(2)WRG.9s13m11-9M

Cullipool

Torsa

Fl.WRG.
6s6-4M

Garvellachs

*p.43*

A'chuli

E. Dubh Mor

*p.44*

Ardinamir
*p.27*

Asknish Bay

Loch

Shuna

Luing

Eileach an Naoimh

Q(9)15s
YBY

Lunga

Sound

Craobh Haven Marina
*p.24*

Fl.6s21m9M
*p.42*

of

Shuna Sound

Shuna

Luing

Grey Dogs

Fl(2)G
G

Ardfern

Ardluing

Scarba

Loch Beag

Gulf of Corryvreckan

Reisa Mhic Phaidean

*p.15*

Loch Craignish

Coiresa

Reisa an t-Sruith
Fl(2)12m7M

Craignish Point

Dorus Mor

*p.12*

Garbh Reisa

Jura

Loch Crinan

0          3

Nautical Miles

Sound of Jura

**Crinan**

Crinan Canal

sail in light weather. It is very easy to be carried off course and although, as I've said, the hazards are quite easily avoided, they are there and a constant check on position must be kept. A branch of the flood stream runs towards Corryvreckan and you need to watch that you aren't being carried into this passage without realising it.

In anything like heavy weather with wind against tide the Dorus Mor and the passage between there and the south end of Luing would be actually dangerous to a small boat. The photograph on page 9 was taken from Craignish Point looking west towards Corryvreckan with a flood tide and a southerly wind about Force 7 (that is, the wind and tide were running the same way).

### Tides

The flood tide runs northwards and westwards, beginning about +0430 Oban (–0100 Dover) at springs; +0515 Oban (–0015 Dover) at neaps.

The ebb runs southwards and eastwards, beginning about –0145 Oban (+0515 Dover) at springs, –0100 Oban (+0600 Dover) at neaps.

Eddies are formed, generally down-tide of any obstruction such as a point of land or a rock, with overfalls where eddies and main tide meet.

At the north end of the Sound of Jura the flood tide sets northwest across the reefs to the NNE of Ruadh Sgeir and this must be allowed for by any yacht coming from the Sound of Jura and making for Loch Craignish or the Dorus Mor. Likewise the ebb sets southeast at the same point. Northwest of the reefs NNE of Ruadh Sgeir there are heavy overfalls on the flood.

### Marks

Unless it is obscured by cloud, the peak of Scarba provides a convenient reference point.

Other marks are Fladda lighthouse at the north end of the Sound of Luing, Reisa an t-Sruith light beacon to the west of the Dorus Mor, and a conspicuous white house on Shuna island, Shuna Cottage.

### Passage notes

*From the Sound of Jura* the passage of the Sound of Luing is straightforward but, especially under sail in light weather, take care to avoid being carried towards Corryvreckan; keep to the east side of the passage. Identify the correct passage by reference to landmarks. Towards the north end of the sound there are two submerged rocks, one on either side of the fairway. These are unlikely to be of any concern except to a deep-draught boat at a low spring tide. The main passage is between Fladda and Dubh Sgeir light beacon.

*From the north* identify Scarba, and Fladda lighthouse will be seen to the east of it – yachts have been known to go west of Scarba by mistake.

### Lights

At night, light beacons at Ruadh Sgeir and Reisa an t-Sruith kept in transit 188° provide a safe line when you are south of Ard Luing. Within the Sound of Luing the only guide is to take compass bearings on Reisa an t-Sruith and on Fladda and Dubh Sgeir light beacons at the north end of the sound.

**Ruadh Sgeir** Fl.6s13m8M.
**Reisa an t-Sruith** Fl(2)12s12m7M
**Fladda** Fl(2)WRG.9s13m11-9M 169°-R-186°-W-337°-G-344°-W-356°-R-026°
**Dubh Sgeir** Fl.WRG.6s9m6/4M 000°-W-010°-R-025°-W-199°-G-000°.

With these sectored lights a night passage of the Sound of Luing is fairly straightforward – but older charts must be amended accordingly.

### Anchorages

*Kinuachdrach (Kinnochtie)* 56°7′.5N 5°41′W
At the northeast end of Jura, either the bay north of the promontory (Port an Tiobairt, see photo on page 17) or south of it (Kinuachdrach Harbour) provides an occasional anchorage according to wind direction.

*Lunga – Poll na Corran* 56°12′.5N 5°41′W
A bay on the east side of Lunga only exposed to the fetch across the sound – holding has been found to be poor, with thick weed. Enter north of the islet there and anchor off the beach.

*Black Mill Bay* 56°13′N 5°39′W
On Luing will give better shelter in easterly winds; just south of the most westerly point on Luing, and north of a ruined timber pier.

*Cullipool,* see page 38.

# Dorus Mor and passage to the Sound of Luing

The Dorus Mor, between Craignish Point and Garreasar (Garbh Reisa), the most northerly of the string of islands and reefs to the SSW of the point, is about a third of a mile wide. It is deep and clean and provides a direct route from Crinan and Loch Craignish to the Sound of Luing.

### Tides

The main stream in the Dorus Mor runs at up to eight knots turning north west at +0330 Oban and turning southeast about –0215 Oban, but at most states of the tide eddies, particularly on the north side, cause small whirlpools at the boundary between the eddy and main stream.

On the flood a strong branch of the stream sets across to Corryvreckan. At certain times, especially early on the flood, an eddy runs southwards on the west side of the Craignish peninsula. At the northwest point of Garreasar an eddy runs northeastwards close to the island. A strong eddy on the north side of the passage runs at the same rate as the main stream, with a sharp line separating them.

On the ebb an anticlockwise eddy runs to the south of the main passage, between Garreasar and Reisa an t-Sruith. As on the flood there is a strong eddy on the north side of the passage. In strong southerly winds there will be heavy overfalls on the ebb from Craignish Point to Ard Luing. In these conditions it would be best to wait for slack water before making this passage.

### Dangers and clearing marks

Half a mile northwest of Craignish Point, towards Coiresa, lies a submerged rock with 0·6 metre of water over it. The Crinan Hotel kept just open north of Garreasar, bearing 140°, leads south of it.

A quarter of a mile west of Reisa Mhic Phaidean, Red Rock (Dearg Sgeir) dries 1·8 metres.

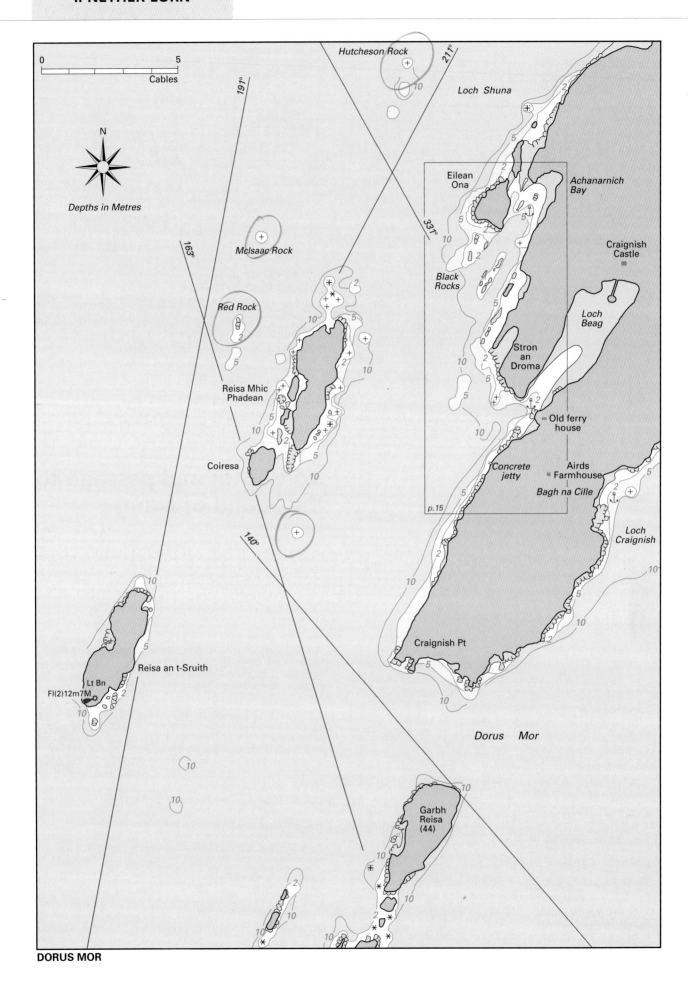

0        5

Cables

N

Depths in Metres

211°

Hutcheson Rock

Loch Shuna

19°

McIsaac Rock

163°

Red Rock

Eilean
Ona

Achanarnich
Bay

Craignish
Castle

Black
Rocks

Loch
Beag

Reisa Mhic
Phadean

Stron
an
Droma

Coiresa

Old ferry
house

140°

Concrete
jetty

Airds
Farmhouse

Bagh na Cille

p.15

Loch
Craignish

Reisa an t-Sruith

Lt Bn
Fl(2)12m7M

Craignish Pt

Dorus     Mor

Garbh
Reisa
(44)

**DORUS MOR**

*Rubha Fiola*

Rubha Fiola open west of the south end of Luing bearing
331° leads southwest of Hutcheson's Rock (2003)

*Ard Luing*

*Airds Farm House*

Airds Farm House at the right of the photo, open west of Sron an Droma
bearing 152° leads south of Hutcheson's Rock (2003)

McIsaac Rock, with less than two metres over it, is 3½ cables northward of Red Rock. Both of these are cleared by keeping Ruadh Sgeir light beacon (to the south) touching or hidden behind the east side of Reisa an t-Sruith, bearing 191°.

To the east of Reisa Mhic Phaidean submerged and drying rocks on both sides of the channel are avoided by keeping near the middle of the channel. If tacking, careful chartwork will be needed.

Nearly a mile to the north of Reisa Mhic Phaidean lies Hutcheson Rock with less – possibly very much less – than two metres, over it.

A long mark for passing southwest of it is to keep Rubha Fiola, the north end of the islands extending north from Scarba, open of the south end of Luing, bearing 331°.

An alternative line to pass southwest of the rock is to keep Aird farmhouse open of Sron an Droma at the west side of Loch Beag, bearing 152°.

To pass east of Hutcheson Rock keep Reisa an t-Sruith touching Reisa Mhic Phaidean, bearing 211°.

### Passage notes

*Going north* it is worth planning to be at the Dorus Mor as soon as, or slightly before, the tide turns northwards; another (lesser) tidal gate lies 20 miles further north, at Duart Point, but with reasonable speed through the water a fair tide can be carried to Tobermory. Note carefully the various clearing marks described above, and take care to avoid being carried towards Corryvreckan, especially under sail in light weather.

*Going south* the tide presents fewer problems except in strong southerly winds when there will be heavy overfalls between Craignish Point and Scarba. If late on the tide at Dorus Mor a skilled helmsman may take advantage of the eddy by keeping close to Craignish Point.

*By night* or if arriving after dark at the end of a passage, Reisa Mhic Phaidean and Ruadh Sgeir light beacon in line bearing 188° lead well clear to the west of Red Rock. You only have a few minutes to identify correctly the light at Crinan, which has a low range, and to turn to keep it in sight through the Dorus Mor. Failing this you have to pass south of Ruadh Sgeir.

### Anchorages

#### West side of Craignish Point

*Loch Beag* a little more than a mile north of Craignish Point, is an occasional or temporary anchorage for settled weather. The greater part of the loch dries, so anchor just within the entrance off the old ferry house (not the concrete jetty a quarter of a mile south of the loch).

Achanarnich, on the west side of the Craignish peninsula,
from southwest (1991)

Gulf of Corryvreckan from Scarba, looking southwest at mid
spring flood, with a light easterly wind, so that there is no
disturbance from the wind (1996)

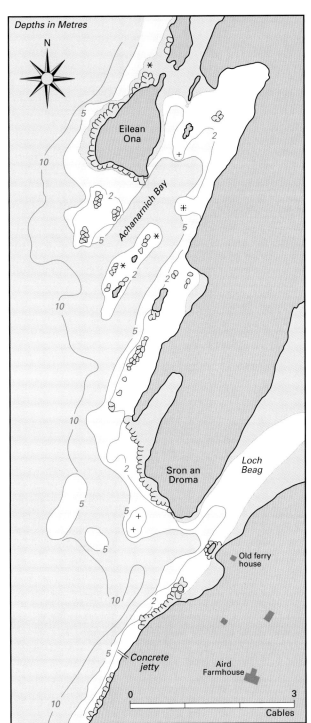

Depths in Metres

N

Eilean
Ona

Achanarnich Bay

Sron an
Droma

Loch
Beag

Old ferry
house

Concrete
jetty

Aird
Farmhouse

0                    3
Cables

**LOCH BEAG AND ACHANARNICH BAY**

## Achanarnich

Tides run strongly across both the entrances, there are many drying rocks, and the south entrance is difficult to identify.

*From the south* find the passage between two lines of long low rocks and keep in mid channel between them on a bearing of 025°; after passing the last rock above water on the west side of the entrance passage, alter course towards the shore to avoid a drying rock at the north end of the west line of rocks (this rock lies to the east of the general line of rocks); then head NNW towards Eilean Ona to avoid a rock awash near the shore.

Anchor either side of an islet in the basin between Eilean Ona and the shore; a submerged rock, on which the depth is about 1·5 metres, lies half a cable south of the islet. The bottom is sand and weed, and the anchorage is reported to be prone to swell.

*At the entrance from the west* by the south side of Eilean Ona the tide sets straight across the entrance. Keep 20 metres off Eilean Ona to avoid rocks close south of it; keep rather further off the southeast point of the island before turning north into the basin.

*Bagh Ban* nearly a mile NNE of Eilean Ona, provides some shelter in settled weather, behind a 4-metre islet north of the middle of the bay. A drying rock lies near the north point of the drying bay east of the islet.

See also Loch Craignish, pages 21–22 and Loch Shuna, pages 23–24.

## Corryvreckan

Before contemplating a passage through the Gulf, see a spectacular DVD from the following: Corryvreckan DVD Sales, Kilmahumaig, Crinan, Lochgilphead, Argyll, Scotland PA31 8SW ☎ +44 (0) 1546 830238 *Email* dvd@whirlpool-scotland.co.uk May also be available from yacht chandlers.

The Gulf of Corryvreckan, between Scarba and the north end of Jura is one of the most notorious stretches of water anywhere around the British Isles, although it is half a mile wide, with no hazards near the surface. With one significant exception it is more than 100 metres deep for the greater part of its width.

The hazardous nature of this passage is due to three factors: the strength of the current, the turbulence at the boundary of eddies on both sides (and overall whenever the tidal stream is opposed to the wind), and the presence of one rock which has a least depth over it of 29 metres.

In addition to the eddies on the surface – as divers know very well – there are also vertical currents, welling up from, and dropping down to, the bottom.

The turbulence is not confined to the gulf itself; even in calm weather it extends several miles WNW as the flood tide meets the relatively stationary body of water further offshore. This is named on the charts as 'The Great Race'.

Because of its width and depth, Corryvreckan takes the bulk of the tidal stream passing backwards and forwards between the north end of the Sound of Jura and the open sea. In addition to this the spring range at Loch Beag, three miles east of the east entrance to the gulf, is 2·1 metres, whereas at Glengarrisdale Bay, three miles SSW of the west entrance, it is 3·1 metres, so that at high and low

Corryvreckan from Scarba (1996)

water springs there is a difference between each end of the Gulf of 0·5 metre.

The turbulence is naturally greatest on the flood, particularly when the tidal stream meets a westerly wind blowing from the open sea with any accompanying swell.

The 29-metre rock rises abruptly from depths of over 60 metres two cables from the Scarba shore and it is located south of the west point of a bay a little west of halfway along the south shore of Scarba. A standing wave builds up around this rock and is said to rise to four metres, and may combine with a westerly swell to rise to twice that height. The east face of the rock is steeper than the west, so that the standing wave is steeper and higher on the flood tide.

An eddy, equal in strength to the main stream, runs down the west side of Scarba on the flood and into Corryvreckan, rejoining the main stream abreast of the 29-metre rock creating, at times, a distinct whirlpool.

On the ebb an eddy of similar strength forms, also on the north side of the gulf, and on both ebb and flood smaller eddies are formed along the south shore of the gulf.

Among the islands on the south side of the west entrance there are further strong currents, especially on the ebb, when an anticlockwise eddy is set up to the west of Eilean Mor; this causes severe overfalls, particularly over a submerged reef which extends a cable WNW of Eilean Mor. There are several submerged and drying rocks among these islands, and most careful chartwork is needed to avoid them.

From the above it will be obvious that the fundamental advice, especially to yachtsmen unfamiliar with the west coast, must be to avoid Corryvreckan and to avoid being drawn accidentally into it, although under certain conditions it is passable and is often used by experienced local yachtsmen as well as by fishermen.

### Tides

The flood tide runs westwards, beginning about +0430 Oban (−0100 Dover) at springs; +0515 Oban (−0015 Dover) at neaps.
The ebb runs eastwards, beginning about −0145 Oban (+0515 Dover) at springs; −0100 Oban (+0600 Dover) at neaps.
The spring rate is at least eight knots.

## Passage notes

The most favourable conditions for passing through Corryvreckan are slack water, a light to moderate fair wind, and no swell.

The ebb is less violent than the flood, and, if heading westwards, it may be better to go through against the ebb, particularly near the beginning or towards the end of the ebb, at the expense of having a foul tide. A further advantage is that you can beat a retreat if you find conditions uninviting at the west end; in the sheltered waters to the east of Jura it is difficult to form any idea of conditions to the west of the gulf.

Bear in mind, however, that if you go through Corryvreckan at the end of the ebb, the Great Race will build up very quickly when the tide turns and you need to be clear of its track.

A passage on the flood should be considered only at neaps with a light to moderate easterly wind, and only if you are sure that there is no swell.

The flood stream sets from the Sound of Jura across the gulf towards the Scarba shore and you must take care to keep within the southern half of the passage.

Remember particularly the flood eddy on the north side at the west end, and keep clear of it if heading northwards.

From west to east the gulf should not be approached while the flood is running and a yacht should not be in the area at all during the flood if there is any swell.

Give the northwest of Eilean Mor a wide berth especially if the ebb is well developed.

From whichever direction you are considering approaching Corryvreckan you must be sure that conditions are suitable for the passage, and unless you are certain of this, avoid it.

Jura, Corryvreckan, Bagh Gleann nam Muc

## Anchorages

*Bagh Gleann nam Muc* is on the south side of the west entrance of Corryvreckan. The tidal stream provides shelter from any swell, except from northwest at slack water.

Owing to the strength and uncertain direction of the currents among the islands this anchorage should only be approached or left within half an hour of slack water at springs, or within an hour at neaps.

A submerged rock lies in mid-channel east of Eilean Beag, and drying rocks lie near the shore on either side; another submerged rock lies 1½ cables east of Buige Rock. The head of the bay is divided by a rocky promontory; the better anchorage is on its west side.

*Bagh Gleann a' Mhaoil* on the southeast of Scarba provides temporary anchorage out of the main tidal stream, in which to wait for a favourable tide through the gulf.

*Kinuachdrach (Kinnochtie)*, on the northeast corner of Jura or **Port an Tiobart**, immediately to the north, provide occasional anchorages to explore ashore or to wait for a favourable tide through the Gulf.

# Grey Dogs
56°12′N 5°43′W

Bealach a' Choin Ghlais on the charts, and sometimes known as Little Corryvreckan, the passage between Lunga and the north end of Scarba is at times more hazardous than Corryvreckan itself. It is less than a cable wide at its narrowest point, with a group of islets and rocks above water in the eastern entrance.

## Tides

The flood tide runs westwards, beginning about +0430 Oban (–0100 Dover) at springs; +0515 Oban (–0015 Dover) at neaps.

The ebb runs eastwards, beginning about –0145 Oban (+0515 Dover) at springs; –0100 Oban (+0600 Dover) at neaps.

That is the principle, but even local fishermen say they don't know to within an hour either side of the expected time when it will turn.

The spring rate is about eight knots. Strong eddies, and standing waves in the fairway, arise, particularly at springs, and of course there is much less space to manoeuvre than in the Gulf.

Except at slack water the eddies make it very difficult to keep a boat under control, and the ebb is more dangerous in that it tends to set a boat onto the islets.

As less volume of water passes through, the race to the west is less extensive than at Corryvreckan.

## Directions

Pass through only at slack water or with the very last of the flood. If necessary wait, on the east side just north of a jetty half a mile south of the north end of Scarba, or on the west side at Camas a' Mhor-Fhir, a deep inlet on the southwest side of Lunga.

Grey Dogs with standing waves at the height of a spring flood tide (1996)

Port an Tiobart, Jura, an occasional anchorage, at which to wait for the tide to approach Corryvreckan (2006)

Grey Dogs (Bealach a'Choin Ghlas) from Scarba. A prawn-fisherman going west
through the *bealach* with a flood (west-going) spring tide has hit the east-going eddy
which runs at 6–8 knots (1996)

# Loch Crinan

56°06′N 5°33′W

Loch Crinan is sheltered from the open sea, but because it is shallow quite a steep chop can build up. The only good shelter outside the canal basin is in Crinan Harbour, a quarter of a mile west of the canal entrance, but this is full of moorings. In anything but heavy weather from north or west, however, good anchorage can be had near the canal entrance on a bottom of sand and clay.

## Tides

**Loch Beag** (56°09′N 5°36′W)
Constant –0100 Oban (+0600 Dover).
*Height in metres*

| MHWS | MHWN | MTL | MLWN | MLWS |
|------|------|-----|------|------|
| 2·4 | 1·7 | 1·4 | 1·1 | 0·3 |

Tidal streams east of the 10-metre contour are slight.

## Landmarks

From north of west the hotel at Crinan, a large white building, is conspicuous. Duntrune Castle, on the north side of the loch, tends to merge into the background.

Four yellow light-buoys near the shores of the loch have no navigational significance.

## Approach

*From southward* keep at least half a cable off Ardnoe Point.

*From the Dorus Mor* make for the hotel.

*From Loch Craignish* either pass southwest of Eilean nan Coinean (Rabbit Island), or east of it, keeping at least a cable off Scodaig, the point of the mainland here, to avoid submerged rocks southwest of the point. A rock half a cable east of Rabbit Island normally stands above water but may be covered by a very high tide.

Black Rock, two cables north of the hotel, stands above water, with a drying reef extending half a cable east of it. The head of the loch dries up to half a mile, the low-water line lying roughly on a line joining Duntrune Castle to the two islands at the head of the loch and continuing to a point two cables east of the canal entrance.

## Lights

At night the light beacon at the canal entrance shows Fl.WG.3s8m4M, white from 114° to 146° and green from 146° clockwise to 280°. The white sector leads close southwest of Rabbit Island and well southwest of Black Rock.

Lights on either side of the sea lock entrance show 2F.R(vert) on the east side and 2F.G(vert) on the west side.

## Anchorages

*Crinan Harbour* west of the hotel, is full of moorings but some are available for visitors. Go alongside the pontoon and ask at the office or call Crinan Boats on VHF.

*Crinan* anchor off the hotel as convenient, keeping clear of the approach both to the canal lock and to the pier. Yachts may berth temporarily at the pier, but a fishing boat may park unceremoniously on top of you. Permission should be sought from the head lock-keeper to remain alongside. The outer part of the pier is smooth concrete without ladders, and the inner part is piled but equipped with ladders. Fender boards are desirable, and there may not be enough depth for larger boats. If anchored off, the best landing is at a slip and concrete jetty on the west side of the canal lock.

*Canal basin* – often very full of fishing boats, especially at weekends and yachts may be subject to minor damage. If staying even overnight it may be best to berth above the next lock. Long term moorings are available for six-month periods at Bellanoch Basin, but there are now no visitors' berths there. For longer periods of berthing yachts have to comply with British Waterways safety standards for which the lock keeper at Crinan or the canal office at Ardrishaig will provide details.

Crinan basin from southwest, with the sea lock at the left of the photo and the pier with the canal to Ardrishaig at the top (1991)

Yachts on a through passage to or from the Clyde are at present exempt.

Winter laying-up at Cairnbaan with craning-out and launching on fixed dates in October and April; preferred maximum size 10m LOA, absolute maximum 12m.

## Crinan Canal

For details of the canal see the *Yachtsman's Pilot, Clyde to Colonsay*.

The sea lock is normally left open, day and night, and you can usually go straight in unless it is filling or emptying or you are directed to stand off. Make ready warps and fenders before approaching. Ladders are fixed on both walls. There is often quite a strong current out of the lock due to the runoff from the canal, so it may be best to get the bow warp ashore first; however if the lock-keeper is standing by to take your warps he may want to take the stern warp, in which case keep some way on to stem the current and avoid being swung across the lock. There may be no-one to take ropes at all, so have a crew member ready to go up the ladder. Ropes should be led well fore and aft to keep the boat under control.

If water is in short supply (which, although it may seem surprising in the Scottish climate, is not uncommon) the use of the sea lock may be limited to half-tide and above.

River Add from southeast (1991)

The lock is operated by a lock-keeper. While the lock is filling keep both warps tight; the bow warp may have to be led to a winch or windlass to control the boat.

At lock 14 the rough masonry has now been faced with timber. At all 'inland' locks it is usual to take the stern warp ashore first to check way on entering the lock, but during and after heavy rain there may be a strong current out of 'uphill' locks.

Hours of operation from mid May to early October 0800–1800 daily; mid-March to mid-May; October to beginning of November, Monday to Saturday 0800–1650; November to mid-March Monday to Friday 0915–1600. These times may vary from year to year, and the sea lock may stay open later; check with canal office, ☎ 01546 603210. The canal is usually closed during parts of October and November for maintenance work.

*River Add* in the southeast corner of the loch is only suitable for shoal-draught boats, and is only accessible in quiet weather, although well sheltered once inside. A bar lies between drying sandbanks at the river mouth, and the position of the channel at the bar marked by two small buoys.

To enter the river (in suitable conditions and with an appropriate boat) keep Black Rock astern in line with the 11-metre islet at the south end of Garreasar (off Craignish Point) bearing 304°; this should lead to the north side of the channel at the bar. When you have almost run out of water turn to head for the tangent of the west side of the river bank and feel your way in. A pool with a depth of two metres lies off the old ferry slip on the west side.

*Gallanach Bay* on the north side of the loch, northwest of Duntrune Castle, is a pleasant anchorage in offshore winds.

### Services and supplies at Crinan

Fully equipped boatyard, chandlery and chart agent (Crinan Boats). Diesel and water from Crinan Boats' pontoon at the mouth of Crinan Harbour. Launderette and showers at Crinan Boats. Diesel also by hose at the west side of the canal basin; ask at the coffee shop. Water hose at corner of coffee shop and above lock 14. *Calor Gas* at chandlery. Refuse disposal; skip at southwest corner of basin. A diver can be arranged. Moorings from Crinan Boats.

Limited range of provisions at chandlery and at coffee shop; greater range at Bellanoch, two miles along canal. Hotel with restaurant, and coffee shop beside canal basin.

*Communications* Phone box beside canal basin. Post office at Bellanoch. Crinan Boats VHF Ch 12, 16, 37. Sea Lock VHF Ch 74.
Telephone numbers:
Crinan Boats ☎ 01546 830232
Crinan Hotel ☎ 01546 830235
Lock-keeper ☎ 01546 830211
Canal Office (Ardrishaig) ☎ 01546 603210
*Fax* 603941.

# Loch Craignish

56°10′N 5°33′W

This is an ideal west coast loch, with easy access, a variety of anchorages, and splendid scenery. The drawbacks are the squalls which come with the scenery and, for those who like solitude, the popularity of the loch. The east side is wild and, in a modest way, mountainous, and the west side relatively highly populated. A string of islands lies on either side, with a navigable channel behind those on the east side but not on the west. There is a well established yacht centre at the head of the loch with pontoons, and moorings are usually available.

The two main islands on the east side are Eilean Macaskin and Eilean Righ, and those on the west side Eilean Dubh and Eilean Mhic Chrion.

There may be severe squalls in easterly and northeasterly winds, especially near the east side of the loch, and westerly winds can produce surprises at times, particularly close under the lee of islands.

## Tides

**Loch Beag** (56°09′N 5°36′W)
Constant –0100 Oban (+0600 Dover).
*Height in metres*

| MHWS | MHWN | MTL | MLWN | MLWS |
|------|------|-----|------|------|
| 2·4 | 1·7 | 1·4 | 1·1 | 0·3 |

The height of tide is very much affected by wind and barometric pressure, and a strong southwesterly may raise the tide one metre higher than predicted in tide tables, and a strong northeasterly depress it, although to a lesser extent. Tidal streams throughout the loch are generally no more than one knot.

I. NETHER LORN

Loch Craignish, looking over Goat Island, between Eilean Macaskin and Eilean Righ from the east shore. Mull stands on the horizon, beyond Luing and Rubha Fiola (1983)

### Approach

The main fairway is almost entirely free from hazards, other than very close inshore, although if coming from Crinan, or tacking, note that a reef extends more than a cable SSW of Eilean Macaskin, but the tip of the reef is normally above water.

In strong southerly winds, particularly on the ebb, there are moderate overfalls abreast of Eilean Macaskin, where the bottom abruptly shoals.

Sgeir Dubh Mhic Lartai 1½ cables SSW of Eilean Dubh is normally above water, but could be covered by a high tide, and needs to be watched out for if tacking. To the east of the northeast end of Eilean Mhic Chrion, Sgeir Dubh, 0·6 metre high, has shoal water extending at least half a cable all round it.

The passage on the east side of the loch (for rocks east of Rabbit Island see page 18) has a number of submerged rocks of unspecified depth, particularly off the southeast side of Eilean Macaskin and off the northeast end of Eilean Righ.

The first are cleared by keeping east of mid-channel when approaching the narrowest part at Eilean Macaskin, and the second by standing well on towards the mainland before altering course towards Sgeir Dubh. There are many fish cages in this channel, and they are thought to be encroaching beyond the area designated for them.

### Anchorages

*Goat Island (Eilean nan Gabhar)* between Eilean Macaskin and Eilean Righ. The anchorage lies between Goat Island and the skerry to the east.

Approach from the eastern channel, although local boats do use the passage through the reef to the north of Goat Island.

If attempting this, note a rock awash ½ cables off the southwest point of Eilean Righ; the least depth between the rock and the point is 2·4 metres.

The passage south of Goat Island has a least depth of 0·9 metre and a bottom of clean sand.

There is limited swinging room and depth between Goat Island and the skerry, but a partly submerged reef extends east from Goat Island. The bottom is sand with some clay.

*Eilean Righ* provides some shelter off the east side of the middle of the island, opposite the old farmhouse.

In easterly winds shelter may be found in bays on the east side of the channel, if space can be found clear of the fish cages. An anchorage area for visiting yachts is marked out by lateral buoys between the entrance and the NW shore. For services and supplies see Ardfern, below.

*Bagh na Cille* on the west side of the loch, about a mile northeast of Craignish Point is a suitable anchorage for quiet weather, but a drying reef lies towards the southwest side of the bay, and a 2·4-metre submerged rock lies one cable off the middle of the bay. See page 12.

*Eilean Dubh* in an area sometimes known as The Lagoon between Eilean Dubh and Eilean Mhic Chrion and the Craignish peninsula. Approach between the two islands, not (for the benefit of anyone foolish enough to be cruising here without a detailed chart) through any opening facing south.

A rock awash lies nearly ½ cable ESE of the 1-metre high rock in the middle of the gap; keep at least a cable offshore until the 1-metre rock is abaft the beam before turning to pass north of the rock. An anchorage area for visiting yachts is marked out by lateral buoys between the entrance and the NW shore. For services and supplies see Ardfern, below.

## Ardfern

Ardfern Yacht Centre lies north of Eilean Mhic Chrion. It is well sheltered except from strong northeast winds; many yachts are left on moorings here over the winter. There is almost no space for anchoring as most of the area is taken up with moorings. An apparently inviting space towards the north end is occupied by a drying rock with a rock awash ¼ cable east of it; these rocks are ½ cable south of the smaller and more southerly of two tidal islets close to the mainland.

### Approach

Note the above-water rock, Sgeir Dubh, with shoal water round it. The passage north of Eilean Inshaig, which is east of the moorings, is straightforward. A Wavebreaker pontoon has been installed at the south end of En. Inshaig, with a G light Fl. on its south end and a red light buoy, Fl.R close to the south shore, and a clear passage between them. Visitors' berths at south and east face of outside pontoons of marina, or at wavebreaker, or as advised by marina staff. A berth can usually be found alongside.

Space is nominally available for anchoring between the northwest side of Eilean Inshaig and the moorings, as well as east of Inshaig, but a good anchor light is needed in the last position.

### Services and Supplies

Ardfern Yacht Centre provides moorings and pontoon berths, and has a 20-ton mobile hoist and laying up space ashore. Trailer-sailers can be launched at the slip. Repairs under cover; engineer. Diesel inshore at south end of pontoons. Water at pontoons; chandlery and *Calor Gas* at head of pier. Refuse disposal. Showers.

Hotel, restaurant, bar, all ¼ mile to the south.

Shop half way to hotel. Bus to Oban.

*Communications* Phone box at marina and beside hotel. VHF at marina Ch 80 during working hours; Ch 16 should not be used.

Yacht Centre ☎ 01852 500247 *Fax* 500624

Galley of Lorn Hotel ☎ 01852 500284

Ardfern from southeast (2003). A wavebreaker pontoon has been added with
a passage between its left-hand end and the shore of Eilean Dubh

# Loch Shuna

56°13′N 5°35′W

The area east of Luing is sheltered except from strong southerly winds, and the surrounding shores are rather more gentle in character than much of the rest of the coast.

Craobh marina with a residential development stands on the east shore.

The east side of Shuna island is clean except for a rock awash northeast of the landing place for Shuna House, towards the north end of the island.

Several dangers lie well off the east shore of the loch, as described below.

The waters to the south of the south end of Luing are described on pages 11–14.

Culbhaie clearing mark – Reisa an t-Sruith just open west of Eilean Mhic Phaidean leads west of Culbhaie 208°

## Tides

**Loch Beag** (56°09′N 5°36′W)

Constant –0100 Oban (+0600 Dover).

*Height in metres*

| MHWS | MHWN | MTL | MLWN | MLWS |
|------|------|-----|------|------|
| 2·4 | 1·7 | 1·4 | 1·1 | 0·3 |

**Seil Sound** (56°17′N 5°36′W)

Constant -0025 Oban (-0555 Dover).

*Height in metres*

| MHWS | MHWN | MTL | MLWN | MLWS |
|------|------|-----|------|------|
| 2·7 | 2·0 | 1·6 | 1·1 | 0·4 |

Tidal streams are generally negligible except in Shuna Sound where they reach one knot on the flood and two knots on the ebb.

## Dangers and clearing marks

At the south entrance to Loch Shuna, Culbhaie, a group of rocks ¼ mile off the east shore, dries 1·5 metres with other rocks within ½ cable of its west side. These are cleared to the west by keeping Kilchoan Farm, a conspicuous white house on the north side of Loch Melfort bearing 011°, open west of Eilean Creagach, which is about a mile south of Arduaine Point. See photo on page 24. Alternatively, the east side of Reisa an t-Sruith bearing 208°, open

| Craignish | Eilean Ona | | Reisa Mhic Phaidean | Reisa an t-Sruith |
|-----------|------------|--|---------------------|-------------------|

Eilean Creagach (2003)

of the west side of Reisa Mhic Phaidean, clears the west side of Culbhaie (see sketch on page 23).

The passage between Shuna and the two main islands to the east is clean except for a rock awash northeast of Shuna. East of these islands careful attention to the chart is needed, although a direct passage from southward of Eilean Creagach to Craobh Haven or to Asknish Bay is straightforward. These will be described under Anchorages, below.

Shuna Sound is generally clean on the Shuna side, but there are rocks off the Luing shore both submerged and drying, notably off its south end and off a drying bay a mile north of the south end; the 15-metre contour will keep you clear of these.

A mile north of Shuna, Scoul Eilean has a rock awash one cable south of its south end and a submerged rock close southeast of the island.

Degnish Point at the south of the entrance to Seil Sound has several drying and submerged rocks off its west and south sides.

### Approach

*From south* see Passage notes for Dorus Mor (pages 11–14). Note the clearing marks described above to avoid Culbhaie which dries 1·5 metres, ¼ mile from the east shore. Pass between Shuna and the islands to the east of it, or through Shuna Sound, to the west of Shuna.

*From west* – unless coming through Cuan Sound – keep two cables off Ard Luing, or outwith the 15-metre contour to avoid rocks inshore. To the north of Shuna and the Arduaine peninsula note the various hazards described above under the heading 'Dangers and Clearing Marks'.

If waiting here for a fair tide in the Sound of Luing, there is a temporary anchorage off a bay ¼ mile north of Ard Luing – not the bay one mile north of the point, in the mouth of which there are many rocks.

## Craobh Haven

56°12′·5N 5°33′W

A substantial development on the east side of Loch Shuna with all conveniences. The name is pronounced 'creuve'.

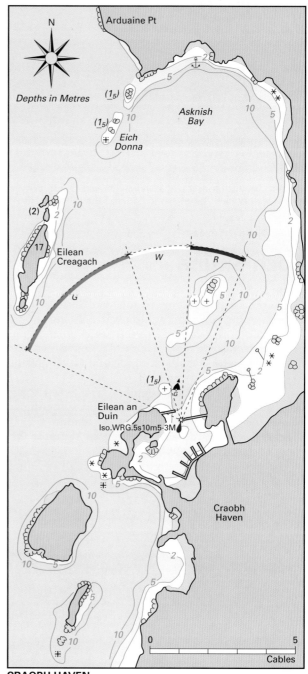

**CRAOBH HAVEN**

Craobh Haven from east (2003)

## Approach

*From west*, leaving the green conical buoy north of Eilean an Duin to starboard.

An extensive patch of drying and submerged rocks lies ¼ mile north of Eilean Buidhe, and many drying rocks lie inshore and to the NNE of Eilean Buidhe.

Inside the entrance a line of red can buoys marks submerged rocks on the east side of the harbour.

In the bay on the west side of the harbour a drying reef projecting more than half the width of the bay from its north side is marked by a perch.

## Lights

A sectored light beacon stands on the head of the east breakwater, Iso.WRG.5s.10m5-3M showing white from 162° to 183°.

## Services and Supplies

Pontoon berths, boatyard with slip and mobile hoist. Divers, refuse disposal, showers, laundrette. Water, diesel, *Calor Gas*, chandlery. Shop, pub/restaurant, coffee shop. Bus to Oban.

*Communications* Phone box.

Craobh Marina ☎ 01852 500222 *Fax* 500252 VHF Ch 37 and 80 call sign *Craobh*.

## Anchorages

*Kilchattan Bay (Toberonochy)* 56°13′N 5°38′W on the east side of Luing, nearly two miles north of the south point of the island, is mostly shoal but it is usually possible to anchor north of the village.

At the north end of Shuna there is a bay with the remains of a stone quay on its west side. Coming from the east, take care to avoid a drying reef which extends ½ cable north of the east point of the bay. Anchor no further in than abreast of the quay, as the head of the bay is shoal, with a drying reef on its southwest side.

*Asknish Bay* 56°14′N 5°33′W

Approach from south, but take care to avoid the drying rocks three cables off the east shore.

A line of drying rocks, Eich Donna, extends three cables SSW from the Arduaine peninsula towards Eilean Creagach, and a drying reef extends more than half a cable NNE from the islet at the north end of Eilean Creagach with a clear passage ¼ mile wide between the reef and Eich Donna.

Some local yachtsmen use a passage between the most northerly rock of Eich Donna, which dries 1·5 metres, and Arduaine, keeping about 20 metres from the shore.

Anchor as convenient, clear of moorings in sand and weed; or, if visiting the hotel, use one of the moorings provided for visitors. The best landing is in a crack in the rocky promontory south of the hotel.

An alternative anchorage north of Arduaine (see below) is preferable in southerly winds.

Loch Melfort Hotel has a restaurant and provides bar lunches and showers. ☎ 01852 200233.

# Loch Melfort

The northeast branch of Loch Shuna, north of the Arduaine peninsula. Campbell Rock in the middle of the loch has 1·8 metres over it, but for most boats this would rarely be a hazard. The south side of Eilean Gamhna touching the north point of Shuna 245° leads southeast of Campbell Rock.

On the north side of the loch, Eilean Coltair has a drying reef extending one cable from its south end and a drying rock one cable from its east side. A rock two metres high stands nearly half a mile east of Eilean Coltair.

Other hazards in Loch Melfort lie within half a cable of the shore, or within bays and anchorages where they will be referred to separately.

### Anchorages

*Arduaine* in a bay ½ mile ENE of the west point of Arduaine (Asknish) Point. A rock in the middle of the bay, ½ cable from the high-water line, dries 1·5 metres and there are visitors' moorings for the hotel to the west of it. For hotel see previous page.

*Kames Bay* on the south side of the loch, nearly two miles from Arduaine Point, lies behind a promontory on which stand several bungalows facing west.

On the south side of the bay a concrete pier stands at the end of a small promontory.

A reef, with intermittent heads just submerged, extends 1½ cable northwest of the pier. Some of the bay is occupied by fish cages.

Melfort Pier and Kilmelford from north west (2007)

Much of the southwest bight of the bay dries but an area of deep water lies between the reef and the drying foreshore, although most of the best water is taken up by moorings. There is said to be space for a few visiting yachts to anchor at the south end of this bight.

Keep away from the pier (even with dinghies) as it is heavily used by the fish farm's workboats.

Services at Kilmelford Yacht Haven, about a mile by road.

# Loch na Cille and Kilmelford
56°15'·5N 5°29'·5W

The head of the loch dries off for two cables, and the inlet is full of moorings, some of which are available for visitors.

### Dangers and marks

At the entrance to Loch na Cille a red perch with a red can topmark stands on the end of a reef on the north side, and a green perch with a green triangular topmark marks a rock awash on the south side of the inlet.

### Services and supplies

The pier, on the south side, has a floating pontoon with diesel and water. Chandlery, *Calor Gas*, repairs to engine, hull and rigging. Moorings for hire; slipping, and winter storage ashore.

Shop, post office, telephone, and hotel at Kilmelford, one mile.

*Communications* VHF Ch 80. Kilmelford Yacht Haven ☎ 01852 200248 *Fax* 01852 200343.

# Fearnach Bay and Melfort Pier
56°16'N 5°30'W

A drying rock lies ½ cable off the west side of Fearnach Bay.

### Lights

Dir FR at head of pier and Dir FG at entrance to boat harbour east of pier.

### Services and supplies

Some berths at pontoons at the end of the pier with two metres depth alongside. Berth at the pier itself with one metre depth. Yachts may dry out alongside the inner end of the pier for repairs (within the limitations of the tidal range); ask first at the office. Space is reserved for visiting yachts to anchor off the pier.

Water, diesel and gas at the pier, and mains electricity can be provided. Showers and laundry are ¾ mile northeast of the pier. Moorings for hire (up to 60′ outer trot, 20′ inner trot).

Pub/restaurant (The Shower of Herring) ☎ 01852 200345 ½ mile east of the pier and Melfort Mermaid, close to pier ☎ 01852 200333 near the pier; shop, post office, telephone, and hotel at Kilmelford, 1½ miles.

*Communications* ☎ 01852 200333 *Fax* 200329. VHF Ch 16, 12.

Ardinamir, with Cuan Sound beyond, from southeast. The more westerly green perch has been demolished, and a red perch, not shown in this photo, stands on the drying rock on the south side of the entrance (1991)

# Ardinamir

56°15′N 5°37′W

A small bay between the northeast side of Luing and Torsa, west of Degnish Point. This is one of the most popular anchorages on the west coast, with a very tricky entrance between drying rocks, marked with perches with triangular topmarks, erected by the CCC. The east perch (green) stands on a rock which dries 0·3m on the north side of the channel, and the west perch (red) stands on a rock which dries 1·5m on the south side of the channel. A rock sill at a depth of 1·2m lies across the channel south of the green perch, and another, which dries 1·1m lies across the channel north of the red perch. The deepest water lies about 15m south of the green perch, and about the same distance north of the red perch.

## Approach

*From the south* keep at least ½ cable offshore to avoid drying reefs inshore. The perches may be difficult to pick out against the shore; take care not to go too far north before identifying them.

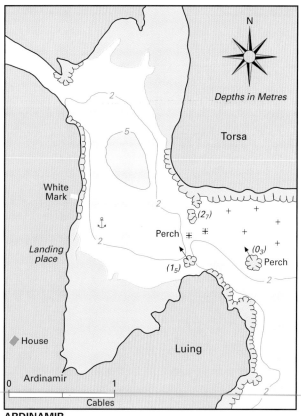

**ARDINAMIR**

*From the north* keep a cable off the southeast side of Torsa and stay outwith the 5-metre contour until the perches have been identified.

Pass 10 to 20 metres south of the east perch, and the same distance north of the west perch; neither of them is on the extremity of the rock which it marks. If the perches are not seen approach very cautiously, keeping a conspicuous white paint mark on the west side of the bay just open of the south point of the entrance, bearing 290° and hold this bearing until the bay opens up.

### Anchorage

Anchor north of a line that joins the rock off the south point of the entrance to a fence on the west shore as most of the bay dries south of this line (see the air photo with cattle standing in the water there). A strong tide runs through the gap between Luing and Torsa Beag at the northwest end of the bay for two hours after HW and the bottom between this gap and the entrance is deep, with soft mud. It is quite usual for yachts there to drag their anchors. Several moorings are laid in the bay for work-boats and yachts.

### Services and supplies

Water may be available from a tap at the house on the north side of the track; shop, post office, phone box and *Calor Gas* at Cullipool, 1½ miles.

# Seil Sound

56°17′N 5°36′W

Entered between Degnish Point and Torsa, Seil Sound runs north between Seil and the mainland, and narrows abruptly to become Clachan Sound.

### Tides

Constant –0025 Oban (–0555 Dover).

*Height in metres*

| MHWS | MHWN | MTL | MLWN | MLWS |
|------|------|-----|------|------|
| 2·7 | 2·0 | 1·6 | 1·1 | 0·4 |

### Dangers

Rocks at the north end of Torsa, both awash and submerged, lie between one and two cables NNE of the point.

Drying rocks extend a cable SSW of Ardmaddy Point on the east side of the sound.

*Balvicar Bay* at the north end of Seil Sound is completely sheltered but much of it dries out. Most of the area west of Eilean Tornal is occupied by moorings.

The channel east of Eilean Tornal is clean except for a submerged rock nearly a cable ESE of the south end of the island.

Two cables beyond the north end of the island drying and above-water rocks lie on both sides of the passage.

Balvicar boatyard: moorings and repairs ☎ 01852 300557.

Balvicar Boatyard from northeast. Eilean Tornal in foreground (2003)

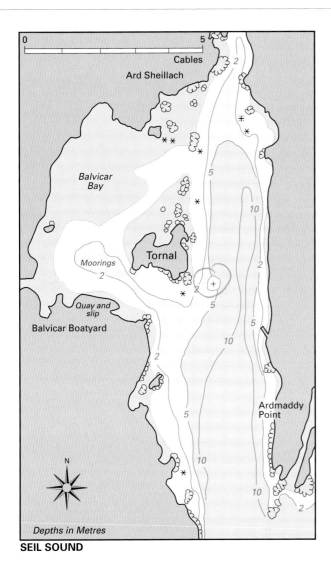

**SEIL SOUND**

### Services and supplies

Petrol at Clachan Bridge. Shop at Balvicar. Pub at Clachan Bridge, two miles. Hotel at Clachan Seil. Bus to Oban.

*Communications* Post office, phone box. Also telephone at pub at Clachan Bridge.

# Clachan Sound

56°19′N 5°35′W

An electricity supply cable crosses the sound north of the bridge. The charted clearance at the bridge is 6·7 metres, and 10 metres under the electricity cable.

A motor boat – or a shoal-draught boat able to lower her mast easily – might find this a painless alternative to the Firth of Lorn on a blowy day, given enough rise of tide to get over the bar at the north end.

### Tides

Tidal streams run strongly between Clachan Bridge and the north end of the sound. Heights and constant are as Oban.

*Height in metres* at Oban

| MHWS | MHWN | MTL | MLWN | MLWS |
|------|------|-----|------|------|
| 4·0 | 2·9 | 2·4 | 1·8 | 0·7 |

The figures for Seil Sound are

Constant –0025 Oban (–0555 Dover).

*Height in metres*

| MHWS | MHWN | MTL | MLWN | MLWS |
|------|------|-----|------|------|
| 2·7 | 2·0 | 1·6 | 1·1 | 0·4 |

Clachan Sound provides a passage for small boats, strictly limited by headroom at Clachan Bridge, and by draft to high tide. The most shoal point is a bar of slate waste from a long-abandoned quarry about ½ mile north of the bridge. This bar is reported to dry 2·4 metres at the north end of the sound (although charted as drying 1·5 metres), so that the passage is available only to shoal draft-boats

Clachan Bridge from northeast (2003)

towards high water. Headroom at the bridge is charted as 6·7 metres, relative to the new HAT datum (see page 7). A further complication is that the tidal range north of the sound is much greater than that south of the Sound, so that at the time when one would probably choose to make the passage, the stream is flowing south, although still rising, and flowing north, at Oban.

For the benefit of owners of shoal-draft boats, the following details are based on observations by David Foster, who lives on the shore of Clachan Sound. The passage is described from south to north.

The Sound is entered east of Ard Sheillach on Seil Island, on which stand several houses. Most of the passage is occupied by permanent moorings for local boats, and several private landing stages, possibly to be supplemented by a further landing stage for a commercial boat. There are no visitors' moorings, or designated anchoring area. To clear a shoal spit, and oyster beds on the west side of the passage, pass ESE of the first group of four moorings, keeping close ESE of the most northerly mooring of this group, heading for a RW pole to the left of a white house on the east shore (photo A). Note that another RW pole on a rocky outcrop further right is easier to identify initially, but is not the one to steer for. A pink buoy to stbd marks the limit of oyster beds there.

Another RW pole marks the HW line of a rock NE of Ard Sheillach on the west side of the passage, and when the pontoon landing stages north of it come into view, steer for them (photo B). A further four moorings lie in this reach, and it is usual to pass west of them. When past these alter course towards the west shore, heading for a conspicuous wall of five courses of stone-filled gabions (a new water-treatment plant, photo C). North of this plant stands a W house (Fasgadh, photo D); when an inconspicuous W drum on a pole is in line with the SE corner of the house (not the conservatory attached to its NE end), steer on this line to clear drying stones on the east side of the channel. South east of Fasgadh stands a round-topped rock which rarely covers, and ESE of the house a rock on the east side of the channel which only uncovers at a low spring tide.

After passing the water treatment plant steer ENE for the largest tree on the right-hand slope of a small flat-topped hill (photo E), until you can see the next group of four moorings clear of 'Fasgadh SE rock'. From here steer north to pass close either side of the moorings. Following this lies a (final) scattered group of moorings, the main line of which lies to the west of mid-channel. Two submerged spits extend from the west side, about 50 and 100 metres south

Clachan Sound from north, at high water (2003)

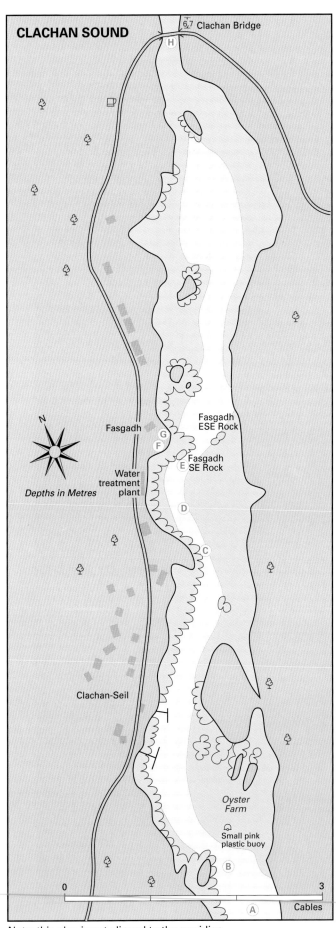

**CLACHAN SOUND**

6.7 Clachan Bridge

Fasgadh

Fasgadh
ESE Rock

Fasgadh
SE Rock

Water
treatment
plant

*Depths in Metres*

Clachan-Seil

*Oyster
Farm*

Small pink
plastic buoy

0                                    3

Cables

Note: this plan is not aligned to the meridian

RW banded pole

A on Clachan Sound plan, east shore

RW banded
pole

Pontoons

Oyster farm buoy

B on Clachan Sound plan

Water treatment plant

Fasgadh

C on Clachan Sound plan

Corner of house

W drum on post

D Clachan Sound plan, Fasgadh

THE ISLE OF MULL AND ADJACENT COASTS **31**

of the bridge. From the south east side of the moorings pass through the gap between the third and fourth mooring from the bridge, heading for the west side of the arch.

Keep in mid channel north of the bridge. The shallowest point lies about ½ mile north of the bridge, apparently drying 2·4 metres at chart datum, followed by a pool, and a further drying bar, where a pair of low W posts on the shore on Seil (astern) lead north east through the deepest water.

After passing through Clachan Sound, to avoid the reef Eich Donna north of Seil, keep Clachan Bridge hidden behind the land on the west side of the Sound (see photo on page 49).

The passage is regularly used by an oyster farmer, in a RIB.

E on Clachan Sound plan, page 31

F on Clachan Sound plan, page 31, channel south of Fasgadh

G on Clachan Sound plan, page 31

H on Clachan Sound plan, page 31

I. NETHER LORN

# Cuan Sound

56°16′N 5°38′W

The dogleg passage between Seil and Luing provides a convenient passage between Lochs Shuna and Melfort and the Firth of Lorn, but it has some dangers and needs much greater care than the Sound of Luing. Tides run strongly with eddies on both sides, and overfalls at the west entrance when a west wind opposes the flood tide. The sound is crossed by overhead power cables which have clear headroom of 35 metres.

From the west the entrance is most easily identified by the pylons of the overhead cable, but they are pale in colour and not always easy to see.

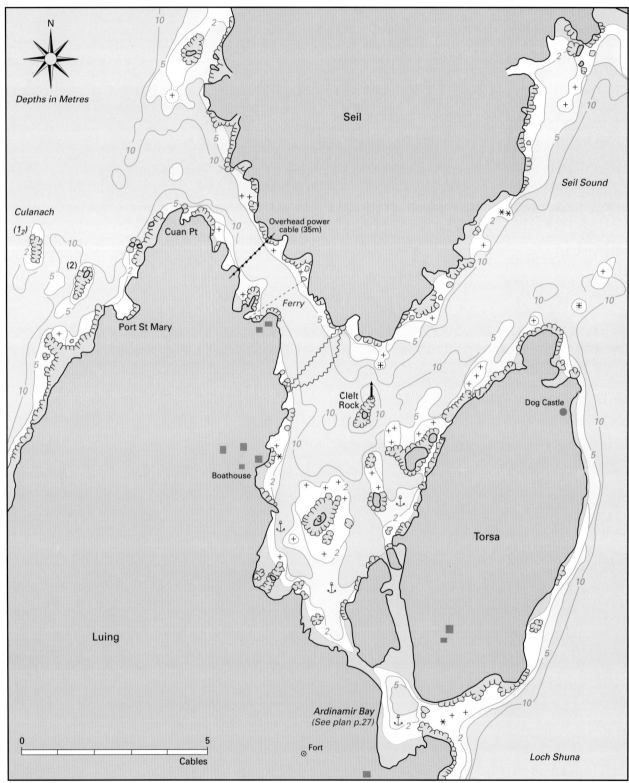

CUAN SOUND

Cuan Sound, from the north end of Luing, at low spring tide. The rocks off Rubha Breac, as well as one off the north end of Torsa, are showing (2000)    *Photo H W King*

### Tides

The flood tide runs westwards, beginning about +0430 Oban (–0100 Dover) at springs, +0515 Oban (–0015 Dover) at neaps.

The ebb runs eastwards, beginning about –0145 Oban (+0515 Dover) at springs, –0100 Oban (+0600 Dover) at neaps.

The stream reaches its greatest strength soon after turning; in the western part of the sound the spring rate in both directions is seven knots.

### Seil Sound

Constant –0025 Oban (–0555 Dover).

*Height in metres*

| MHWS | MHWN | MTL | MLWN | MLWS |
|------|------|-----|------|------|
| 2·7  | 2·0  | 1·6 | 1·1  | 0·4  |

### Firth of Lorn (as Carsaig, Mull)

Constant –0010 Oban (–0540 Dover).

*Height in metres*

| MHWS | MHWN | MTL | MLWN | MLWS |
|------|------|-----|------|------|
| 4·1  | 3·1  | 2·4 | 1·8  | 0·6  |

Cuan Sound, from the north end of Luing, at extra low spring tide, with both of the rocks north of the Cleit Rock showing    *Photo H W King*

## Dangers and marks

Rocks at the north end of Torsa, both awash and submerged, lie between one and two cables NNE of the point. In the east reach many submerged and drying rocks lie up to ¾ cable off each shore.

At Rubha Bhreac, the south point of Seil, the sound takes a pronounced bend northwards.

On the south side of the channel, Cleit Rock, a drying reef extending NNE from the islet An Cleiteadh, lies 1½ cables south of Rubha Bhreac. Cleit Rock is marked by a yellow perch with a triangular topmark, maintained by the CCC. The perch was reported in the past as not easy to see when approaching from the east, but it should be in line with the south end of a group of houses on the Luing shore ahead. Cleit Rock is separate from An Cleitadh at HW, and extends a few metres north of the perch.

Between the perch and Seil a rock awash lies slightly nearer to Seil than to the perch, and a submerged rock lies between the awash rock and Seil. The clear passage between Cleit Rock and the awash rock is, at the most, ¾ cable, and the currents will make it difficult to hold a steady course.

At the north west entrance of the sound, a submerged rock, at a depth of 1·1 metres, lies one cable west of the north point of the entrance, and one cable SSW of the above-water rock Sgeir nam Faiolean. The awash rock claims several victims each year, reported to have amounted to nine groundings in 2006.

## Directions

At the east end, to wait for a fair tide through the sound, anchor off the ruins of Dog Castle, two cables from the north end of Torsa.

*From east*, going westwards keep ¼ cable northeast of the north point of Torsa to pass inshore of the rock awash one cable off the point, or alternatively at least ¼ mile off the point to pass outside both rocks. If taking the inshore passage keep on a course north of west from the point to avoid a submerged rock 1·8 metres, a cable west of the point.

Keep in mid-channel in the east reach of the sound.

Cleit Rock beacon must be identified approximately in line with the south end of a group of houses on the shore of Luing, ahead. Pass ¼ to ½ cable north of the beacon, where eddies will make steering particularly difficult, and keep heading for the Luing shore until the west reach is well open.

Keep in mid-channel in the west reach and at the west entrance head about 280° for half a mile towards a point midway between the south end of Easdale Island and the islet Dubh fheith, before altering course (if making for Easdale Sound). Be ready for overfalls at the west entrance if there is much westerly wind, and beware of the rock on the north side (before 'Directions' above).

Cleit Rock in Cuan Sound, looking north from the islet An Cleitadh at about half ebb on a spring tide. Already the stream is less spectacular than during the early part of the ebb, when the rock was unapproachable

Cuan Sound – Cleit Rock from ENE. The perch is not at its outer end

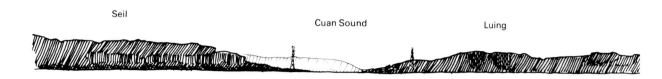

Seil          Cuan Sound          Luing

Cuan Sound from westward. The pylons are pale in colour and may not be easy to see

*From west* identify the entrance by the electricity cable pylons and approach with the entrance bearing about 100°. If approaching from Easdale Sound, keep west of a line joining Easdale Sound to the south pylon, to clear the submerged rock north of the entrance.

Cleit Rock beacon is easier to identify from this direction. Steer towards it and alter course to pass north of the rock; however, because of the orientation of the rock, the ebb tide is deflected to set strongly across the north end of Cleit Rock.

Keep in mid-channel in the east reach and, if heading south after leaving the sound, you can take the passage inside the rocks off the north end of Torsa as described above.

In either direction you can pass south of Cleit Rock, but submerged rocks lie half a cable southeast of the rock, so keep within ¼ cable of Cleit Rock on that side.

## Anchorages

See also photo on page 27.

*In Cuan Sound* in the bight south of Cleit Rock there are several well protected anchorages clear of the tidal stream. The most straightforward approach is along the Luing shore keeping more than half a cable off the shore to clear a drying rock off the boathouse. South of this, close the shore to ¼ cable to clear submerged rocks off the 3-metre islet and pass west of the ferry mooring, a spar buoy. A submerged rock, 1·3 metres, lies half a cable southwest of the islet. If anchoring south of the islet use a tripping line to avoid fouling old moorings.

*Other anchorages* in this bight are between the two islets off the west side of Torsa, and northwest of Torsa Beag which is the island southwest of Torsa; these anchorages are partly obstructed by fish farming.

## Services

Phone at Cuan Ferry, Calor Gas at Cullipool.

# Anchorages West side of Luing

## Poll Gorm

56°14'·35N 5°39'·4W

The approach to Poll Gorm, which lies NE of Eilean Mhic Chiarain, is best made around slack water. With Fladda Lighthouse bearing roughly NW astern, follow the coast of Eilean Mhic Chiarain as it bears away to the SE and S. The deeper water lies closer to Eilean Mhic Chiarain and shoal and drying rocks south of Diar Sgeir must be avoided. As the coast trends south a light coloured rock appears on the slopes of Eilean Mhic Chiarain. Here turn approximately east towards a perch which should be visible about two cables further east at the entrance to a passage between the inner reefs.

About one cable east of Eilean Mhic Chiarain, Poll Gorm opens to the north. Anchor so as to leave clear access to the lobster pond to the north of the pool, used by local fishermen to store their catches. Shelter is excellent but the tide runs strongly in the approaches.

The pool known as Back o' the Pond lies further in behind Fraoch Eilean, east of Poll Gorm. The perch referred to above marks the south end of a low rocky spit at the entrance to the very narrow entrance channel. Shave this perch close to port and follow the channel to the SE clearly visible between rocks. One of the former leading marks is still visible on the opposite shore but the other has disappeared. Once through the channel turn to port and proceed carefully towards the north. Deeper water lies towards Cullipool and anchorage may be found at the north end of the anchorage. The pool is very sheltered. For access from the north see page 38.

Poll Gorm, Cullipool, from northeast with Eilean Mhic Chiaran at the top and the narrow passage to Back of the Pond at bottom left (2003)

# Cullipool

56°15'N 5°39'W

The former slate-mining village on the west coast of Luing to the east of Fladda lighthouse has an occasional anchorage from which to visit the Garvellachs, begin a passage to Iona, or to wait for the tide in the Sound of Luing.

### Tides

Firth of Lorn (as Carsaig, Mull)
Constant –0010 Oban (–0540 Dover).
*Height in metres*

| MHWS | MHWN | MTL | MLWN | MLWS |
|------|------|-----|------|------|
| 4·1 | 3·1 | 2·4 | 1·8 | 0·6 |

### Approach

*From west*, with Fladda lighthouse bearing 270° astern in line with the highest point of Garbh Eileach, identify and keep in line ahead two beacons on shore with triangular topmarks 090°. Do not anchor on this line around HW, to avoid obstructing the passage of fishing boats to their moorings east of Fraoch Eilean, which they can only approach at that time.

*From north*, to pass inside Sgeir Bhuidhe, keep very close (about 10 metres) to Rubha Buidhe, heading for the skerries 1½ cables south of the point; increase the distance off to about 20 metres at the south end of the point. Do not attempt to pass between Sgeir Bhuidhe and the rocks on its east side.

### Anchorages

Photos page 37 and 39.

*Black Quay* southeast of Rubha Buidhe. From south hold onto the leading line described above until the passage west of Rubha Buidhe is clearly open, to avoid the rock awash a cable south of Sgeir Bhuidhe. Steer with Rubha Buidhe bearing about 011° to pass close west of the skerries south of the point and anchor between the quay and the skerries southwest of it in about four metres, black mud. The tide runs through this anchorage at about one knot. There are rings on the skerries to which to take a warp, but take care not to obstruct the passage.

*Fraoch Eilean* in the mouth of an inlet between Fraoch Eilean and the islet northeast of it. Access to the pool east of Fraoch Eilean is impracticable for anyone without intimate local knowledge; it can only be entered close to HW and the tides are very unpredictable.

### Supplies

Shop (with post office) ¼ mile along road to southeast. Water at standpipe in Cullipool old village, ½ mile north.

*Port St Mary* WSW of the entrance. Culanach, a large rock drying 1·2 metres lies about ¼ mile from the shore. An above-water rock inshore of Culanach should not be mistaken for the drying rock.

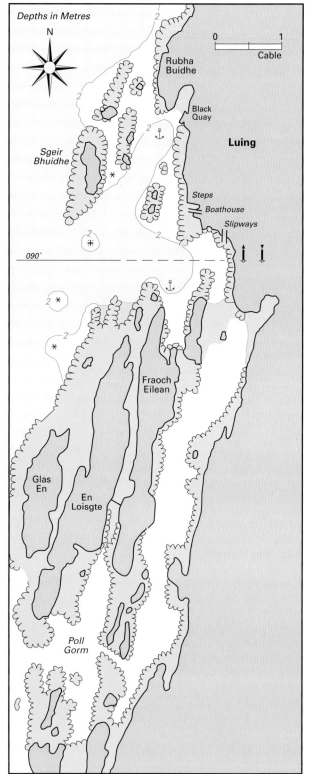

CULLIPOOL

*To wait for a fair tide* At the west end of the sound, Port Mary, three cables south of the south point of the entrance in a bay inshore of the 2-metre skerry.

**I. NETHER LORN**

Fladda from above Cullipool, Luing.
Note the submerged rocks beyond the reefs and islets off Cullipool itself (2000)   *Photo H W King*

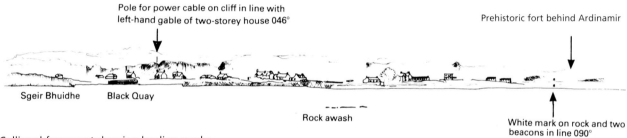

Pole for power cable on cliff in line with
left-hand gable of two-storey house 046°

Prehistoric fort behind Ardinamir

Sgeir Bhuidhe      Black Quay

Rock awash

White mark on rock and two
beacons in line 090°

Cullipool from west showing leading marks

Cullipool from the north end of Luing at a low spring tide.
Note the rocks in the approach to Cullipool (2000)   *Photo H. King*

# II. The Firth of Lorn

The Firth of Lorn is open to the Atlantic to the WSW and any sea from that direction becomes higher and steeper as the shores of the firth close in. If the ebb tide is running against an onshore wind conditions may be very unpleasant, particularly in contrast to the protected passages of the Sound of Luing and southward.

The main fairway of the firth is clean and it is only to the east and southeast of the Garvellachs that there are any significant unmarked rocks.

Slate for the roofs of Glasgow, Edinburgh, Dundee, Belfast and even America came from a small group of islands in this area during the 18th and 19th centuries. At first, of course, it was all carried in fairly unhandy sailing vessels, loading at islands in the tideway such as Belnahua. Building stone was also quarried, for example at Carsaig on Mull; there was no wharf and vessels were loaded at the base of the cliff where the stone was quarried. It's worth remembering these earlier seamen when we find it difficult making our way around in our handy modern cruiser-racers.

For the purpose of this Pilot the Firth of Lorn is taken to begin at Frank Lockwood's Island, close inshore south east of cliffs on Mull, east of Loch Buie. Carsaig and Loch Buie are described at the beginning of Chapter VII, on pages 124 and 125.

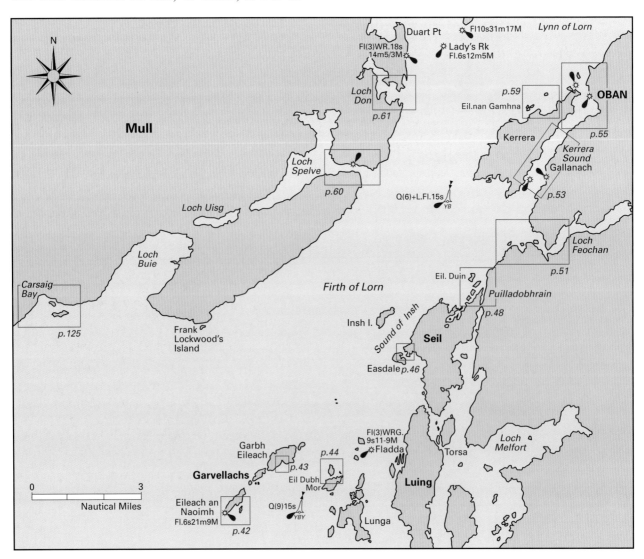

## Charts

*2386* and *2387* respectively cover the south and north parts of the Firth of Lorn at 1:25,000. The approach to the firth is also covered, together with waters further south and west on *2169* at 1:75,000, and the remainder on *2171*.

## Tides

In the fairway of the firth the stream turns progressively clockwise, setting northeastwards about +0430 Oban (–0100 Dover); southwestwards about –0155 Oban (+0500 Dover). Tidal streams generally run at one to 1½ knots but southeast of the Garvellachs the spring rate is two to three knots with an eddy setting southwestwards after half-flood. Between Fladda and Easdale the spring rate is three knots.

Constant averages –0010 Oban (–0540 Dover).

*Height in metres* at Carsaig (Mull)

| MHWS | MHWN | MTL | MLWN | MLWS |
|------|------|-----|------|------|
| 4·1 | 3·1 | 2·4 | 1·8 | 0·6 |

## Dangers and marks

The two main dangers are separate submerged rocks, six miles apart, both named Bogha Nuadh, and both marked by buoys. One, halfway between Fladda and Easdale has a red can light buoy on its east side, and swell usually breaks on it. To distinguish it from the other its buoy is named on the chart as Bono Rock. Another rock, Bogha Ghair ¼ mile NNE of the buoy, with four metres over it should also be avoided if there is any sea running.

The second Bogha Nuadh, nearly two miles southwest of Kerrera, is marked by a south cardinal light buoy, positioned south east of the rock.

Conspicuous marks are: Scarba, at 446m the highest land to the south of the Firth of Lorn; the Garvellachs; Insh Island (Sheep Island) west of Seil; and Lismore lighthouse at the north end of the firth.

Dubh fheith, an isolated rock 12-metres high, 1½ miles northeast of the Garvellachs, is a useful reference point.

Southeast of the Garvellachs there are several dangerous rocks, of which the most hazardous is Bogha an t' Sagairt which dries 0·3m, approximately halfway between Lunga and the Garvellachs. It is cleared to the ESE by keeping the west side of Eilean Dubh Beag touching the east side of Insh Island 025°, and to the WNW by keeping Dubh fheith in line with the west side of Insh Island 026°. Bogha an t' Sagairt is now marked by a W car light buoy.

## Directions

The passage northwest of the Garvellachs and Dubh fheith presents no problem other than from steep seas when the wind is against the tide.

On a passage from or to the west side of Jura the Great Race which extends several miles to the west of Corryvreckan should not be crossed on the flood, particularly at springs or in strong west winds. Southeast of the Garvellachs use the clearing marks described above to avoid Bogha an t' Sagairt. Other drying rocks are out of the way of a direct passage, but careful chartwork is needed if exploring within this area.

Passing from or to the Sound of Luing pass east of Bono Rock red buoy. From the north identify Scarba and then Fladda lighthouse to find the right passage.

North of Insh Island drying rocks lying more than a cable northeast of Dubh Sgeir (a rock above water half a mile northeast of the island), would be a hazard if tacking, or if heading from the Sound of Insh to the Sound of Mull.

Bogha Nuadh, two miles southwest of Kerrera, lies a cable northwest of the south cardinal buoy which marks the rock, and the buoy should not be passed less than ¼ mile on its northwest side.

Directions for Loch Linnhe, the Lynn of Lorn, and Loch Etive are given in the following chapter (page 63); and in Chapter IV for the passage between Lismore and Mull as well as for the Sound of Mull (page 87).

## Lights

**Bogha an t' Sagairt** W car light buoy Q(9)15s

**Garvellachs** Fl.6s24m9M (not visible from NE between 215° and 240°).

**Fladda lighthouse** Fl(2)WRG.9s13m11-9M 169°-R-186°-W-337°-G-344°-W-356°-R-026° showing red over Bono Rock bearing 169°-186°, white from eastward, and not visible from west of the red sector.

The boundary between the red and white sectors leads close west of the southwest tip of Easdale Island.

**Bono Rock** buoy Fl.R(4)12s.

**Dubh Sgeir** Fl.WRG.6s9m6/4M (000°-W-010°-R-025°-W-199°-G-000°) less than half a mile ESE of Fladda is visible all round except where obscured by Belnahua.

**Bogha Nuadh** light buoy, two miles SW of Kerrera, Q(6)+LFl.15s.

**Lismore** lighthouse Fl.10s31m17M is very distinctive.

**Lady's Rock** Fl.6s12m5M ½ mile SW of Lismore.

**Black's Memorial** Fl(3)WR.18s14m5/3M, on Mull, one mile west of Lady's Rock, showing red over Lady's Rock and west of 353° to shore, and white elsewhere; not very bright.

# Garvellachs, or Isles of the Sea

56°13′N 5°48′W

The Garvellachs are well worth visiting in settled weather but the anchorages are too exposed to be often suitable for staying overnight.

On Eileach an Naoimh (Neave) there are extensive remains of 9th-century monastic buildings, and a grave reputed to be that of St Columba's mother.

## Tides

Constant –0010 Oban (–0540 Dover).

*Height in metres* at Carsaig, Mull

| MHWS | MHWN | MTL | MLWN | MLWS |
|------|------|-----|------|------|
| 4·1 | 3·1 | 2·4 | 1·8 | 0·6 |

On the southeast side of the Garvellachs, an eddy on the flood runs southwestwards from about +0130 Oban.

## Eileach an Naoimh (Neave)

The most southwesterly island of the group.

### Approach

*From east or southeast* make for the southwest side of a gap in the skerries, keeping closer to that side to avoid a reef, part of which is awash, on the northeast side of the gap.

*From southwest* it is possible to pass between the skerries and the island, but keep closer to the skerries to avoid drying rocks on the island side.

The northeast end of the channel between the skerries and the island is awash at chart datum, with dense weed, but there do not appear to be any individual rocks at a higher level, so that if there is no swell a boat of moderate draught might pass through this channel above half-tide.

Anchor off the old landing place southwest of the ruins, or behind the drying rock at the northeast end of the inlet. When the rock is covered it can usually be seen showing white underwater, but note that submerged rocks extend beyond both ends of it.

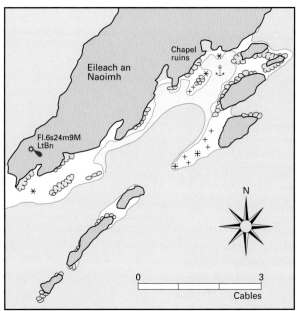

**EILEACH AN NAOIMH**

Eileach an Naoimh (2003)

Eileach an Naoimh anchorage from east. Note drying rocks towards left-hand side of photo, which lie at the edge of the approach from south and southeast (2003)

## Garbh Eileach

The largest of the group, towards their northeast end. The landing place in the middle of the southeast side of the island provides an occasional anchorage. Keep the cottage open west of the west end of Sgeir a' Phuirt; a submerged rock south of the islet lies on the line shown on the plan – it is not a clearing mark. There are mooring points on the west end of Sgeir a' Phuirt and on the shore to the north of it, and at the concrete slip on the west side of the bay. The old stone slip is reported to have been been washed away.

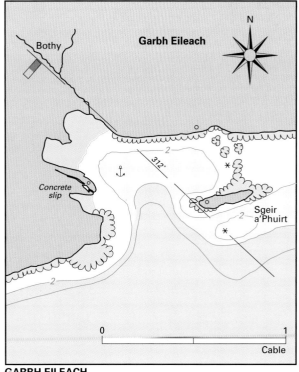

**GARBH EILEACH**

II. THE FIRTH OF LORN

# The Black Isles

56°14′N 5°43′W

Eilean Dubh Mor and Eilean Dubh Beag, 1½ miles southwest of Fladda provide reasonable and very secluded anchorage on the east side of the narrows between the two islands. This channel probably never dries right across, but a large rock just south of mid-channel dries at least three metres. Local fishermen say the basin east of the narrows is sheltered from swell but I have only anchored there in calm conditions.

### Approach

*From north* keep only half a cable off the east side of Eilean Dubh Beag to avoid a drying rock a cable off the island.

*From east* pass either close south of the islet off the north end of Eilean Dubh Mor, or not less than half a cable north of it. If taking the southern passage keep to the north side at the east end of the channel to avoid a submerged rock half a cable northeast of the point of Eilean Dubh Mor.

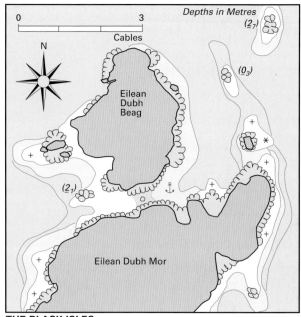

**THE BLACK ISLES**

The Black Isles (Eileanan Dubh) from southeast, showing submerged hazards in the approach (1991)

## Anchorages

Anchor between the two islands as near the narrows as will give you swinging room between the reefs (where the bottom is sand), or off the east side of Eilean Dubh Beag.

Both of the bays on the north side of Eilean Dubh Mor are foul with submerged and drying rocks, but it is possible to anchor off the promontory between them.

Fishermen use the passage through the narrows, north of the drying rock (so show a riding light); to try the passage for the first time take it from east to west, but only if there is no swell and you are sure of the position of the rock. Another rock, drying 2·1 metres, lies 1½ cables west of the narrows.

*Fladda* 56°15′N 5°41′W provides a temporary anchorage NNE of the island during flood tide.

*Belnahua* four cables WNW of Fladda has the remains of very extensive slate quarries, which penetrated far below sea level. Over a hundred people, including the families of the quarrymen, lived on this island which is less than ¼ mile across. It makes an interesting visit on a quiet day, but anchoring there needs care as the tide runs at five knots at springs. On the ebb, anchor in the tidal lee at the south end of the island. On the flood anchor as close inshore as possible on the east side. Keep an eye on your boat all the time; the bottom is mostly slate waste.

# Easdale

17′·5N 5°39′·5W

For at least two centuries Easdale was one of the two main centres of the Scottish slate industry, so that its character is that of derelict industry, with miners' rows converted to holiday homes. It also has what must be one of the largest tourist shops on the west coast, fed by a steady flow of coaches from Oban.

Easdale Island has more industrial archaeology and fewer visitors than Ellanbeich, and a small drying harbour. A museum on Easdale Island has an excellent collection of photographs and exhibits showing the industrial and social life of the place when it was a working community.

For the last 60 years it has been said that Easdale Sound was silting up, but a survey by a resident yachtsman shows that for the most part it is as deep as ever, except in the southwest corner.

Ellanbeich, on the north side of the sound, was originally separated from Seil by a channel, later filled in by waste from the quarries, which themselves are now flooded.

The southeast end of Easdale Sound from above Easdale Island. The harbour at bottom left is no longer used by cargo vessels, but would only be suitable for a yacht able to take the ground (1987)

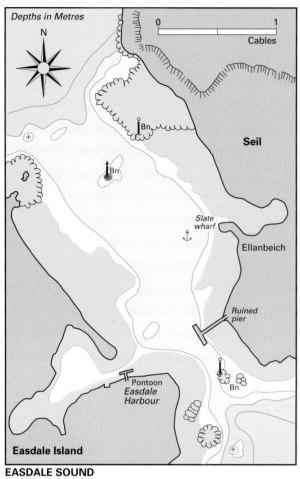

**EASDALE SOUND**

The beacon in the NW entrance has been restored by the Easdale Island Trust. Note that the green beacon on the reef at the north side of the passage stands several metres inshore of the edge of the reef.

**Tides**

Constant –0010 Oban (–0540 Dover).

*Height in metres at Carsaig, Mull*

| MHWS | MHWN | MTL | MLWN | MLWS |
|------|------|-----|------|------|
| 4·1  | 3·1  | 2·4 | 1·8  | 0·6  |

### Dangers and marks

The sound is very narrow and the shoals and rocks are best seen from the plan (note the large scale).

The remains of the pier are conspicuous.

### Approach

*From southeast* keep the south end of Insh Island just open south of the head of the ruined pier 320°. This entrance is very narrow, the clear passage at low tide being no more than 20 metres wide. After passing the pier alter course to the north, and before the slate wharf comes abeam, alter course to north west to pass about 30 metres south of the beacon on the reef on the north shore. Continue on this heading until clear of the entrance.

*From northwest* identify the entrance to the sound by the cliff on its north side, about a mile southeast of the south end of Insh Island.

Easdale from north. The outline of Scarba is conspicuous on the skyline (1991)

Approach to Easdale Sound from east. Keep close to the line of the face of the pier at this point to avoid rocks on the south side of the channel (2003)

Take care not to cut the corner, but when you have identified the beacon approach with the south point of Insh Island astern, to pass about 30 metres south of the beacon. Steer first for the slate wharf bearing 130° and, after passing the beacon, towards the head of the ruined pier, bearing 155°.

### Anchorage

Anchor off the slate wharf, about 50 metres off the head of the wharf, leaving a clear space for the passenger ferry to the island, as well as for boats passing through the sound.

Shoal-draught boats may find a berth in Easdale Harbour, especially if able to take the ground. The bottom is stony in places.

### Supplies and services

Shops at Ellanbeich. Bus to Oban.

*Communications* Post office, phone box.

Easdale Sound from west.
Note that reef extends as much as 10m south of the beacon (2003)

# Ardencaple Bay

56°19′N 5°36′W

An occasional anchorage lies close east of Rubha Garbh Airde, the northwest point of Seil. There is usually a fish cage just inside the point, but still room for small vessels to anchor there.

Shelter in settled weather or moderate southerly winds may be found in the south corner of the bay, off Ardfad Point. The bottom here is thick weed and mud, but may be cleaner in depths of more than six metres.

There is usually a fish cage just inside the point, but still room to anchor there for small vessels.

**II. THE FIRTH OF LORN**

# Puilladobhrain

56°19′·5N 5°35′W

Puilladobhrain is not named on charts, but is three cables southeast of Eilean Duin at the northeast end of Seil.

The name, pronounced approximately 'puldohran', translates as 'the pool of the otter', although, no doubt, any otters have long since been frightened away by the yachts. Almost as sheltered as any anchorage on the west coast and only seven miles from Oban, this is one of the west coast's most popular anchorages and you will be lucky to find less than a dozen and a half yachts there on any evening in July. Double that number is about the limit and it does sometimes overflow. 58 yachts are recorded to have taken part in the RHYC Spring Meet 1998.

As in many other anchorages, a shoal-draught boat able to take the ground will be at an advantage in being able to use the areas at the head of the pool which other yachts cannot reach. The islets on the west side of the pool are low enough to let you watch the sun (if any) set over Mull.

For shoal draft boats able to lower their masts see page 29 for the passage through Clachan Sound at high tide.

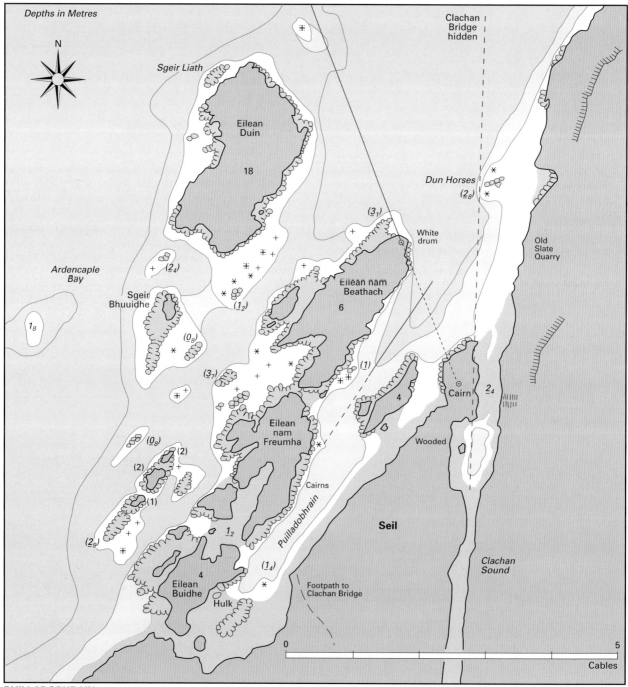

**PUILLADOBHRAIN**

Puilladobhrain from north west, with the drying passage of Clachan Sound and the 'Bridge over the Atlantic' at the upper left (1991)

## Tides

Constant as Oban (–0530 Dover).

*Height in metres*

| MHWS | MHWN | MTL | MLWN | MLWS |
|------|------|-----|------|------|
| 4·0 | 2·9 | 2·4 | 1·8 | 0·7 |

## Dangers and marks

Eilean Duin, which looks like a ruined castle 18 metres high although it is in fact a natural rock formation, is the key to identification from any direction.

A rock, awash, lies one cable off the north point of Eilean Duin.

A drum (orange to NW, white to SE) stands at the northeast end of Eilean nam Beathach. An inconspicuous cairn built of slate near the north end of Seil open north of the drum bearing 160° leads clear of a rock awash off the north end of Eilean Duin.

The Dun Horses, which dry 2·8 metres, lie near the mainland shore.

A drying rock close to the east shore of Eilean nam Beathach is easily avoided by keeping in mid-channel. Two white cairns in line below the high-

When Eilean Dun is approached from northward, Clachan Bridge appears through the entrance to Clachan Sound. When the bridge is hidden by the west side of the sound it is safe to turn towards the shore clear of the Dun Horses (2007)

Puilladobhrain leading line – the white painted cairns.
A white cross on the shore to the right marks the position of a drying rock

water line of Eilean nam Freumha lead clear of this rock, but very close to a spit at the west end of the islet southeast of Eilean nam Beathach. The cairns are difficult to see unless they have been freshly painted, and almost cover at HW.

Another drying rock, on the leading line, close to the shore of Eilean nam Freumha is marked by a painted cross on the shore.

Other rocks at the head of the pool are shown on the plan, which is based on a detailed survey by Ian Wallace (of BorroBoats).

### Approach

*From south* pass the northwest point of Seil and identify Eilean Duin, the outermost island about a mile to the northeast. Keep at least a cable NNE of the island to avoid the submerged rock (whose position will usually be obvious from lobster pot buoys), and round the end of Eilean nam Beathach, three cables further SSE, about half a cable (but no more) off that island to avoid the Dun Horses.

*From north* Eilean Duin is less easy to identify against Seil, but when you have picked it out, steer for it until you can see the bridge through Clachan Sound. Continue on the same heading until the sound is shut in, when it is safe to alter course to starboard avoiding the Dun Horses.

### Supplies

Pub at Clachan Bridge, half a mile by footpath from a signpost on the shore near the head of the pool; the ground to the east is boggy – land as near to the head as possible. Petrol at the pub; post office and phone box at Clachan Seil, a mile further south. The nearest shop is at Balvicar, three miles south.

The 18th-century Clachan Bridge, popularly known as 'The Bridge over the Atlantic' and incorrectly attributed to Telford, is well worth a visit even for those for whom the pub holds no interest.

There is a variety of curious geological formations on Eilean Duin, and a herd of wild goats.

## Barrnacarry Bay

56°21′N 5°33′W

An occasional anchorage on the south side of the entrance to Loch Feochan for settled weather or moderate southerly winds.

### Approach

*From south and west* keep ¼ mile offshore to avoid a 1·5-metre shoal ½ mile west of Barrnacarry, as well as drying rocks off the west point of the entrance. Approach the bay with the farm buildings in line with the west side of the largest

Barrnacarry from north. The farmhouse in line with the west edge of the 2-metre rock leads clear of drying rocks on the west side of the bay (2007)

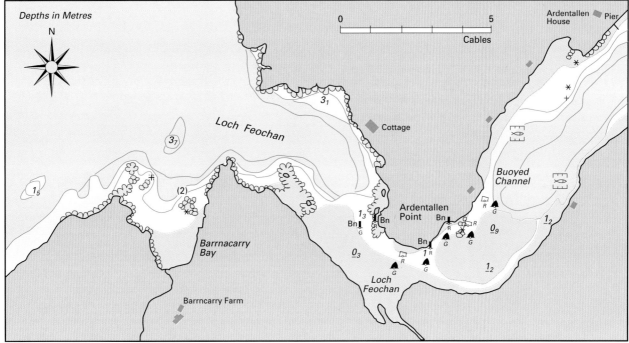

**LOCH FEOCHAN AND BARRNACARRY BAY**

above-water rock in the bay bearing 182° to pass east of the drying rocks. Anchor towards the southwest side of the bay.

# Loch Feochan

56°21′N 5°31′W

A mile and a half southeast of the south end of Kerrera, this loch has become more popular since the tortuous entrance was buoyed by Ardoran Marine.

A shallow sand bar lies across the entrance to the west of Ardentallen point. Southeast of the point the channel is almost blocked by banks and drying rocks, but a tortuous channel close southeast of the point is marked with six pairs of buoys (or buoys and perches) of which the first lie west of the point (see photo on page 52).

### Tides

HW as Oban. The ebb continues until two hours after LW Oban at springs, but rather earlier at neaps. The tidal stream has been measured at five knots.

### Approach

As the flood begins after the tide has risen for two hours, it might be thought appropriate to enter the loch at the beginning of the flood. However, weed is troublesome around low water, and it is recommended to approach during the last quarter of the flood, although local boat owners familiar with the entrance take it at all states of tide.

Note that the second and third port-hand marks are perches on shore. The flood tide sets across the banks to the east of the channel and the helmsman should be prepared to counter this set, particularly at the second and third pair of marks and take the middle of the channel between each pair at right angles.

The strength of the tide sometimes pulls the buoys under water, and this must also be watched for.

Four cables NNE of the inner end of the entrance channel a rock which dries 0·5 metre lies more than a cable SSW of the promontory at Ardentallen House with a shoal extending south of it.

Otherwise the loch is clean as far as Ardoran Marine, about a mile northeast of Ardentallen Point. This rock is marked by a Y beacon, with a golden mermaid as a topmark.

Three cables southeast of Ardoran, Eilean an Ruisg in the middle of the loch has rocks all round it. The north side is cleaner, but ¾ cable NNW of the island a rock dries 0·6 metre, and the best passage lies closer to the island.

### Services and Supplies

40 swinging moorings with one designated visitors' mooring, loading pontoons dredged to two metres at all states of tide. Fresh water and diesel on the pontoon with gas at the office.

Light engineering, small diesel and outboard repairs, basic chandlery. The Barn Bar 30–45 minute walk depending on thirst and pace.

The buoyed channel at the entrance to Loch Feochan at low water. The flood tide sets
a yacht strongly to the east at the first bend – onto drying banks (1991)

# Kerrera Sound

56°24′N 5°31′W

A sheltered approach to Oban from the south, with
most, but not all, of the hazards well marked and lit.
Several reasonable anchorages can be found in the
sound, but all of them are likely to be disturbed by
passing traffic. Gylen Castle at the south end of
Kerrera can be visited from Little Horseshoe Bay, or
in quiet weather one can anchor in the bay south of
the castle.

### Tides

Tidal streams run at one to two knots turning about 1½
hours before HW and LW Oban.

*Height in metres* at Oban

| MHWS | MHWN | MTL | MLWN | MLWS |
|------|------|-----|------|------|
| 4·0  | 2·9  | 2·4 | 1·8  | 0·7  |

### Dangers and marks – from south

Sgeirean Dubha, one cable off the Kerrera shore, ¾
mile northeast of the south end of the island, is
marked by a white light beacon.

Cutter Rock, which covers at half-tide, lies more
than 1½ cables SSW of the beacon.

An unmarked reef drying 0·9 metre lies ½ cable
from the mainland opposite the light beacon.

Little Horseshoe Shoal, ½ mile NNE of Sgeirean
Dubha, is marked on its south side by a port-hand
light.

A rock drying 0·3 metre, ½ cable off Oban Marine
Centre at Gallanach on the mainland, ½ mile
northeast of Little Horseshoe Shoal, is surrounded
by buoys marking a diving practice area.

Ferry Rocks, more than ½ mile further northeast,
lie in mid-channel, some of them drying and some
submerged. The northwest side, where the main
channel lies, is marked by a starboard-hand light
buoy, and the southeast side by a port-hand light. A
separate rock two cables further northeast is marked
by a starboard-hand light.

Underwater cables cross the sound from the south
end of Horseshoe Bay, as well as immediately
northeast of the ferry.

### Directions

There is little to add to the above except to
emphasise that you must not pass between the more
southerly of two buoys at Ferry Rocks, or west of
Heather Island unless you have a large-scale chart.
There is considerable traffic in the sound; yachts
should observe the rules of the road, but at the same
time look out for other vessels which may not do so.

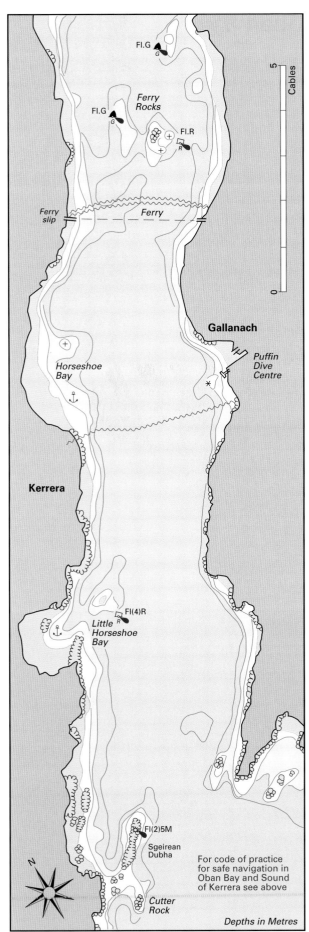

**KERRERA SOUND**
Note: this plan is not aligned on the meridian

### VOLUNTARY CODE OF PRACTICE

1. A voluntary Code of Practice has been developed to promote safety of navigation in the Oban Bay area and its approaches. The attention of owners, masters and crew of all vessels is drawn to the International Regulations for Preventing Collisions at Sea 1972, as amended, and in particular Rules 2, 5, 6, and 9.

2. The area is bounded to the N by a line from the NW tip of Kerrera to the NW tip of Maiden Island and to the S by a line drawn E-W through Dubh Sgeir Light.

3. For the purposes of this code the N and S entrances to Oban Bay are deemed to be Narrow Channels (see COLREG Rule 9) and a large vessel is defined as a vessel of more than 20m in length, or of more than 3m in draught.

4. Large vessels leaving Oban Bay have the right of way over all vessels entering Oban Bay. Small vessels, including sailing vessels, are not to impede the passage of large vessels entering or leaving Oban Bay.

5. Small vessels entering or leaving Oban Bay are required to keep as near to the starboard side of the channel as is safe and practicable.

6. Vessels within the Oban Harbour limits are not to exceed 5 knots, except in case of an emergency. Outwith the Oban Harbour limits, displacement vessels are not to exceed 7 knots N of the Kerrera Ferry Slips, except in case of an emergency.

7. Vessels operating in Oban Bay should listen on VHF and those of more than 40m in length should make a brief safety announcement prior to entry or departure.

### Lights

At night the following lights give you just enough guidance, but you will need to take bearings or use the echo sounder to keep clear of unlit dangers. The 15 or 20-metre contours generally clear all dangers but a 7-metre shoal ¼ mile northeast of Sgeirean Dubha may cause some anxiety.

**Sgeirean Dubha** light beacon Fl(2)12s7m5M.
**Ferry Rocks** west buoy Q.G.
For lights further north see Oban Bay, page 54.

### Anchorages

*Little Horseshoe Bay* Note the position of the shoal in relation to the buoy, and the drying reef which extends nearly a cable NE from the south point. The bay dries out fairly level, but it would be risky to dry out there because of possible damage from wash.

*Puffin Dive Centre, Gallanach*; most of the space is taken up by moorings although the boatyard usually keeps some for visitors.

　Go alongside to enquire (keep clear of the buoys round the drying rock). The quay dries alongside but has about 1·2 metres at LW neaps.

### Services and Supplies

Diesel, water, showers, slip, winter storage
　☎ 01631 566088

**Horseshoe Bay** is partly occupied by moorings. Inshore of them is drying foreshore; to the north lies a 1·8-metre submerged rock, and further north the bay is mostly very deep, but you might find a place to anchor close inshore towards the ferry slip.

Little Horseshoe Bay

Kerrera Sound and southern entrance to Oban Bay; the main fairway lies west of Ferry Rocks NW (green) buoy at the left of the photo. Ferry Rocks SE (red) buoy lies in the centre of the photo; do not pass between these two buoys. Ardbhan buoy, immediately above Ferry Rocks SE buoy, marks shoal ground off the mainland shore, and Heather Island immediately beyond that, with fish cages further beyond again. The tower of the cathedral stands on the far side of Oban Bay at the extreme right of the photo (2003)

# Oban Bay

56°25′N 5°29′W

See *Voluntary Code of Practice* notes on page 53. The Oban Harbour limit referred to in Rule 6 of the *Voluntary Code of Practice* extends approximately 190° from Dunollie Lt Bn to a point W of 'Pulpit Hill'. Seaplanes are now regularly operating in Oban Bay.

### Charts

*2387* (1:25,000), *1790* (1:10,000); *2171* (1:75,000).

### Tides

Oban is a standard port (–0530 Dover).

*Height in metres*

| MHWS | MHWN | MTL | MLWN | MLWS |
|------|------|-----|------|------|
| 4·0 | 2·9 | 2·4 | 1·8 | 0·7 |

For tidal streams in the Sound of Kerrera see above.

In the north entrance tidal streams run at 2½ knots springs, turning about 1½ hours before HW and LW Oban. The flood stream runs northwards.

### Identification

In poor visibility the town may not be easily seen from the west, being largely obscured by Kerrera. Conspicuous features are a radio mast close south of the town, and Hutchesons Monument, a stone obelisk at the north end of Kerrera.

### Dangers and marks

Sgeirraid (Sgeir Rathaid), a reef at the south entrance to Oban Bay, is marked at its south end by a south cardinal light buoy, and at its north end by a north cardinal light buoy.

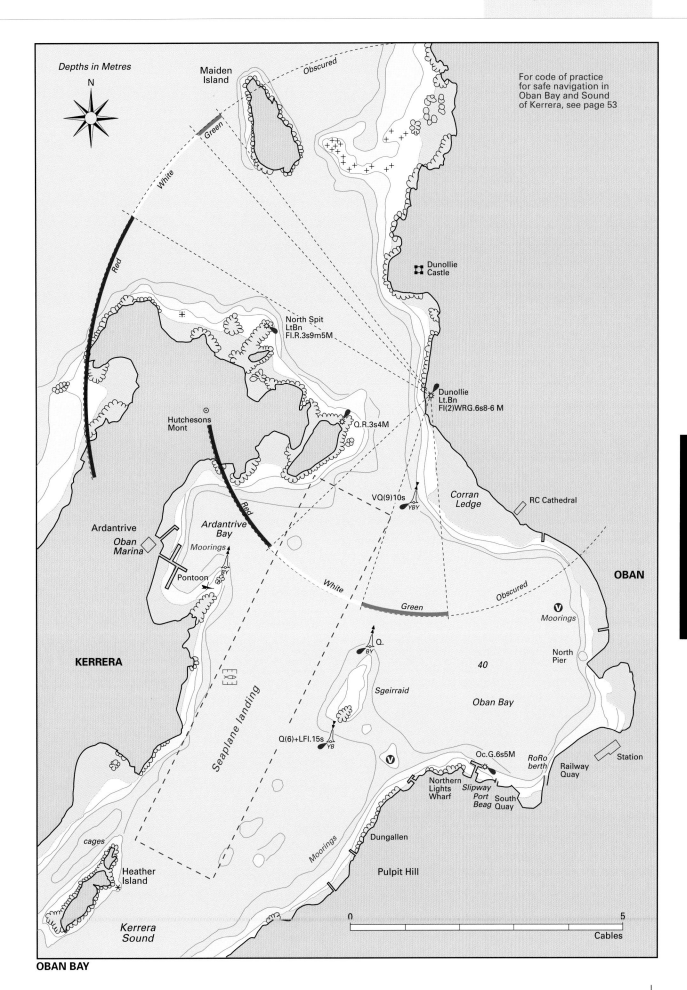

Depths in Metres

N

Maiden Island

Obscured

Green

White

Red

For code of practice
for safe navigation in
Oban Bay and Sound
of Kerrera, see page 53

Dunollie
Castle

North Spit
LtBn
Fl.R.3s9m5M

Dunollie
Lt.Bn
Fl(2)WRG.6s8-6 M

Hutchesons
Mont

Q.R.3s4M

Red

VQ(9)10s
YBY

Corran
Ledge

RC Cathedral

Ardantrive
Oban
Marina

Ardantrive
Bay

Moorings

White

Green

Obscured

OBAN

Pontoon

BY

Moorings

V
Moorings

North
Pier

KERRERA

Seaplane landing

Q.
BY

Sgeirraid

40

Oban Bay

Q(6)+LFl.15s
YB

V

Oc.G.6s5M

RoRo
berth

Station

cages

Heather
Island

Northern
Lights
Wharf

Slipway
Port
Beag

South
Quay

Railway
Quay

Dungallen

Moorings

Pulpit Hill

0                                                    5

Kerrera
Sound

Cables

**OBAN BAY**

Oban Bay from west. Visitors' moorings at right foreground
North Pier at upper left (1991)

Corran Ledge towards the north entrance on the mainland side is marked at its outer end by a west cardinal light buoy. A sewer outfall pipe encased in concrete runs across the ledge towards the buoy, in places standing 0·5 metre above the ledge.

Kerrera North Spit on the south side of the north entrance, is marked by a cylindrical light beacon with red and white bands.

At Rubh' a' Cruidh at the northeast corner of Kerrera a small framework beacon stands just inshore of the end of a reef.

Heather Island lies on the west side of the sound, and the southeast shore of the island should be given a berth of at least 20 metres to avoid a detached rock which dries 1·6 metres, known as the Soldier's Rock, about 15 metres off the most easterly point of Heather Island. An unmarked shoal lies west of the south point of Heather Island.

Seaplanes may be encountered, landing and taking off in the area designated at the west side of the bay on the plan.

### Approach

*From south* pass either side of Sgeirraid, preferably to the east if making for Oban.

*From north* the main passage lies south of Maiden Island; the passage east of the island, which is used by the car ferry to Lismore, is partly obstructed by submerged rocks extending from the mainland to within half a cable of Maiden Island.

A particularly good lookout should be kept, especially if under sail, for large commercial vessels, fast-moving car ferries in particular, as they have limited scope to manoeuvre.

Corran Ledge buoy stands further off shore than one might expect, and both yachts and fishing boats go aground on the wrong side of the buoy.

### Lights

At night lights may not be easy to make out against those of the town; also, for the same reason, keep a particularly good lookout for other vessels.

**Sgeirraid** buoys show the usual lights for cardinal buoys, Q(6)+LFl.15s to the south and Q at the north.

**Corran Ledge** buoy shows Q(9)10s.

**Dunollie** light beacon, two cables north of **Corran**

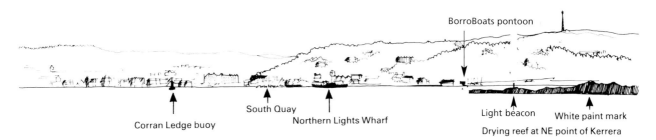

Oban Bay north entrance, from northwest of North Spit beacon

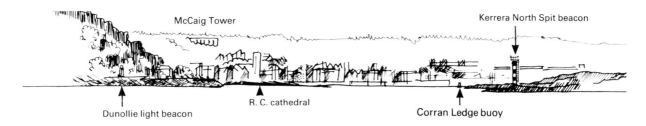

Oban Bay from north, from east of North Spit beacon

**Ledge** shows a sectored light, Fl(2)WRG.6s7m8-6M, white over the fairways to SSW and NW, red over Kerrera and green to the mainland side, obscured from the east side of the bay.

**Rubh' a' Cruidh** Q.R.3m4M.

**Kerrera North Spit** light beacon Fl.R.3s9m5M.

**North Pier** and **South Quay** both show 2F.G(vert).

**Car ferry** terminal at the south end of Railway Pier.

**Northern Lights Wharf** shows Oc.G.6s10m5M.

*From south* pass either side of Sgeirraid.

*From north* approach in the white sector of Dunollie light; Corran Ledge light buoy should appear before Kerrera North Spit is abeam. After passing the beacon come round gradually to starboard but don't get closer to Kerrera than the 10-metre contour. Pass west of Corran Ledge buoy and make for the berth chosen.

## Anchorages, moorings, berths alongside

The piermaster's office is often unmanned, and the Railway Quay and South Quay are controlled by separate organisations, so that R/T calls to 'harbourmaster' or 'harbour control' are unlikely to be answered.

Except for a short stay a visiting yacht should use either the red visitors' moorings off BorroBoats' pontoon, or a mooring at Ardentrive.

Large yachts may be able to berth at the North Pier.

*Railway Quay* Yachts may berth alongside but you take your chance with fishing boats, and may not be able to get near a ladder. The quay is constructed of steel sheet piling with timber facings so fender boards are essential. It is best to approach a boat larger than your own and ask permission to lie alongside. You can usually lie here overnight on Saturday. To check before berthing at the Railway Quay, call Calmac Oban.

Keep out of the way of car ferries approaching or leaving the RoRo berths at the south end of the Railway Quay.

Note that the back-wash makes it very uncomfortable to lie alongside the quay with NW wind.

See *Codes of Practice* on page 53.

*North of North Pier* there are both visitors' and private moorings, and an obstruction on the bottom about one cable NNW of North Pier. It may be possible to anchor, but the foreshore dries off about 60 metres, beyond which the bottom quickly drops away. Space to anchor can sometimes be found in the northeast corner of the bay, off a concrete slip southeast of the Roman Catholic cathedral.

*Ardantrive Bay* New moorings have been laid by Oban Marina, and berths may be available at the pontoon; consult yard manager. Showers, toilets, launch to Oban. VHF Ch 80.

From the south take care to avoid the drying spit which extends a cable NNE from the south point of the bay, with a wreck on it which rarely covers.

*Cardingmill Bay*, ¼ mile southwest of Northern Lights Wharf, is completely occupied by private moorings. Visitors' moorings, red with pick-up rings, have been laid to seaward of former BorroBoats' pontoon and there may be space to anchor inshore of these, but do not obstruct access to the pontoon.

Ardantrive Bay and north entrance to Oban Bay from SSW (2007)   *Mark Fishwick*

Wreck                    N cardinal buoy

Oban Marina from ESE (2007)

### Services and Supplies (Ardantrive)

Diesel, water, mains electricity, showers, bar/grill (summer months), regular ferry to Oban.

Additional pontoon 2008. Winter storage.

Petrol in town. Calor Gas at Oban Marina, or at Nancy Black. Slipping, moorings, hull and engine maintenance and repairs at Oban Marina, Ardantrive; drying out on concrete slip alongside pier by arrangement. Divers.

Chandlery and chart agent (Nancy Black) in Argyll Square near the Railway Quay; some chandlery at Oban Marina.

Supermarkets, shops and hotels in Oban.

Launderette beside Royal Hotel and at Oban Marina.

Train and bus to Glasgow. Car ferries to Mull, Lismore, Coll, Tiree and Colonsay. Seaplane service from Glasgow. Car hire. Tourist information office.

*Communications* Post office, phone boxes at railway station and elsewhere.

Caledonian MacBrayne ☎ 0631 562285
Coastguard ☎ 01631 563720
Nancy Black (chandlery) ☎ 01631 562550
Loch Lomond Seaplanes ☎ 0870 242 1457
Oban Divers ☎ 01631 566618
Oban Marina ☎ 01631 565333 *Fax* 565888
Oban Marina VHF Ch 80
Piermaster (North Pier) ☎ 01631 562892
Tourist information ☎ 01631 563122
Vale Engineering ☎ 01631 564513

## West side of Kerrera

*Oitir Mhor Bay (Otter More)* 56°25′N 5°31′W, on the northwest side of Kerrera, a mile from its north end, provides reasonable shelter in moderate summer weather, away from the disturbance of passing traffic in Oban Bay. The approach is straightforward, except from southwest between Eilean nan Gamhna and Kerrera where drying rocks reduce the navigable channel to a width of about 30 metres on its north side; drying areas on either side make it necessary to take an indirect course to the east of the narrows. The southwest side of the bay dries off one cable, allow for this when anchoring.

Fish cages.

Oitir Mhor, Kerrera, west side (2003)

# Loch Spelve

56°23′N 5°42′W

On the west side of the Firth of Lorn, Loch Spelve is completely landlocked and surrounded by an impressive range of hills, which sometimes produce correspondingly impressive squalls.

In the narrow entrance tidal streams run at about 3½ knots at springs.

A drying reef extends about ¼ cable south from Rubha na Faoilinn, the north point of the entrance. A series of white cairns and marks on the north shore is now redundant.

A rock which dries 0·5 metre, less than ½ cable from the north side is marked by a light-beacon.

A shoal extends more than halfway across the entrance from the south side.

Near the outer edge of this shoal a rock, known as The Mushroom because it is undercut on its seaward sides, stands 1·5 metres above the general level of the shoal and only 0·3 metre below chart datum. This rock lies only just south of mid-channel and very much in the way of any boat cutting across the edge of the shoal when the tide might seem to have risen enough.

### Tides

Constant and heights as Oban
*Height in metres*

| MHWS | MHWN | MTL | MLWN | MLWS |
|------|------|-----|------|------|
| 4·0 | 2·9 | 2·4 | 1·8 | 0·7 |

### Approach

Hold a cable off Rubha na Faoilinn and steer for the second point on the north side, bearing about 300° and keep the vertical cliff on Rubha na Faoilinn just

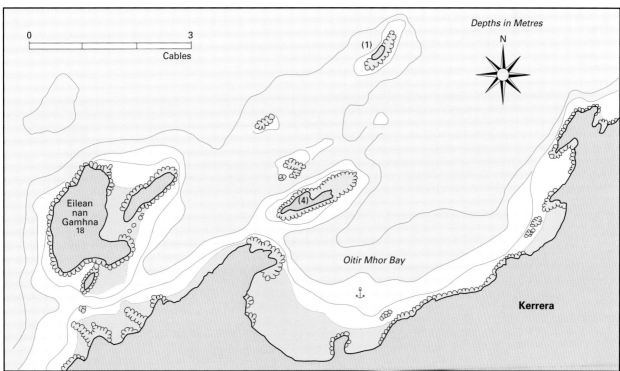

OITIR MHOR BAY, KERRERA

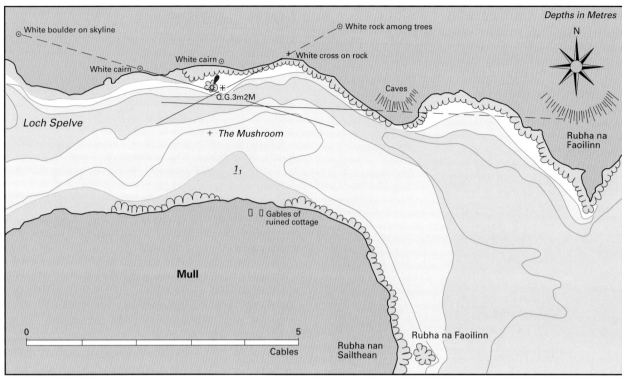

**LOCH SPELVE ENTRANCE**

open of the dark shoulder of the second point, bearing about 092°.

Keep about ¼ cable from the north shore, and the same distance south of the light beacon, and steer for the pier at Croggan on the south shore.

*Loch Spelve is heavily obstructed by fish farms (2003)*

If tacking the north shore can be approached until just before the first white cairn. Above half-tide a mid-channel course may be taken but the south shore should not be approached closely as several boulders stand above the general level of the bottom.

### Anchorages

Head of southwest arm of the loch provides reasonable shelter. The bottom rises abruptly from

Duart castle from the slipway at Torosay (2000)

12 metres to a foreshore which dries more than ½ cable on the south and southwest sides.

*Camas an-t Seilisdeir*, on the west side of the loch, southwest of Rubha Riabhach, where there are several fish cages.

*Ardura* at the west side of the north arm, as far into its southwest corner as depth permits. Extensive drying foreshore, and fierce gusts in westerly winds.

*In the Northeast Bay* the bottom is mostly rock, and not good holding, and a broad drying rock lies towards the head of the bay.

On the east shore there is some shelter in the bay northeast of Eilean Amalaig, which lies about a mile north of the entrance, but it may be partly obstructed by mussel lines.

In easterly winds the unnamed bay q mile south of Eilean Amalaig is reported to provide good holding but is shoal inshore and an uncharted drying rock lies off the south point of the bay.

The skerry one cable offshore north of the entrance should not be mistaken for Eilean Amalaig, but in quiet weather anchorage may be found north of the skerry.

Good anchorage in offshore winds is found at Croggan, southwest of entrance, where there is a phone box.

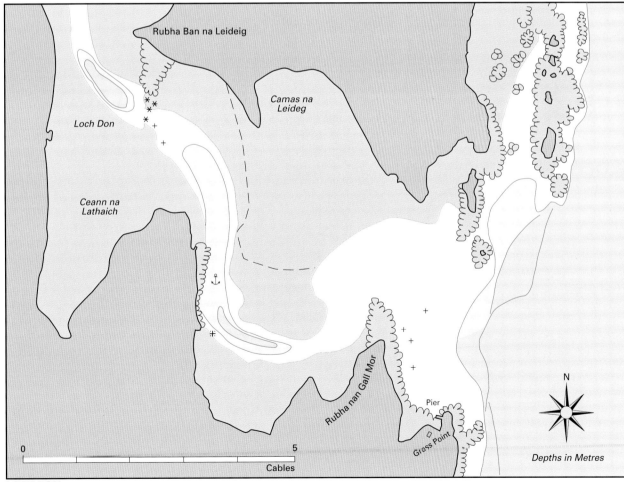

**LOCH DON**

Loch Don from southeast (2003)

# Loch Don

56°25′N 5°40′W

A curious place of shoals and drying banks, rather like a river from the east coast of England set down among mountains. The entrance is identified by a conspicuous white house at Grass Point, about two miles south of Black's Memorial light beacon.

## Approach

There are no marks to guide you round the twists of the channel, and the best you can do is to feel your way in on a rising tide, watching the echo sounder as you approach the edges of the channel. Don't try to cut across the bank in the middle of the loch, which extends east further than it would appear to do, and has large boulders scattered over it; pass well north of Rubha nan Gall Mor and hold towards its west side (the east side of the channel).

## Anchorage

There is a useful temporary anchorage off the pier at Grass Point (which was originally the main ferry pier for Mull). Leave room for tourist launches to approach the pier.

There is a phone box at Grass Point.

# III. Loch Etive and Loch Linnhe

These lochs together with the branches of Loch Linnhe are set in some of the most dramatic scenery on the west coast including, of course, Britain's highest mountain, and many others which drop sheer into the sea. Parts of the shore have no access by road and this is an ideal area for co-operative ventures between yachtsmen and climbers. By contrast, Lismore in the middle of the mouth of Loch Linnhe is green and fertile, consisting mainly of limestone. Yet another contrast is the new super-quarry on the west side of Loch Linnhe, feeding 65,000-ton bulk carriers.

### Charts

Admiralty *2389, 2379, 2380* cover the whole of Loch Linnhe and its branches at 1:25,000. A new Admiralty chart *2388* covers the whole of Loch Etive, with a large-scale plan of Dunstaffnage Bay. Imray chart folio *2800* covers Loch Linnhe and its branches adequately and economically.

## Dunstaffnage Bay and approaches to Loch Etive

56°27′N 5°25′W

Much of Dunstaffnage Bay dries out and towards the west side there are moorings, and fish cages belonging to the Scottish Marine Biological Association laboratory.

Dunstaffnage Yacht Haven has pontoons and swinging moorings on the southeast side of the bay. Shoal-draught yachts may find a space to anchor inshore of the moorings.

An extensive housing development stands at the head of the bay, with the SMBA laboratory on the west side.

Dunstaffnage Castle (which is well worth visiting) stands on Rubha Garbh, the northwest point of the bay. The pontoon pier below the castle has a gate which is normally locked.

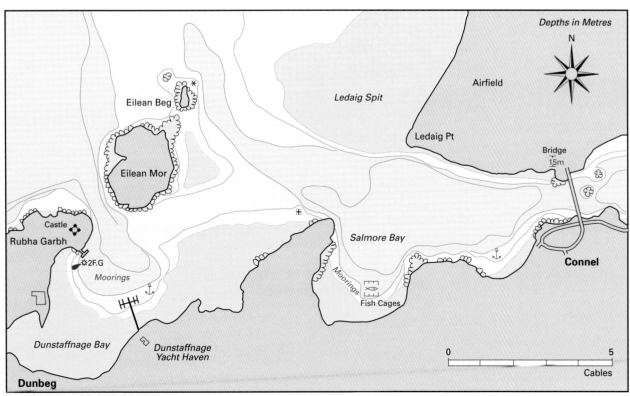

**DUNSTAFFNAGE AND CONNEL**

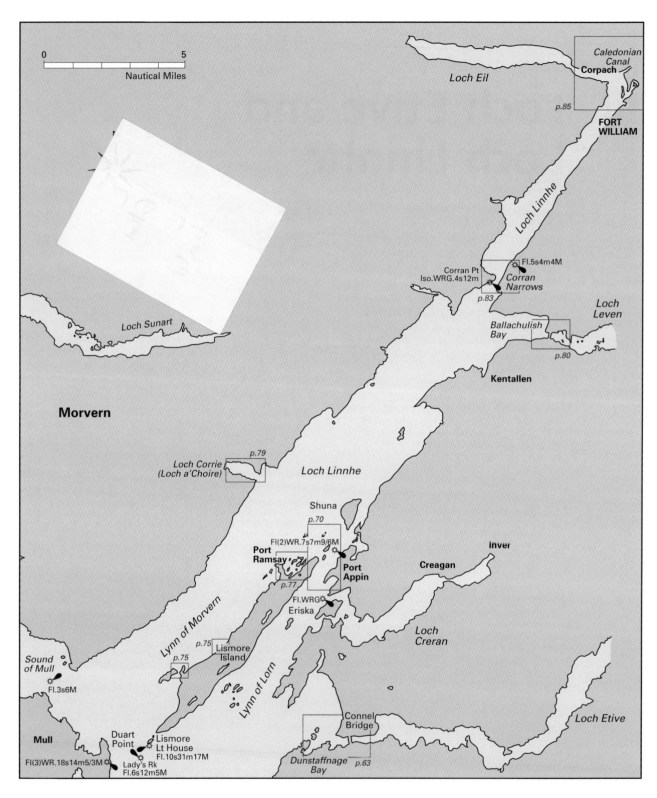

## Tides

At Dunstaffnage Bay the constant is as Oban (–0530 Dover).

*Height in metres*

| MHWS | MHWN | MTL | MLWN | MLWS |
|------|------|-----|------|------|
| 4·1 | 3·0 | 2·4 | 1·9 | 0·8 |

Tidal streams in Dunstaffnage Bay normally circulate counter-clockwise but may, unpredictably, run in the reverse direction.

## Identification and Approach

The entrance can be identified by Connel Bridge when the loch opens up from (or heading for) north of west. The approach from southward is clean, but if coming from, or heading for, the Lynn of Lorn keep at least ¼ mile off Rubha Garbh-Aird, the point immediately west of Ardmucknish Bay, 1¼ miles northwest of the entrance. A clearing mark for rocks off this point is the village of Achnacroish on Lismore open of Rubha Fion-Aird bearing 339°; also

Dunstaffnage and the entrance to Loch Etive from the west. The yacht haven is at the right beyond the castle, and Connel Bridge and Ben Cruachan at upper left (1987)

keep clear of a drying reef off Rubha Fion-Aird itself. Pass southwest of Eilean Mor, but keep clear of shoal water on the south side of the entrance.

At night (or dusk) do not mistake Dunbeg village, which can be seen over low ground south of Dunstaffnage Castle, for the entrance.

To continue further east keep towards Eilean Mor at first to avoid drying banks extending more than halfway between the mainland and the island. Steer 075° for the low-lying Ledaig Point on the north side of Connel Sound to avoid drying banks east of the island as well as a rock awash half a cable northwest of Rubha Ard nan Leum. From here onwards there are eddies all over the place and steering needs close attention.

Connel Sound may also be entered by the north side of Eilean Beag, but keep clear of a half-tide rock half a cable northwest of the island.

A drying spit off Ledaig Point extends three quarters of the way across the channel, so pass about a cable east of Eilean Beag and come round gradually to head for the bridge. A post on the south side of the spit stands well to the east of its outer end.

## Anchorages

*Dunstaffnage Bay* Visiting yachts can anchor between Eilean Mor and the moorings, clear of the fairway to Loch Etive and to the pier, or at neaps inshore of moorings after taking careful soundings. Moorings or pontoon berths are available at Dunstaffnage Yacht Haven. There is usually more space for visitors at the beginning of the week as charter boats should be away.

*Salmore Bay* (Camas Bruaich Ruaidhe), east of Dunstaffnage Bay, is entirely occupied by fish cages and permanent moorings.

*South Connel Bay* east of Salmore Bay is almost full of moorings and is more affected by the tide, but is more convenient for stores.

*Dunstaffnage Marina* See the note about tidal streams on previous page. When approaching observe how boats on moorings are lying and allow for the tide. Note that the direction of the stream changes abruptly in the middle of the bay. Steer to leave all the moorings to starboard and approach the pontoons from northeast. Call the marina on Ch 37 (or mobile phone) on

**III. LOCH ETIVE AND LOCH LINNHE**

Dunstaffnage Yacht Haven from southeast. Several more rows of pontoons have been added since this photo was taken (2003)

approaching, but if there is no response, make for the fuel berth at the head of the third pontoon from the right.

Two stbd-hand light-buoys are established NE of the moorings at Dunstaffnage Marina. These must both be left to stbd before turning to approach the marina.

### Lights

Lateral lights should have been established in the passage south of Eilean Dubh by the time this is published.

Stbd-hand light-buoys Fl.(2)G6s, Fl.(4)G10s
**Connel Bridge** south tower FR

### Services and Supplies

Dunstaffnage Yacht Haven on the southeast side of Dunstaffnage Bay has slip with mobile hoist, water, Calor Gas. Mechanical, electrical and hull repairs. Engineer; Sailmaker (Owen Sails) will collect sails for repair. Diesel.

General store at Dunbeg. Shop and hotels at Connel. At Dunstaffnage Yacht Haven, chandlery, restaurant, accommodation, bar.

Local bus service to Oban from Dunbeg. Train and bus at Connel.

*Communications* Post office and phone box at Dunbeg and Connel. Phone box also at yacht haven. Dunstaffnage Yacht Haven ☎ 01631 566555 *Fax* 01631 567422.

# Falls of Lora and Lower Loch Etive

56°27′·5N 5°23′W

### Charts
*2388* (1:25,000)

Apart from the usual crop of unmarked rocks there are three specific obstacles which discourage visitors from entering Loch Etive. The first in order of appearance is the bridge at Connel, with a charted clearance at MHWS of 14 metres. Next, immediately east of the bridge a drying reef extending more than halfway across the channel from the north side holds back the water and causes a tidal fall, known as the Falls of Lora. Lastly, at Bonawe, five miles east of the bridge, a very high-voltage electricity cable crosses the loch, with a safe clearance at its lowest point of 13 metres.

The shores of the lower part of the loch are pastoral and well wooded. Beyond Bonawe the loch is overshadowed by high mountains with no road except at its head, and the few farms are supplied by mail boat. Fish farming is expanding rapidly. On the north side of Bonawe narrows there is a quarry from which granite is taken away by sea. On the south shore at Bonawe the buildings of a late 18th-century iron foundry have been restored; all the iron ore was brought from Wales and Cumbria by sailing coasters which had to negotiate the falls under sail or with sweeps.

### Tides

Tidal streams run at up to six knots in the narrows at Connel.

The east-going stream begins about –0345 Oban (+0310 Dover).

The west-going stream begins about +0200 Oban (–0330 Dover).

Meteorological conditions may cause these figures to vary by up to 1½ hours with a tendency to be early rather than late, owing to the greater frequency of, and exposure to, westerly winds. There is almost no slack water. This information is based on research by the SMBA laboratory at Dunstaffnage.

The reefs to the east of Connel Bridge hold back the water so that at HW springs the level is 0·5 metre higher outside the loch than inside, and at LW springs it is 1·2 metres higher inside than outside. Again, there is virtually no slack water, and the stream runs very strongly through the channel south of the reef with eddies on either side. Recommended times to pass the falls vary from half an hour either side of the turn of the tide to two hours, one figure being given by the owner of a sailing yacht with a small engine, the other by the skipper of a fishing boat. A F.R light is established at the south tower of Connel Bridge.

Connel Bridge at the entrance to Loch Etive, with the ebb tide in full cry at the Falls of Lora immediately east of the bridge

### Approach

*From the west* the best approach is to be at the narrows a little before the tide turns eastwards so as to go through at fairly slack water. Read the notes about tides above, and allow for the tide turning up to 1½ hours early in strong southwesterly winds or if the barometer is low, or up to 1½ hours late in the opposite conditions. If you are early anchor off a blue-painted pub on the

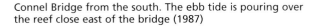

Connel Bridge from the south. The ebb tide is pouring over the reef close east of the bridge (1987)

III. LOCH ETIVE AND LOCH LINNHE

Falls of Lora from a Victorian chart

Kilmaronag Narrows, showing the rock which uncovers at the south side of the channel

south shore (no longer the Dunstaffnage Arms).

Steer for the space between the bottom of the first and second oblique struts of the bridge from its south tower. There is no satisfactory mark for clearing the south end of the reef, but at low tide it is uncovered.

Turn to steer diagonally across to the north shore; A submerged rock lies a little south of mid-channel nearly half a mile east of the bridge.

Rocks lie off the end of Dunfiunary, a point on the south shore on which stands a house with a round tower, and violent eddies beyond it.

The tide sets strongly towards rocks on the south shore at the east end of the channel.

At Kilmaronag Narrows, 1½ miles east of Connel Bridge, the tides turn about ten minutes later than at Connel and runs at nearly the same rate as at the falls.

Abbot's Islands, Stonefield Bay, Loch Etive   *John Shepherd*

Strong eddies run westward along the south shore east of the narrows on the flood, and west of the narrows on the ebb, flowing east.

Rocks, of which the outermost is submerged, extend more than halfway across the channel from islets on the southeast shore, and the foreshore on the northwest side dries off 50 metres southwest of the narrowest part of the passage.

Kilmaronag Shoal, 0·6 metre, lies one cable northwest of Kilmaronag Point.

Several rocks and banks drying up to a cable from the shore lie between these narrows and Bonawe, about four miles further east.

Ardchattan Shoal, 2¼ miles east of Kilmaronag Narrows, with a charted depth of two metres, lies rather north of mid-channel off the jetty at Ardchattan House on the north shore.

### Anchorages

*Achnacreemore Bay* North of the narrows. Except in onshore winds anchor at the north end of the bay's west shore, but keep clear of a rock which dries 0·6 metre, a cable south of the mouth of a burn.

*Stonefield Bay (Linne na Craige)* 56°27'·5N 5°19'W is on the south shore a mile west of the narrows. Anchor east of Eilean Traighe, towards the head of the bay.

Alternatively, east of Abbot's Isles on the east side of the bay. The channel there is rather deep and the bottom rocky, and an eddy sets through it on the flood; anchor in the bight close to the islands. There may be lost moorings here.

*Auchnacloich Bay*, the next bay east of Stonefield, provides some shelter. Leave clear access to the pier which is used by workboats from the SMBA laboratory.

*Sailean Rubha*, west of Airds Point, three miles from Kilmaronag Narrows, provides good shelter in four metres, but there are rocks towards the head of the inlet.

*Airds Bay*, southwest of Bonawe Narrows has a foreshore drying out for more than half a cable beyond which the depth increases very quickly.

At the concrete jetty east of the river mouth in the southeast corner of the bay underwater cables run WNW from the head of the pier and northwest from a point on shore north of the pier.

Areas on either side of the approach to the pier have been leased for permanent moorings, and the area allocated for anchorage is off the SW shore, about ¼ mile west of the pier.

### Supplies

Shop, post office, phone box, hotels; petrol at Taynuilt, ¾ mile from Bonawe Pier.

The 18th-century ironworks at Bonawe are an outstanding example of the industrial archaeology of the period (near Airds Bay). Gardens at Ardchattan Priory on the north shore of the loch are open to visitors.

# Bonawe and Upper Loch Etive

56°27'N 5°13'W

Overhead power cables cross Bonawe Narrows with a safe clearance of 12 metres at their lowest point but greater, although unspecified clearance towards the north side.

In case any shoal-draught boats should enter the mouth of River Awe on the south side of the narrows, note that power cables cross the river, ¼ mile from its mouth, with a safe clearance of four metres.

### Tides

The constant at Bonawe is +0200 Oban (−0330 Dover).
*Height in metres*

| MHWS | MHWN | MTL | MLWN | MLWS |
|------|------|-----|------|------|
| 2·0  | 1·2  | 1·0 | 0·5  | 0·2  |

Tidal streams at these narrows run at 2½ knots springs on the flood, 1½ knots on the ebb.

### Dangers

A drying bank extends up to a cable northeast of the old ferry slip on the south shore.

The upper loch is mostly clean except for drying rocks extending more than ¼ mile from the north point of Inverliever Bay on the southeast shore, 3½ miles from Bonawe Narrows.

Winds tend to be erratic unless the true wind is straight along the loch.

### Anchorages

Most bays are very deep and there are many fish cages. The best anchorage is at the head of the loch between the ruined pier on the west shore and a tidal islet northeast of it, but this is exposed to southerly fetch.

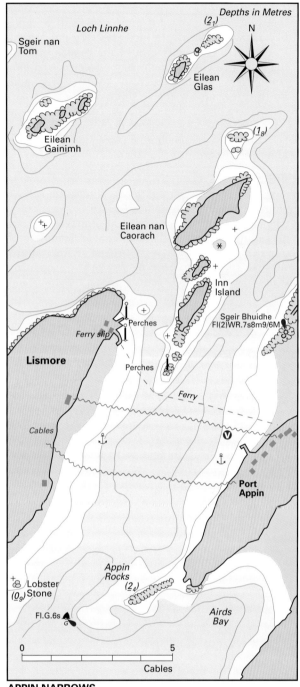

**APPIN NARROWS**

# Lynn of Lorn

56°30′N 5°28′W

The passage from Oban to Loch Linnhe by the east side of Lismore is sheltered from the west but tides run strongly and careful pilotage is needed at the north end.

### Charts

The passage can be negotiated with these directions and chart *C65*, but *2379 and 2389* at 1:25,000 will be needed for exploring inshore.

### Tides

The constant at Port Appin is –0005 Oban (–0535 Dover).
*Height in metres*

| MHWS | MHWN | MTL | MLWN | MLWS |
|------|------|-----|------|------|
| 4·2 | 3·1 | 2·5 | 1·9 | 0·8 |

At the south end of the Lynn of Lorn the tidal stream turns NNE at +0445 Oban (–0045 Dover); SSW at –0140 Oban (+0515 Dover).

Southwest of the group of islets off the southeast side of Lismore an eddy on the flood sets southwestwards.

At the north end of the Lynn of Lorn, the tidal stream turns NNE at +0600 Oban (+0030 Dover); SSW at –0015 Oban (–0545 Dover).

The rate of tidal streams in the Lynn of Lorn varies from one knot at the south end to 2½ knots at the north end at springs.

### Dangers and marks

Drying rocks extend one cable WSW of Rubha Fionaird, the east point of the south entrance.

Over a mile west of this point is a group of islets, the Creags, the shores of which are generally clean, but a rock drying four metres lies between the most easterly islands of the group.

2½ miles NNE of the Creags, rocks above water extend two cables west of Eilean Dubh, with drying rocks SSW and NNE of them, and shoal water between them and the island.

A submerged rock lies one cable NNE of the north end of Eilean Dubh.

Branra Rock, which dries 2·7 metres, six cables NNE of Eilean Dubh, has an iron beacon with a barrel topmark.

A light beacon stands on Dearg Sgeir, 1¾ cables southwest of Airds Point at the north side of the entrance to Loch Creran.

Appin Rocks, which dry at half-tide, extend two cables southwest of the next point to the north, in which there is a natural arch. A starboard-hand buoy is moored four cables WSW of the point. The flood tide sets NNW across these rocks which might affect a yacht tacking, or entering Airds Bay.

The Lobster Stone, 1½ cables off Lismore WNW of Appin Rocks buoy, dries 0·9 metre.

Inn Island lies in the channel between the mainland and the north end of Lismore, with Sgeir Bhuidhe, on which is a light beacon, on the mainland side of the channel.

Drying rocks extend more than 1½ cables SSW of Inn Island, with a perch with a radar reflector near their south end.

Drying rocks also extend more than 1½ cables southwest of Sgeir Bhuidhe.

In the passage west of Inn Island a drying spit on the Lismore side is marked at its outer end by another perch with a radar reflector, and further north the ferry slip has a red perch with a spherical topmark on it.

A submerged rock lies ¾ cable east of the north point of Lismore.

North end of the Lynn of Lorn, with perches marking rocks in the foreground and the spit extending east from Lismore (2003)

## Directions

*From south* keep outwith a cable off Rubha Fion-aird on the east side of the entrance and pass east of Eilean Dubh, and at least ¼ mile off the mainland shore here; pass either side of Branra Rock beacon. Pass within a cable to the west of Appin Rocks starboard-hand buoy, to avoid the Lobster Stone. Pass in mid-channel between Inn Island and Sgeir Bhuidhe light beacon.

There is also a clean passage between Lismore and both the Creags and the rocks west of Eilean Dubh.

To continue the passage north, and for the north and west of Lismore, see pages 73–78.

*From north* keep at least a cable off the shore of Shuna and outwith the 5-metre contour to avoid submerged rocks there.

Keep closer to Shuna than to rocks above water between Shuna and Lismore, as drying rocks extend 1½ cables from the above-water rocks towards Shuna. Keep to the middle of the channel between Inn Island and Sgeir Bhuidhe.

## Lights

At night, given enough visibility to see the outline of islands and Branra Rock beacon, it should be possible to negotiate this passage with the help of the following lights, but the large-scale chart would be needed, with the bearings over which each light is obscured by islands carefully plotted.

**Branra Rock Beacon**
*of Iron 18 feet*

**Lismore lighthouse** Fl.10s31m17M; obscured NW of 237°.
**Sgeir Bhuidhe** light beacon Fl(2)WR.7s8m9/6M.
**Airds Point** light beacon Fl.WRG.2s2m3-1M.
**Appin Rocks** buoy Fl.G.6s.

## Anchorages

Apart from Port Appin there are no regular anchorages within this sound but charts *2379* and *2389* will show several possible occasional anchorages.

*Achnacroish,* Lismore 56°31′N 5°29′W, temporary anchorage clear of the pier and car ferry slip.

*The Creags,* off Kilcheran, Lismore, constitute the major part of a SSSI for seals and seabirds; several occasional anchorages may be found according to wind direction, the easiest being NE of Eilean na Gamhna or off the isthmus between Eilean na Cloiche and Eilean Dubh.

*Airds Bay,* north of the entrance to Loch Creran. The head of the bay dries off for ¼ mile. Exposed to southwest, and the flood tide sets strongly across Appin Rocks.

*Port Appin* 56°33′N 5°25′W Most of the area around the pier is occupied by moorings; and cables cross the channel both north and south of the pier as shown on the plan; make sure of anchoring clear of the cables.

Visitors' moorings for yachts up to 40′ are provided for its customers by the Pier House Hotel ☎ 01631 730302.

### Supplies

Shop, post office, phone box, hotel, Calor Gas. Water tap 200 metres northeast of pier. Diesel, petrol.

# Loch Creran entrance

56°31′N 5°24′W

The entrance, through which the tide runs at four knots at springs, needs to be taken with care.

Tidal streams turn as at the north end of the Lynn of Lorn (page 70).

A Marine Special Area of Conservation (mSAC) has been established in Loch Creran, and boat owners are asked to anchor only in designated anchorages, to avoid disturbing unique features on the seabed.

The Marine Resource Centre at Barcaldine Pier provides moorings, storage under cover as well as in the open, a loading pontoon, a hoist and the usual repair services ☎ 01631 720291 MRC visitors' mooring buoys are numbered: D12, D13, D14, E13, E14, E15.

Creran Marine, at the west side of Barcaldine Pier, provides moorings and storage ashore ☎ 01631 720253.

### Dangers and marks

Glas Eilean, four cables WSW of the entrance, has a submerged reef off its southwest end.

Dearg Sgeir which dries 3·7 metres, on the northwest side of the entrance, is marked by a red light beacon.

On the southeast shore opposite this beacon, a submerged reef runs obliquely out from the shore, ending in a drying rock almost in mid-channel, ESE of the beacon.

On the northeast point of Eriska stands a green light beacon. Opposite this point lies an unmarked drying reef, about a third of the width of the channel from the east shore.

Two cables SSE of this rock is a rock above water with an extensive drying reef round it.

Sgeir Caillich, a long ridge of rock above water, extends northeast from the south shore of the loch four cables southeast of Eriska, ending in a drying reef marked by a green conical light buoy.

### Directions

In the entrance keep closer to Dearg Sgeir red beacon than to the shore of Eriska, and after passing a cable beyond the beacon keep in mid-channel. A clearing mark for the rocks on the southeast side of the entrance is Branra Rock beacon in line with the north high-water mark of Glas Eilean.

On rounding the north end of Eriska the tide will tend to carry you north of the channel; keep closer to the northwest point of Eriska than to the mainland opposite to avoid the drying rock there.

### Lights

Dearg Sgeir light beacon Fl.WRG.2s2m3-1M, shows white over the fairway in both directions, green over Eriska and Eriska Shoal, and red over Glas Eilean and over dangers on the NW side. It is obscured between 093° and 196°.

Eriska NE Point light beacon shows Q.G.2m2M obscured between 128° and 329°.

Sgeir Caillich buoy Fl.G.3s.

Approach in the white sector of Dearg Sgeir light. Appin Rocks buoy (Fl.G.6s) on the port beam will give some indication of how near to the beacon you are; the echo sounder will not be much help. Pass close southeast of the beacon until in the white sector again, and when Eriska beacon appears steer to pass close northeast of it with the Fl.G light buoy ahead. There are no lights further up the loch.

### Anchorages

*South Shian* between Eriska and Sgeir Caillich. The southwest side of the bay dries off for two cables. Anchor off the east side of Eriska outwith the 5-metre contour (there are shoal patches close to it), and clear of moorings and fish cages; subject to disturbance from frequent boats to and from Glensanda Quarry day and night.

South Shian from west (2003)

# Loch Creran - inner part

Beyond Sgeir Caillich the loch extends for four miles to Caolas Creagan, and the foreshore dries off up to two cables in several places.

Two cables east of Sgeir Caillich buoy submerged rocks extend more than half a cable from the northeast shore.

### Tides

The constant at Barcaldine is +0015 Oban (–0515 Dover).
*Height in metres*

| MHWS | MHWN | MTL | MLWN | MLWS |
|------|------|-----|------|------|
| 4·1 | 3·0 | 2·4 | 1·8 | 0·8 |

### Directions

Pass northeast of the buoy off Sgeir Caillich, but keep at least a cable off the northeast shore beyond it. In the main part of the loch keep outwith the 10-metre contour.

### Anchorage

*On the south side* of the loch close west of Barcaldine Pier (56°32′N 5°19′W) Creran Marine has a slipway at which trailed boats may be launched, and a mooring for visitors with a capacity of 10 tons. Mechanical repairs can be arranged. ☎ 01631 720253.

### Supplies

Water, showers, shop, bar meals, rubbish disposal. At Barcaldine, a post office (early closing Wednesday and Saturday), phone box, shop and Calor Gas at caravan site, all within ½ mile.

Boathouse Grill. Sea Life Centre nearby.

Caolas Creagan (56°33′N 5°17′W) the bridge headroom is charted as 9·5 metres. The northern span and its approaches are obstructed by rocks, and within three cables east of the bridge shoal spits and drying rocks encroach on both sides of the fairway. Tidal streams run at up to five knots.

Black Rocks which dry 3·7 metres, extend over a cable off a promontory four cables WSW of the narrows.

Occasional anchorage, except in fresh to strong westerlies, off Creagan Inn on the north shore, west of the bridge. Pub, bar meals.

# Lynn of Morvern

56°31′N 5°33′W

This is the main entrance to Loch Linnhe, between Lismore and Morvern, and it is generally clean and deep. There are only occasional anchorages until the north end of Lismore. Coming from southward the strong tidal streams between Lismore and Mull have to be taken into account, but otherwise there are neither the pilotage problems nor the interest of the Lynn of Lorn.

### Dangers and marks

Liath Sgeir, which dries three metres, lies a little more than a mile north of Lismore lighthouse, halfway between the lighthouse and the southwest end of Bernera Island, and slightly to the west of a line joining these two points. This is a hazard if tacking, or making direct for the Lynn of Morvern from south of Lismore.

The super-quarry at Glensanda on Morvern, west of the north end of Lismore, is a landmark on an otherwise featureless shore.

Both ends of a loading jetty are marked by lights Fl.R.3s. A boat harbour south of the loading jetty is not available to yachts except in emergency. Very

Achadun Bay and castle on the west side of Lismore, looking south (1991)

large bulk carriers operate from Glensanda to the open sea, normally by way of the Sound of Mull. An announcement of their departure is usually made on VHF Ch 16.

At the northwest point of Lismore a white beacon stands on the promontory west of Port Ramsay.

### Tides

Constant as Oban (–0530 Dover).
*Height in metres*

| MHWS | MHWN | MTL | MLWN | MLWS |
|------|------|-----|------|------|
| 4·3  | 3·2  | 2·5 | 1·8  | 0·7  |

The north-going stream begins –0545 Oban (+0110 Dover).
The south-going stream begins +0025 Oban (–0505 Dover).

In the Lynn of Morvern the main body of the tidal stream runs at one knot, but on the flood a narrow stream runs northwards from Lismore lighthouse across to the Morvern shore and then northeast towards Shuna island, at 2½ knots.

On the ebb an eddy sets into Bernera Bay. Also on the ebb, at springs only, a strong stream off the Morvern shore northwest of Bernera, runs at four knots to the southeast, with overfalls.

### Directions

Except for Liath Sgeir there are no specific hazards and the main consideration is to carry a fair tide. With wind against tide there are steep overfalls between Lismore and Mull, and on a passage between the Firth of Lorn and Loch Linnhe, the Lynn of Lorn may be a more comfortable choice.

### Lights

**Lismore** lighthouse Fl.10s31m17M is obscured NW of 237°.

**Glensanda** jetty Fl.R.3s5m4M.

**Sgeir Bhuidhe** light beacon at Appin, Fl(2)WR. 7s8m9/6M, provides a cross bearing when bearing more than 100°.

**Corran Narrows** lighthouse, Iso.WRG.4s12m10-7M, shows red to the west of 030°.

Achadun Bay from the castle (2003)

Port na Moralachd is partly occupied by a large fish cage (1987)

## Anchorages

*Achadun Bay, Lismore* 56°30′N 5°34′W Occasional anchorage on the west side of the bay east of a promontory northeast of Bernera Island.

Alternatively in the bay at the northeast end of Bernera itself.

*Bernera Bay,* southeast of Bernera is a further alternative in northerly winds. A submerged rock lies one cable east of the rocks standing above water on the west side. Achadun Castle ruins are a short distance from each of these bays.

*An Sailean* 56°31′N 5°31′W about the middle of the northwest side of Lismore is a shallow inlet, suitable as an overnight anchorage only for shoal-draught boats or for those of moderate draught at neaps. There are remains of extensive limestone quarries and limekilns from which lime was shipped out in the first half of the 19th century.

Grogan Dubh, a rock with a perch just above HW springs, is the north end of a drying reef extending from the southwest point of the entrance. The deepest part of the pool is abreast of the high-water mark of this point.

*Port na Moralachd* 56°33′N 5°28′W south of the northwest point of Lismore provides reasonable shelter close inshore at the south side of the bay. There is no clear passage between the off-lying islands, and the only approach is from the southwest.

If coming from northward, note that submerged rocks extend over half a cable southwest of the most southerly islet.

A large raft of fish cages lies off the north point of the bay.

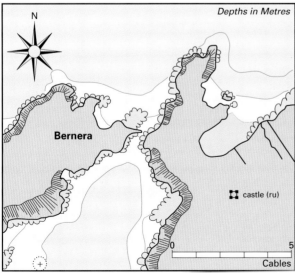

**ACHADUN BAY, LISMORE**

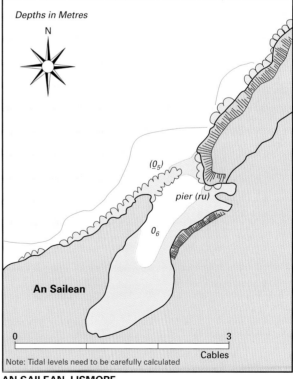

**AN SAILEAN, LISMORE**

# Port Ramsay

56°33′N 5°27′W

A good anchorage at the north end of Lismore, with many rocks in the approaches; two of the rocks north of the bay have been marked for the benefit of workboats from the Glensanda quarry.

In the approach from the north, a perch with white encapsulated radar reflector stands on the rock which dries three metres on the west side of the entrance, and on the rock which dries 2·4 metres, two cables northeast of Eilean Ramsay. Neither of these perches is at the extreme edge of the rock. There are ruins of several limekilns, and the lime-burners' cottages on the east side of the bay are now nearly all used as holiday cottages.

### Tides

Constant at Port Appin –0005 Oban (–0535 Dover).

*Height in metres* at Port Appin

| MHWS | MHWN | MTL | MLWN | MLWS |
|------|------|-----|------|------|
| 4·2 | 3·1 | 2·5 | 1·9 | 0·8 |

### Approach

At the west point of the bay a rock above water stands at the end of a reef extending northeast of Eilean nam Ban.

Eilean nam Meann extends north from the south side of the bay with an islet at the north end joined to it by a drying reef; a rock ½ cable north of the islet probably only covers at HW springs. Drying rocks

Port Ramsay; the shallow channel east of Eilean Droineach from northeast. A boulder spit lies east of mid channel parallel to the shore (2003)

*Below* Port Ramsay, at the north end of Lismore. The island left foreground is Eilean nam Ban. Eilean nam Meann is the long thin island right of the centre (1987)

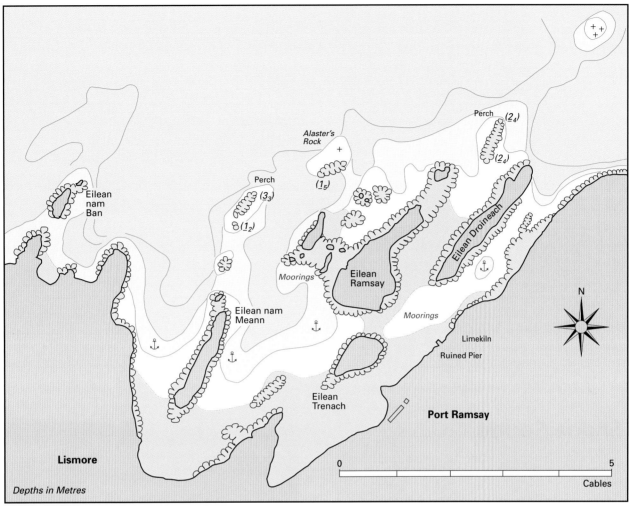

**PORT RAMSAY**

continue north to a perch with white encapsulated radar reflector standing on the rock which dries three metres.

If the drying rock north of Eilean nam Meann is showing, pass either side of it, but not more than ½ cable from its north side, to avoid a rock which dries 1·2 metres further north. If it is covered pass 30 metres north of the islet north of Eilean nam Meann, then rather further off the northeast point if coming round to the east side of that island.

*From north* many rocks and islets lie up to a mile north of the anchorage, of which Sgeir nan Tom is furthest to the northwest, with drying rocks 1½ cables southwest of it. Pass more than ¼ mile southwest of Sgeir nan Tom or not more than a cable east of it and identify the perch on the drying rock on the west side of the entrance.

Pass ½ cable east of the perch to avoid Alaster's Rock, a cable northeast of the perch, and pass half a cable east of the perch, heading for the east side of Eilean nam Meann.

*From east* pass a cable north of the perch on the rock which dries 2·4 metres northeast of Eilean Ramsay, but no further off to avoid a submerged rock further northeast.

Sgeir Bhuidhe light beacon just open of the northeast point of Lismore bearing 100° leads between these two rocks. Steer to pass well north of the next perch, keeping north of the 10-metre contour until the perch bears 200°, before turning to pass east of it as above.

## Anchorages

The best is off the east side of Eilean nam Meann, but no further south than the middle of the island as the head of the bay dries off nearly two cables.

Alternatively, anchor between the west end of Eilean Ramsay and Eilean Trenach. The bay west of Eilean nam Meann is also suitable, although less sheltered.

With sufficient rise of tide it is possible to enter by the southeast of Eilean Droineach, but a sand bar lies across the entrance with a depth of only 0·3 metre, and a stony spit roughly parallel to and near the centre of the apparent channel. The course to take is about a quarter of the width of the channel away from Eilean Droineach. Anchor in a pool abreast of the south part of the island; further southwest it is shoal, with some moorings.

Water at standpipe behind cottages; phone box.

Shuna Sound. The traditional leading line leads to the south end of the buoyed channel (1987)

# Shuna Sound

56°35′N 5°23′W

The shoal passage between the island of Shuna and the mainland, 1½ miles NNE of Sgeir Bhuidhe light beacon has been buoyed by Linnhe Marine.

The channel is less than straight, but regular surveys by Linnhe Marine show a least depth of 2·5 metres. It is marked with a pair of lateral buoys at its south end, followed by five pairs of lateral buoys with radar reflectors.

A shoal spit extends three quarters of the width of the channel from Shuna, and there are shoals south of the spit on the mainland side.

The traditional line to lead through is to keep the left-hand side of Appin House above Knap Point, although the deepest water lies to the east of this line. It is best avoided within two hours of LW.

## Anchorages

*Dallens Bay,* on the east side of Knap Point dries out at the head for nearly two cables and there are several commercial and private moorings. The east shore dries off for a cable further north.

Linnhe Marine have a few visitors' moorings and a pontoon in deep water ☎ 07721 503981. Alternatively, anchor in Shuna Sound, towards the island, southwest of Knap Point.

## Services

Water, showers, repairs, slip, diesel and petrol from garage, refuse disposal.

Linnhe Marine landing stage (2007)

# Loch Linnhe – central part

56°38′N 5°24′W

Off the northwest shore of the loch there are several drying and submerged rocks and shoals, of which the most southerly is about four miles northeast of the entrance to Loch Corrie (Loch a' Choire).

Sallachan Point is marked by an unlit red beacon.

## Tides

As in the Lynn of Morvern.
The north-going stream begins –0545 Oban (+0110 Dover).
The south-going stream begins +0025 Oban (–0505 Dover).
Constant as Oban (–0530 Dover).
*Height in metres*

| | MHWS | MHWN | MTL | MLWN | MLWS |
|---|---|---|---|---|---|
| | 4·3 | 3·2 | 2·5 | 1·8 | 0·7 |

## Directions

No specific directions are needed except to keep clear of the rocks and shoals on the northwest side of the loch. These are all avoided by keeping ½ mile offshore or outwith the 30-metre contour or, if these marks can be seen, keep Corran Point light beacon (page 83) open-east of Sallachan Point red beacon, bearing 048°, on the point about two miles further southwest open-east of Rubha na h-Earba, off which stands a rock 2m high, bearing 234°.

# Loch Corrie

56°37′N 5°30′W

The name of this inlet on the northwest shore (Loch a' Choire on the charts) may be translated as 'a cauldron', which probably derives from the squalls which drop into the loch from the splendid ring of mountains surrounding it. Like several other potential anchorages most of it is either too deep or too shallow, and there are many fish cages on its north side. The head of the loch dries out for more than ¼ mile. It is worth visiting for the scenery, preferably in settled weather.

The anchorage east of a jetty and boathouse on the north side at the head of the loch is now occupied by moorings. It is possible to anchor outside them in 10 metres, but there have been reports of anchors fouling discarded chain here. A rock which dries at LWS half a cable offshore is marked by a perch with a diamond topmark.

An alternative anchorage is off a cottage on the south side of the loch, but there is also a permanent mooring there.

*Eilean Balnagowan* on the east side of Loch Linnhe, about three miles northeast of Shuna, provides some shelter on its east side, to the north of a reef which shows above water at MHWS. A drying rock lies one cable northeast of the north point of the island.

# Ballachulish Bay and Loch Leven

56°40′N 5°10′W

Loch Leven is one of the most spectacular of west coast lochs, with hills over 800 metres high crowding in on both sides. The upper five miles of the loch average less than ¼ mile wide but, apart from the scenery, would hold little attraction for a sailing yacht's crew.

The narrows, between Ballachulish Bay and Loch Leven, are crossed by a road bridge of bold or brutal design, depending on your point of view.

Two miles east of the bridge on the south shore Ballachulish slate quarries continued in operation until about the 1950s, being easier to work than those at Easdale, and having rail transport.

The area between the quarries and the shore has now been cosmetically landscaped.

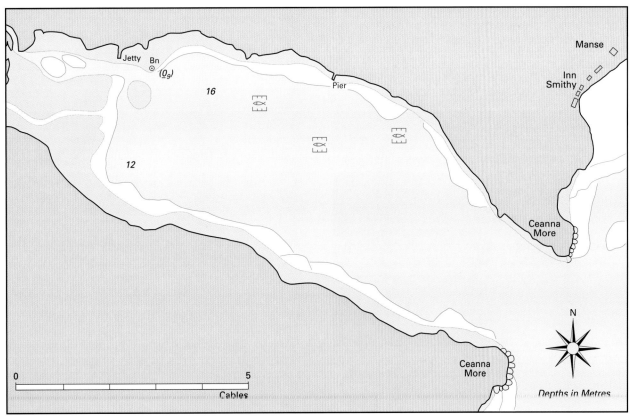

**LOCH CORRIE**

III. LOCH ETIVE AND LOCH LINNHE

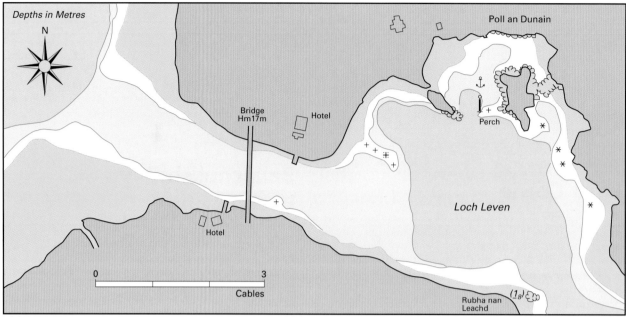

**LOCH LEVEN**

One of the earliest aluminium smelters powered by hydroelectricity was established in 1908 at Kinlochleven, at the head of the loch.

**Chart**

*2380* (1:25,000)

**Tides**

In the main body of the loch the tidal streams run at up to one knot, but at the narrows, and at Caolas nan Con, five miles further east, they run at more than five knots.

At the narrows the in-going stream begins at –0515 Oban (+0115 Dover).

The out-going stream begins at +0100 Oban (–0430 Dover).

At Caolas nan Con the in-going stream begins ¾ hour later, but the out-going stream begins at the same time as at the narrows.

The tidal constant at Corran, just north of the entrance to Loch Leven is +0005 Oban (–0525 Dover).

At the head of Loch Leven the constant is +0045 Oban (–0445 Dover).

*Height in metres* at Corran

| MHWS | MHWN | MTL | MLWN | MLWS |
|------|------|-----|------|------|
| 4·4  | 3·3  | 2·5 | 1·7  | 0·7  |

There are no official figures for heights within Loch Leven, but the range is likely to be substantially less than outside the narrows.

Moderate overfalls occur west of the narrows on the ebb with a westerly wind.

### Dangers and marks

Cuil-Cheanna Spit starboard-hand light buoy lies south of the middle of the entrance to Ballachulish Bay, more than a mile from the north point, and the spit shoals very gradually from the buoy towards the land.

On the south side of the bay rocks lie close inshore, and 1½ miles west of the bridge, Sgeir nan Ron, a drying rock lies ½ cable offshore.

Ballachulish Bridge, at the narrows, has a charted headroom of 17 metres. West of the narrows there are drying banks of stones on both sides of the channel with a bar between them on which the greatest depth is only three metres.

Half a cable east of the bridge a submerged rock lies 50 metres off the south shore. East of the narrows both shores dry out up to ½ cable, and there are rocks in the bay northeast of the narrows.

At Eilean Choinneich, a mile east of the bridge drying and submerged rocks lie up to three cables east of the island, and in the bay to the north of it. There are rocks southeast of the next group, St Mungo's Islands, but their north side is clean.

At Caolas nan Con, about five miles from the bridge, drying banks on the south side of the channel are marked by a decaying timber beacon at the west end.

Ballachulish Bridge; Rubha na Leachd, the point on the south side beyond the bridge, in line with the mid point of the bridge leads between drying banks in the approach from the west (1990)

Bishop's Bay, North Ballachulish (2003)

## Directions

Pass south of Cuil-cheanna Spit buoy, which is slightly south of the middle of the entrance to Ballachulish Bay.

Approach the narrows from north of west, with Rubha nan Leachd, the south point beyond the bridge, under its midpoint, bearing about 110°.

A mile east of the bridge pass south of Eilean Choinneich, and continue east for half a mile to avoid the rocks east of the island; the 20-metre contour should keep you clear of these rocks. Pass north of St Mungo's Islands (Eilean Munde), ¾ mile further east. At Caolas nan Con, five miles east of the bridge, keep within a quarter of the apparent width of the channel from the north side.

Ballachulish; the visitors pontoon at the Isles of Glencoe Hotel (2003)

### Lights

At night Cuil-cheanna Spit buoy is lit Fl.G.6s, and there are street lights on Ballachulish Bridge.

### Anchorages

*Port Eoghainn* ENE of the bridge, is occupied by moorings, and the bottom, which consists of boulders, is said to be unsuitable for anchoring.

*Kentallen Bay*, on the south side of the entrance to Ballachulish Bay, is very deep almost to the low-water line and there are many moorings. The rocky promontory at the head of the bay stands on the low-water line.

*In Ballachulish Bay* there are only occasional anchorages for use in settled weather or to go ashore for stores. All of them are exposed to onshore winds, and the best is probably at Onich on the north side, to the east of the ruined pier. The broken stumps of a timber extension may remain around the head of the pier, which dries.

Diesel, petrol, *Calor Gas*, some chandlery, and mechanical and electrical repairs at garage. Shop, post office, phone box.

*Poll an Dunain (Bishop's Bay)* east of the narrows on the north shore. A reef, part of which dries, extends a cable from the west shore of the bay, and the ebb tide, which runs anticlockwise round the bay, sets across this reef see plan.

Much of the inner pool is shallow and most of it is occupied by moorings, but it is usually possible to find space to anchor. A drying rock in the middle of the entrance to the pool is marked by a thin steel perch which almost covers at HW with drying rocks lying east of it. A drying reef extends almost ¼ cable off the west point of the entrance. The stone pier dries at LWS and the skipper of a yacht wishing to lie alongside must make prior arrangements with the chairman of the Moorings Association, Derrick Thom ☎ 01855 821554. A charge is made for this facility. A scrubbing berth with a clean bottom lies on the east side of the pier, with bollards and mooring hooks. All the moorings in the bay are private and there are no visitors' moorings. Limited space for anchoring may be found north or NW of the perch. Note that the west side of Bishop's Bay dries.

The hotel at Ballachulish Bridge is reached by a shore path.

*Ballachulish* (on the south shore) The Isles of Glencoe Hotel provides pontoon berths for its customers in the north-west facing inlet 1½ miles ESE of the bridge.

### Services and supplies (at hotel)

Water, diesel, petrol, showers, swimming pool.

At Ballachulish (south) there are shops, bank, post office, phone box, fish-and-chips.

*Eilean Munde* Occasional anchorage south of the islands, between the largest and most westerly (St Mungo's Island, on which is a graveyard and ruined chapel) and the islet on its east side.

A large drying rock lies ¾ cables southeast of the next islet, with a submerged rock ½ cable further southeast.

Fish cages lie between the drying rock and the most easterly island.

*Loch Leven Seafoods* on the north shore, about four miles east of the bridge, has four visitors' moorings with pick-up buoys, a pontoon landing stage, and a cafe-restaurant ☎ 01855 821048 www.Lochlevenseafoods.co.uk

*Eilean nam Ban* beyond the narrow passage at Caolas nan Con, a rather constricted pool lies behind an island close to the north shore, where a small boat can anchor.

*Kinlochleven* off the wharf on the south side towards the head of the loch. Private moorings are reported to occupy all the water with suitable depths for anchoring. Beyond this the loch is shoal and drying for ¼ mile.

Kinlochleven now lives by catering for walkers on the West Highland Way.

Supermarket, garage, post office, phone box in Kinlochleven.

Eilean nam Ban, east of Caolas nan Con, with space for one small boat to anchor (2003)

Eilean nam Ban, Loch Leven

# Loch Linnhe – upper part

56°47′N 5°10′W

The upper part of Loch Linnhe is impressive, with high mountains on each side, but offers little interest to the crew of a sailing yacht unless going to or from the Caledonian Canal, which leads to the east coast of Scotland, although the lochs along the canal itself are worth visiting on their own account.

The wind is normally funnelled along the axis of Loch Linnhe, one way or the other. In general, the longer a loch and the higher the mountains at its head, the greater is the rainfall. Loch Linnhe is one of the longest, with the highest mountain.

Fort William has nothing to offer the yachtsman except the convenience of shops and some services.

An expedition to the top of Ben Nevis, the highest mountain in Britain, can be made, although its head is not often clear of cloud.

The continuous staircase of locks on the canal, Neptune's Staircase, is worth seeing.

Another expedition which might take you out of the rain is the railway journey to Mallaig, and the coast on the way – particularly if you don't have time to go there by sea.

Loch Eil, to the west of the head of Loch Linnhe, is more open and unusually featureless.

### Charts

*2380* (1:25,000). *2372* shows both Corran Narrows and the head of the loch at 1:10,000 and 1:6,250 respectively, but is hardly necessary for yachts.

Corran Narrows from south (1991)

# Corran Narrows

56°43′N 5°14′W

### Dangers and marks

Shoals on both sides up to two miles SSW of the narrows are marked, on the east side by a green conical light buoy at the south end of Cuil-cheanna Spit, and on the west side by red can light buoys. Note that both port-hand buoys are lit.

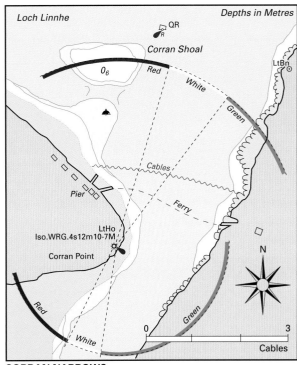

**CORRAN NARROWS**

An unlit red beacon stands on Sallachan Point, two miles southwest of the narrows.

A white lighthouse stands at Corran Point, on the west side of the narrows.

Corran Shoal, north of the lighthouse, is marked by a red can light buoy, northeast of the shoal and nearly ½ mile north of the lighthouse.

A white rectangular light beacon stands on the east shore, ½ mile northeast of the lighthouse.

### Tides

The tidal stream in the narrows runs at more than five knots at springs, with eddies on both sides, mainly north of the narrows on the flood and south of them on the ebb.

The in-going stream begins –0600 Oban (+0055 Dover).
The out-going stream begins +0005 Oban (–0525 Dover).
The constant is +0005 Oban (–0525 Dover).

*Height in metres*

| MHWS | MHWN | MTL | MLWN | MLWS |
|------|------|-----|------|------|
| 4·4  | 3·3  | 2·5 | 1·7  | 0·7  |

### Directions

Between the more southerly port-hand buoy and the east point of the entrance keep towards the buoy as the east shore dries off for 1½ cables.

With chart *2380* and carefully watching the echo sounder it is feasible to sail west of the buoys on the west side of the channel.

### Lights

**Corran Point** lighthouse, Iso.WRG.4s12m10-7M, shows red to west of the fairway, white over the fairway and the shore to SE of the fairway, and green between 215° and 305°.
**Pier** NNW of Corran Point Fl.R.5s7m3M.
**Cuil-cheanna** buoy Fl.G.6s.
**Red buoy** Fl(2)R.15s.
**Red buoy** Fl(4)R.10s.
**Corran Shoal** buoy Q.R.
**Corran north beacon**, on east shore, Fl.5s4m4M.

### Anchorages

*Corran Point*, north of the pier, clear of ferry moorings, and avoiding both the shoal and very deep water on either side. Avoid also the underwater power cables crossing the narrows.

*Camas Aiseig*, ½ mile north west of the pier. There are many fish cages, but the best anchorage is about halfway between a stone slip and a group of houses at the mouth of a burn three cables further north. Don't go closer in than the 5-metre line, as there are drying rocks on the low-water line.

There is a shop, and petrol, at Clovulin, one mile south from the pier.

# Upper Loch Linnhe

56°49′N 5°07′W

The loch north of Corran Narrows is generally clean except for drying banks at the mouths of burns on either side.

Fort William stands on the east side of the loch towards the head. North of the town a long pier extends from the east shore.

North of the pier, Lochy Flats dry out half a mile from the east shore. Their outer edge is marked by a green conical light buoy.

Three cables north of Lochy Flats buoy, a red can light buoy marks McLean Rock which dries 0·3 metre, on the west side of the fairway.

North and west of this buoy are several low islands with drying areas up to ½ cable round them. Beyond Rubha Dearg on the west shore the pulp mill is very conspicuous.

South of the most westerly island a submerged rock lies ¾ cable off the south shore.

North of Eilean na Creich the entrance to the Caledonian Canal is marked by a cylindrical white tower with a conical slate roof.

Between Eilean na Creich and the canal entrance is a red can light buoy.

### Tides

The constant is +0022 Oban (–0508 Dover).

*Height in metres*

| MHWS | MHWN | MTL | MLWN | MLWS |
|------|------|-----|------|------|
| 4·1  | 3·1  | 2·5 | 1·9  | 0·9  |

### Directions

After passing the long pier at Fort William the two light buoys must be identified and passed on the appropriate hand. After passing the island off Rubha Dearg, if heading for Loch Eil, keep midway between the south shore and the islands to the north, to avoid the submerged rock off the south shore.

If making for the canal entrance, pass at least ½ cable northeast of Eilean na Creich and either side of the red buoy.

### Lights

**Lochy Flats** buoy Q.G.
**McLean Rock** buoy Fl(2)R.12s4M.
**Buoy south of canal** Fl.R.3s4M.
**Light tower at canal entrance** Iso.WRG.4s6m5M; white over fairway 310°–335°, green to east, red to southwest. Obscured from west of 030°.

### Supplies

Water, diesel, petrol, showers, refuse disposal.
☎ 01397 703786 *Fax* 704969. VHF Ch 16.

### Anchorages

A temporary anchorage is between the small town pier and the long pier to the north. Shoal and drying inshore of a line between the heads of these piers.

Lochaber Yacht Club has a single visitor's mooring, capacity six tons. ☎ 01397 702370 *Fax* 703360.

*Camusnagaul*, nearly a mile northwest of Fort William on the west shore. Keep clear of McLean Rock, ½ cable northwest of the red buoy, as well as a submerged rock halfway between the buoy and the shore to the west. There are many moorings in the bay. Occasional ferry to Fort William.

Camusnagaul from NNE (2003)

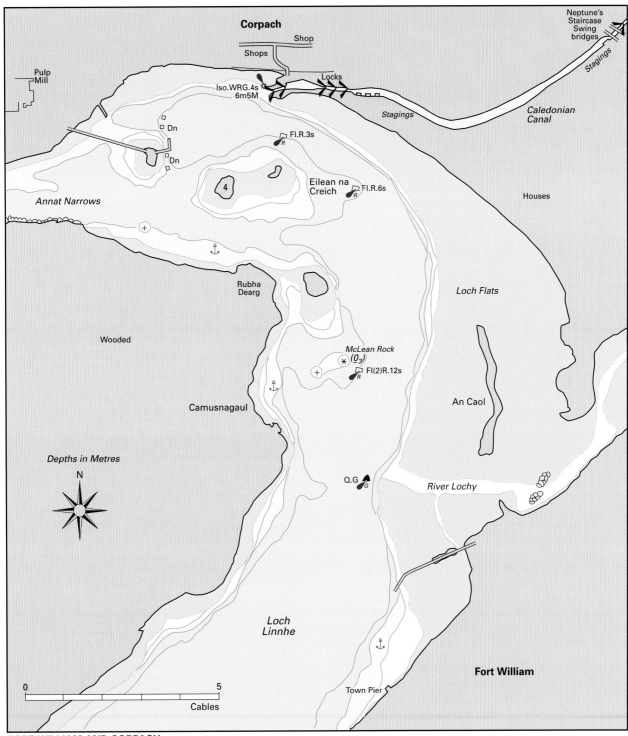

**FORT WILLIAM AND CORPACH**

Corpach Sea Loch (2003)

***Fort William Underwater Centre*** at the long pier north west of the town has pontoon berths as well as visitors' moorings. A temporary berth, for a brief visit ashore, alongside sheet piling at the car park at the southwest end of town there are ladders but nowhere to make fast, do not leave a yacht unattended.

***Rubha Dearg*** Anchor off shore west of the point, avoiding the submerged rock noted above. Trees on shore provide some shelter from southerly winds. A yacht at anchor may be held by the tide across the wind.

***Corpach*** anchor west of canal entrance, clear of moorings and the approach to the canal. A port hand light buoy Fl.R.6s is established east of Eilean na Creich.

A pontoon has been provided for yachts waiting to enter the canal, and the staging has been faced to make it more user-friendly.

The canal basin, above the sea lock, is used by commercial vessels; yachts are not normally allowed to stay there and have to go through two more locks to lie at stagings; these are now on the north side and less liable to interference than in the past.

In the canal basin the water level varies so that fenders of yachts moored there are likely to be pushed over the edge of the quay, leaving the hull to chafe.

The canal is open seven days a week from mid May to early October, 0800–1800; from mid-March to mid-May, and October to beginning of November, Monday to Saturday 0800–1650; November to mid-March Monday to Friday 0915–1600. The sea lock is only open four hours each side of HW. The opening times should be checked by phone, particularly near the ends of the season.

For details of the Caledonian Canal and East Coast see *The Yachtsman's Pilot to North and East Scotland* and Imray's *Map of the Inland Waterways of Scotland*.

VHF R/T: call sea lock on Ch 74. Corpach lock office, Corpach ☎ 01397 702249; Canal office, Inverness ☎ 01463 233140.

### Supplies and services

Shops, hotels and garages in Fort William. Early closing Wednesday. In Corpach, a shop on the north side of the main road is open late some evenings, and open on Sunday. *Calor Gas* at garage. Bus to Glasgow, Mallaig and Inverness, train to Glasgow and Mallaig.

*Communications* Post office, phone boxes.

## Loch Eil

56°51′N 5°14′W

Entered through Annat Narrows, south of the pulp mill.

In the narrows the tide runs at five knots at springs.
The west-going stream begins –0435 Oban (+0220 Dover).
The east-going stream begins +0130 Oban (–0400 Dover).

The shore generally dries up to ½ cable, and more in places, usually off the mouth of a burn. Shoals extend two cables off the north shore at the west end of the narrows. The head of the loch dries off two cables, and then quickly becomes deep.

# IV. Sound of Mull

This is the usual route to the north and west, the alternative being along the exposed south side of Mull. The Sound of Mull is straightforward and the fairway is well marked and adequately lit. If you want to explore (or tack) close inshore you will need a large-scale chart, but if you keep generally at least two cables from the shore you could manage without it.

The southeast half of the sound has high hills on both sides, particularly on Mull, and the wind tends to funnel along the sound, with occasional squalls through valleys. About halfway along the sound, at Salen, there is a gap in the Mull hills and a southwest

wind often divides, blowing northwest and southeast from there. The converse may happen as well – in a generally northeasterly wind two yachts approaching this point from opposite directions may both be under spinnaker.

On the Morvern shore at the southeast end of the sound there are cliffs up to 250-metres high, and it is not uncommon for waterfalls on these cliffs to be blown upwards in strong southwest winds.

**Charts**

*2390* (1:25,000); *2171* Sound of Mull and Approaches (1:75,000).

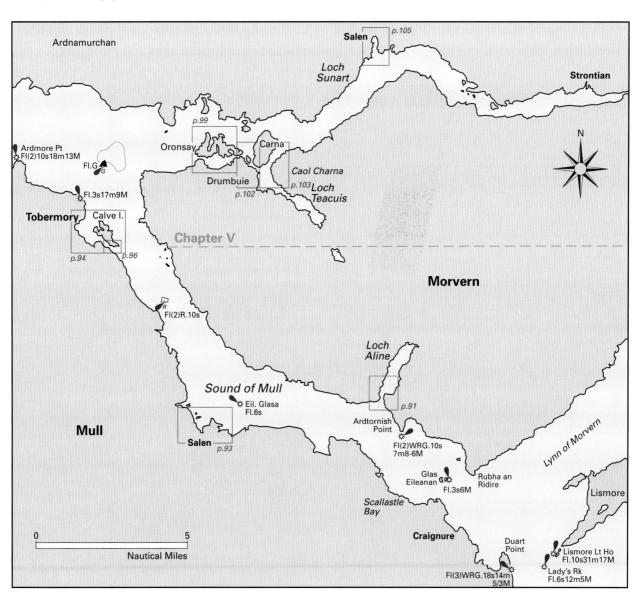

**Yeoman Bridge** is one of five very large bulk carriers serving the superquarry at Glensanda (2007)

## Southeast entrance to the sound

56°30′N 5°42′W

The southeast entrance to the sound is between Rubha an Ridire on Morvern and Scallastle Point on Mull, but for convenience the passage between Lismore and Mull is included here.

### Dangers and marks

Lismore lighthouse on Eilean Musdile, southwest of the south end of Lismore, is a very distinctive mark. Half a mile southwest of the lighthouse is Lady's Rock, above water but with drying rocks up to half a cable round it, and a white light beacon on it, not always easily seen on a dull day.

Black's Memorial Tower, low on the Mull shore, is a miniature mock castle, nearly a mile west of Lady's Rock.

Duart Castle, also on Mull, is a classic picture-postcard castle on a low cliff six cables WNW of Black's Memorial tower; it is not visible from southeast.

Liath Sgeir, drying three metres, is just over a mile north of Lismore lighthouse halfway between the lighthouse and the southwest end of Bernera, and slightly to the west of a line joining these two points. This is a hazard if tacking, or making direct for the Lynn of Morvern from south of Lismore.

### Tides

Constant +0015 Oban (–0515 Dover).

*Height in metres* at Craignure

| MHWS | MHWN | MTL | MLWN | MLWS |
|------|------|-----|------|------|
| 4·0 | 3·0 | 2·3 | 1·7 | 0·6 |

The north-going stream begins –0545 Oban (+0110 Dover).

The south-going stream begins +0025 Oban (–0505 Dover).

In the fairway between Lady's Rock and Mull tidal streams run at three knots springs, with overfalls at the windward end of the passage if the wind is against the tide. Between Lady's Rock and Lismore the ebb reaches four knots.

On the flood there are eddies and severe turbulence northwest of Lismore lighthouse, which can be very uncomfortable in heavy weather.

On the ebb an eddy sets into Bernera Bay.

### Directions

Apart from Liath Sgeir there are no specific hazards until the Sound is entered between Rubha an Ridire and Scallastle Point. The main consideration is to carry a fair tide.

With wind against tide there may be steep overfalls between Lismore and Mull.

Especially in southerly winds there is often a wind shadow off Duart Point.

### Lights

At night the passage is well lit.

**Lismore** lighthouse Fl.10s31m17M.

**Lady's Rock** Fl.6s12m5M.

**Black's Memorial** Fl(3)WR.18s14m5/3M, showing red over Lady's Rock and from 353° to the shore, and white elsewhere.

### Anchorages

*Duart Bay*, Mull 56°27′N 5°40′W. Both parts of the head of the bay dry off nearly four cables and it rapidly becomes deep beyond the low-water line.

Drying and submerged rocks lie one cable NNE of the slip at Torosay on the west side of the bay.

Occasional anchorage off the slip in five metres, clear of the rocks, and leaving clear access to the slip for tourist launches.

Alternative temporary anchorage in very quiet weather off the stone jetty at Duart Castle on the east side of the bay, leaving clear access to the jetty. Both Torosay Castle, which is a Victorian mansion, and Duart Castle, which is ancient, are popular tourist attractions.

*Craignure Bay, Mull* 56°28′N 5°42′W. This is the main car ferry terminal for Mull so the anchorage is likely to be disturbed. The west side of the bay dries and shoals for 1½ cables, but some shelter can be found anywhere in the bay in offshore winds; leave space for ferries manoeuvring to the pier.

A drying berth may be found at the stone pier in the south corner of the bay.

Light, F.R, at head of ferry pier. Leading lights 244°.

Shop, post office, phone box, hotels, *Calor Gas*, refuse disposal. Ferry to Oban; bus to Tobermory and southwest Mull.

*Bernera Bay* 56°29′·5N 5°34′·5W southeast of Bernera is suitable for anchoring in northerly winds – see page 75.

# The Sound of Mull

56°32′N 5°54′W
A listening watch should be kept on VHF Ch 16 for information about very large ships passing through the Sound to or from Glensanda – when laden they draw 14m.

## Dangers and marks

The direction of buoyage is northwestward.

Throughout the sound unmarked rocks lie up to two cables off both shores.

In the middle of the southeast entrance, between Rubha an Ridire (Morvern) and Scallastle Point on Mull are the Grey Rocks (Glas Eileanan), two islets with a light beacon on the east one; the fairway is to the north.

Off Scallastle Point a group of rocks stands above water. Sgeir nan Gobhar is the most northerly of these, and a rock drying 0·5 metre lies two cables east of it.

Seven cables WNW of Grey Rocks light beacon a red can light buoy marks the north side of Yule Rocks, which are submerged.

Ardtornish Point, nearly two miles northwest of Grey Rocks at the west end of the cliffs on the Morvern shore, has a ruined castle and a small white light beacon low on the point itself.

The entrance to Loch Aline is about a mile northwest of Ardtornish.

A red can light buoy a mile WSW of Ardtornish Point near the Mull shore marks Avon Rock over which the depth is 2·2 metres.

Green Island (Eileanan Glasa) is the largest of a group of islets 5½ miles west of Ardtornish, with a light beacon on the north islet. The main fairway is on the north side.

A mile ENE of Green Island light beacon a green conical light buoy four cables off the Morvern shore marks Fiunary Rocks, which can be a hazard because of their position on the inside of the bend of the sound.

¾ mile SSW of the light beacon another green conical light buoy Bogha Rock marks the south side of a group of rocks, on the north side of a channel between these rocks and Mull.

A red can light buoy 3½ miles northwest of Green Island, near the Mull shore, marks a wreck with 2·7 metres over it, and a green conical light buoy Bogha Bhuilg more than a mile further north marks drying rocks near the Morvern shore.

Inninmore N cardinal light buoy, between Yule Rocks and Ardtornish Point marks a bank which is only of concern to large ships.

There are no other specific dangers outwith two cables from the shore until the sound opens out at the mouth of Loch Sunart. The west entrance to the Sound of Mull is described on page 97.

### Tides

Tidal streams run at up to two knots at the southeast entrance to the sound, and up to one knot elsewhere.

At the southeast end of the sound:

The northwest-going stream begins about –0600 Oban (+0100 Dover);

the southeast-going stream begins about –0045 Oban (+0615 Dover).

Three miles southeast of Calve Island:

The northwest-going stream begins about +0500 Oban (–0030 Dover);

the southeast-going stream begins about –0045 Oban (+0615 Dover).

Note that the stream runs northwest for about 5¼ hours at the southeast end and 6¾ hours at the northwest end of the sound.

The constant throughout averages +0015 Oban (–0515 Dover).

*Height in metres at Craignure*

| MHWS | MHWN | MTL | MLWN | MLWS |
|------|------|-----|------|------|
| 4·0 | 3·0 | 2·3 | 1·7 | 0·6 |

*Height in metres at Tobermory*

| MHWS | MHWN | MTL | MLWN | MLWS |
|------|------|-----|------|------|
| 4·4 | 3·3 | 2·5 | 1·8 | 0·7 |

The times quoted are all interpolated from more comprehensive data, for which refer to almanacs or Admiralty tide tables.

### Directions

The passage is straightforward but, unless you have the large-scale chart, keep north of Grey Rocks and Green Island and at least two cables offshore.

### Lights

At night, the following lights give sufficient guidance.

**Lismore** lighthouse Fl.10s31m17M.
**Grey Rocks** light beacon Fl.3s6M.
**Fiunary Rocks** buoy Fl.G.6s.
**Bogha Rock** light buoy Fl(2)G.6s and

**Bogha Bhuilg** light buoy Fl.G.5s

**Inninmore** N card light buoy Q

**Ardtornish Point** Fl(2)WRG.10s8-6M; white over fairway in both directions with green sectors to the north and red sectors to the south, with a further white sector between the red.

**Avon Rocks** light buoy Fl(4)R.12s

**Green Island** light beacon Fl.6s8M.

**Yule Rocks** light buoy Fl.R.15s

Red buoy Fl(2)R.10s.

**Rubha nan Gall** lighthouse Fl.3s9M (obscured by Calve Island southwest of the centre of the sound).

Ardtornish light beacon is not very bright and in poor weather the coloured sectors may not be visible from the west from as far as Eileanan Glasa.

### Anchorages – southeast part of the sound

*Rubha an Ridire* 56°30´N 5°42´W; an occasional anchorage, at the northeast point of the island west of Rubha an Ridire, the north point of the entrance to the sound.

The island has drying rocks off its east and northwest sides: approaching from southeast keep closer to the mainland than to the island; approaching by the north of the island keep at least a cable off it.

Anchor in five metres near the northeast tip of the island with Grey Rocks beacon over the northwest tangent of the island.

*Scallastle Bay*, Mull 56°29´N 5°44´W. Good anchorage in offshore winds but the approach from eastward needs care. There are drying patches two cables off the west side of the bay and up to one cable elsewhere.

Approaching from southeast steer towards Grey Rocks to avoid the rock which dries 0·5 metre referred to above, and keep northeast of the middle of the channel between Grey Rocks and Sgeir nan Gobhar.

Approaching by the north of Grey Rocks needs more careful chartwork to avoid Yule Rocks.

From northwest there is little problem.

*Ardtornish Bay*, east of Ardtornish Point on Morvern, provides good shelter from southwest to northeast, and is an inviting place to wait if the weather is particularly unpleasant further up the sound, although a north-westerly funnels through a gap from Loch Aline. Anchor off the boathouse in the northwest corner. The head of the bay is shoal.

# Loch Aline

56°33´N 5°46´W

**Charts**

A new edition of chart *2390* includes a plan of Loch Aline. In 2006 there were no fish farms within the loch.

The best anchorage between Oban and Tobermory, and better in many ways than either, Loch Aline has a variety of sheltered places within and is fairly easy to enter, even at night, and can provide most essential supplies. The shores are steep and thickly wooded.

The entrance is a cable wide but the least depth in the fairway is only 1·7 metres, and the tide runs at about 2½ knots in the narrows. Just inside the loch a mine produces high quality silica sand, and coasters load sand several times a week from a jetty on the west shore. Look out for the coasters, which have no room to manoeuvre once they are in the narrows, as well as for the car ferry which runs frequently to Mull from a slip on the west side of the narrows.

Ardtornish Estate appears to positively welcome visitors and there are several pleasant walks, particularly to the west side, and to Ardtornish Castle, southeastward along the Sound of Mull. The gardens of Ardtornish House are usually open to visitors; a box is provided at the gate for donations.

Respect the courteously worded notices by which access to parts of the estate is restricted at certain times, so that visitors will continue to be welcome.

The church, half a mile northwest of the village, has an excellent collection of medieval carved stones. Visits to the sand mine, which has 30 miles of tunnels, can be arranged for groups of people in mid-week.

**Tides**

Constant +0012 Oban (–0518 Dover).

*Height in metres*

| MHWS | MHWN |
|------|------|
| 4·5 | 3·2 |

**Dangers and marks**

Outside the entrance Bolorkle Reef (Bogha Lurcain), which dries nearly a cable from the east shore, is unmarked but leading marks at the root of the loading jetty at the mine lead clear of it. The front

Coasters are often encountered in Loch Aline

Loch Aline entrance from southwest

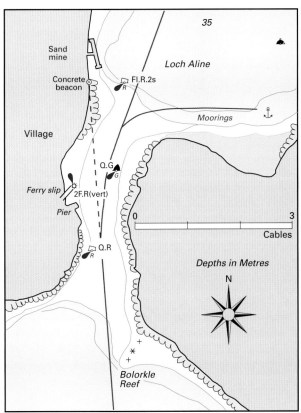

**LOCH ALINE**

mark is a concrete pillar, originally painted orange, but faded, and the back mark is an orange stripe on the structure of the jetty.

Three light buoys in the narrows are usually easier to pick out than the leading marks. The marks lead east of the first red can buoy, which is often the best guide to finding them.

Half a mile within the loch a yellow iron beacon with a spherical topmark marks the end of a reef on the east side, and half a mile further a similar beacon marks the east end of a more extensive reef on the west shore. The head of the loch dries for about half a mile.

**Approach**

*From southeast* keep two cables offshore until the leading line is identified before turning in to the entrance.

*From west* keep a cable offshore until the leading line is seen to the east of the first red buoy. Each buoy should be left on the appropriate side; they are intended for commercial vessels, but there is little space for yachts to tack inshore of them.

*By night* the buoys are lit (Q.R, Q.G, Fl.R.2s) and there are fixed white lights on the leading marks, but a much brighter light stands on the head of the jetty. It has sometimes been known, on a quiet night, for a helmsman to steer for this light, carefully keeping it in line above its own reflection.

The line of the southeast face of the screen at the ferry slip bearing about 220° astern leads through the deepest water at the north end of the narrows between the second and third buoy.

Loch Aline provides shelter in a gale

## Anchorages

*Lochaline Pier* is outwith the loch, three cables west of the entrance; yachts can berth temporarily alongside, but should not be left unattended as coasters load timber at the pier. Water is laid on.

*An alternative temporary berth* is at the old stone pier on the west side of the entrance narrows, except within an hour of LW springs; however, the face of this pier is very rough.

*The most convenient anchorage* is on the west side, north of the loading jetty. The immediate surroundings are rather industrial and there are several private moorings, but the wooded shore provides good shelter in westerly winds and it is convenient for the village. There is reported to be less water than charted. Keep clear of the approach to the jetty.

*Miodar Bay* in the southeast corner of the loch. It is best to anchor beyond the moorings, but the bottom shelves abruptly just off the low-water line, so take care not to swing over it at low tide.

*East shore* There is also a good anchorage beyond the first beacon, towards the slipway and moorings. Leave swinging room clear of shoal water inshore.

*West shore* A stony shelf extends a cable off the mouth of a burn to the SSW of the second yellow beacon, but there is a good anchorage between the burn and the beacon.

*Beyond the beacon* there is an anchorage between the beacon and a stone jetty on the west shore further north, but there are rocky patches on the bottom with poor holding.

After heavy rain the outflowing stream from the river here will hold a yacht's stern to a strong southwest wind – even a ketch with the mizzen set, which can be discouraging if rain is still falling.

The heavily wooded shore provides excellent shelter, but the steep hillside cuts out any sun quite early in the evening.

## Supplies and services

Shop in the village, on the west side of the narrows.

Ardtornish Estate ☎ 01967 421288 has an engineer, and can supply diesel in cans in emergency. Divers may be available – ask piermaster or at shop. Calor Gas at the shop. Water hose at the stone pier. Water also at slipway on east side of loch (by containers). Showers at Dive Centre near pier. Whitehouse Restaurant ☎ 01967 421777. See www.thewhitehouserestaurant.co.uk Snack Bar on pier.

Yachts can be dried out at the north side of the stone pier at the narrows.

Ferry to Mull; the quickest way to Oban may be to take this ferry, then a bus or a lift, and then a ferry at Craignure.

*Communications* Post office and phone box in the village.

## Anchorages – middle part of the sound

*Fishnish Bay*, Mull 56°31′N 5°50′W, occasional anchorage in offshore winds. The head of the bay dries off ¼ mile and the sides of the bay are steep-to, and there are many fish cages. Anchor towards the head of the bay in about five metre.

# Salen

56°31′·5N 5°57′W

Southwest of Green Island, this is a fairly good anchorage, but it needs to be approached carefully because of several groups of rocks in the way.

## Approach

*From east* keep at least ¼ mile offshore to avoid drying banks at the mouth of the Forsa river. The 10-metre contour is close to the low-water line here.

Salen (Mull). More rocks, which are covered, lie beyond those which show here (1991)

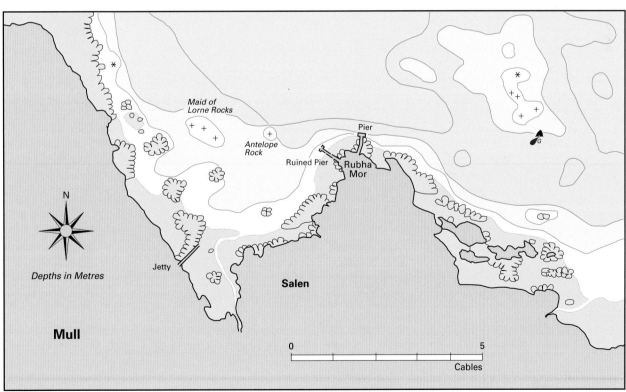

SALEN, MULL

Taking into account that it may range around its mooring, the green conical buoy in line with houses at the root of the pier on the north side of Rubha Mor at the east side of the bay lead clear of this bank.

Pass either south of the buoy, which is on the south side of a group of submerged and drying rocks, or at least ¼ mile north of it, keeping north of the 5-metre contour.

Land at the stone jetty west of the river mouth on the south side of the bay.

Antelope Rock is marked by an unofficial yellowish buoy (if you expected a red can buoy you were using an uncorrected old chart).

### Supplies

Shops, post office, hotel, phone box. Bus to Tobermory and Craignure. Airstrip one mile east. Diesel from filling station 100m along Loch na Keal road from junction in the village.

# Tobermory

56°37′N 6°03′W

Few yachts pass by Tobermory without stopping there. It is one of the few attractive towns on the west coast of Scotland – there are few towns of any sort. The selection of pubs is one of its main attractions, and it has the best range of shops between Oban and Stornoway.

A fairway which must be kept clear to Old Pier from the northeast is marked by small plastic buoys. Additional visitors' pontoons have been established at the landing stage.

MacBrayne's Pier is used by fishing boats, divers' and tourist boats and the Kilchoan Ferry lies alongside overnight. Yachts may go alongside to take on fuel and water but the pier is of piled construction.

Old Pier is the property of Mull Fishermen's Association and dries completely. It should not be used by yachts or tenders except in emergency.

Land has been reclaimed at the west side of the bay, and a floating landing stage installed as well as a launching slip.

### Tides

Constant +0020 Oban (–0510 Dover).
*Height in metres*

| MHWS | MHWN | MTL | MLWN | MLWS |
|------|------|-----|------|------|
| 4·4 | 3·3 | 2·5 | 1·8 | 0·7 |

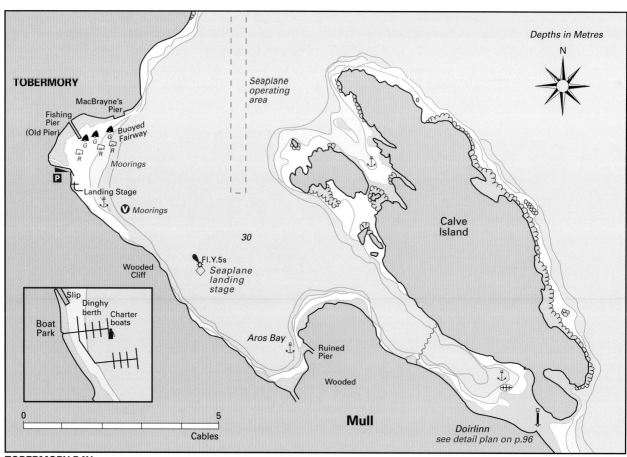

**TOBERMORY BAY**

Tobermory Harbour from east. Visitors' moorings and landing stage at upper left, MacBraynes' Pier at upper right (2003)

## Approach

In the main entrance, north of Calve Island, there are no dangers other than fishing boat and ferry traffic.

*The Doirlinn*, the passage southwest of Calve Island, dries at its southeast end.

Two beacons mark rocks, a tripod in the middle of the southeast entrance and a cylindrical beacon on the northeast side.

Additional visitors' pontoons were installed in 2007
*N Vitelli*

Tobermory waterfront

Doirlinn Narrows from south east about half tide (1987)

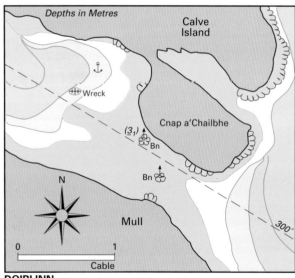

**DOIRLINN**

The passage between the beacons is charted as drying 1·0 metre, so that there should be 1·5 metres at half-tide. The solid bases of the beacons cover at about three metres rise.

The traditional leading line is the church spire at Tobermory with the high-water line on the southwest side of the channel.

The submerged wreck of a fishing boat close northeast of the leading line is no longer a hazard to a yacht passing directly through the narrows.

## Anchorages

Visitors' moorings are laid southeast of the landing stage as well as one off MacBrayne's Pier.

An anchoring area is designated inshore of the visitors' moorings.

*Aros Bay*, at the south end of the bay, is mostly very deep, but reasonable depths can be found off the ruined pier on the west side. Part of the bay may be occupied by fish farming.

*The Doirlinn* The anchorage is near the southeast end, but you have to be sure of clearing the fishing boat wreck. Show an anchor light – fishing boats sometimes come through at HW by night.

## Services and Supplies

Shops, bank, hotels. Chandlery and chart agent (Seafare). Water and electricity at pontoons. Diesel at fuel berth, provided by Mackay's Garage ☎ 01688 302103. Calor Gas from Mackay's, at car park adjacent to pontoons, and from Highland Services ☎ 01688 302296. Showers, launderette at new Harbour Association building. Seaplane service from Glasgow. Divers available (ask at Seafare). Bus to Craignure, ferry to Kilchoan (Ardnamurchan).

*Communications* Post office, phone box.
Piermaster ☎ 01688 302217.
Seafare ☎ 01688 302277 (also VHF Ch 37).
Maclean (fuel) ☎ 01688 302175.
Harbour Association (Jim Traynor) ☎ 07917 832497.
Loch Lomond Seaplanes ☎ 0870 242 1457.

# Northwest entrance to the Sound of Mull

56°39′N 6°04′W

### Charts

*2171* (1:75,000) *2392* 1:25,000. *2394* (see next chapter, Loch Sunart) includes the main group of rocks.

### Tides

Off Rubha nan Gall,
the northwest-going stream begins +0400 Oban (–0130 Dover);
the southeast-going stream begins –0045 Oban (–0615 Dover).
The spring rate is about one knot.

### Approach

The entrance itself is completely clear, but north of Tobermory in mid-channel there is a large area of rocks, with a clear passage nearly a mile wide between Mull and a green conical light buoy which marks their south side. The buoy is about five miles from the entrance and the passage should present no difficulty in moderate weather.

If tacking, look out for the most southeasterly rock, Little Stirk, which dries 3·7 metres. Even when uncovered it is not easily seen if there is a slight sea. For the passage north of New Rocks, see Chapter V. Loch Sunart.

Kilchoan (2001)

### Lights

**Rubha nan Gall** lighthouse Fl.3s17m9M.
**Ardmore Point** Fl(2)10s18m13M (2¼M WNW of Rubha nan Gall).
**New Rocks** buoy Fl.G.6s (NNE of Rubha nan Gall).
**Mingary Pier** (Kilchoan) Q.R8m3M

### Anchorages

56°41′·5N 6°07′W

*Kilchoan Bay* is on the east side of Sron Bheag, the east end of the cliffs which stand on the south side of Ardnamurchan Point.

A drying rock in the middle of the bay, with a shoal area ½ cable west of it is marked by an isolated danger beacon.

Drying rocks lie up to a cable off the west shore, and up to 1½ cables off the east shore.

Pass a cable west and northwest of the isolated danger beacon.

Hotel ☎ 01972 510222, restaurant and shop. Water, petrol, diesel, showers, toilets, rubbish disposal.

Visitors' moorings, pay at box at head of slip.

*A pier 1½ miles east of Sron Bheag* on the northeast side of a small promontory is used by the ferry from Tobermory.

*Mingary Castle* stands half a mile east of the ferry pier. There is temporary anchorage in settled weather on the northeast side of a promontory, Rubh' a' Mhile, close east of the castle.

# V. Loch Sunart

56°41′N 5°48′W
For index plan see previous chapter, page 87.

One of the most picturesque of west coast lochs, with successive ranks of mountains and islands arranged as in a Victorian engraving of Highland scenery.

There are several attractive anchorages and some spectacular bits of rock-dodging for those who have a taste for that sort of thing.

Even in the main fairway of the loch a lot of anxiety will be spared by having chart *2394*. However, the popular anchorage at Drumbuie on the south side of the loch can be reached without any difficulty.

**Chart**

2394 (1:25,000)

**Tides**

Streams run generally at less than one knot.
The in-going stream begins about –0500 Oban (+0200 Dover);

the out-going stream begins about +0130 Oban (–0400 Dover).

At Salen (Loch Sunart) the constant is as Oban.

*Height in metres*

| MHWS | MHWN | MTL | MLWN | MLWS |
|------|------|------|------|------|
| 4·6 | 3·4 | 2·6 | 1·7 | 0·6 |

**Dangers**

*From the south*, and from Tobermory, two rocks, the Stirks, six cables off the west end of Morvern, must be identified.

Big Stirk, the more northerly of the two, is above all except extra high spring tides.

Little Stirk, which dries 3·7 metres, two cables south of Big Stirk, lies east of a line from Tobermory to the Big Stirk, and so is very much a hazard.

*From the west* the main dangers are Red Rocks and Sligneach Mor and Sligneach Beag.

Red Rocks, the most northerly of the group of rocks at the junction of Loch Sunart with the Sound of Mull, nearly a mile ENE of the green conical buoy, dry 2·8 metres, showing about half-tide.

Sligneach Mor lies ¼ mile southwest of Rubha Aird Shlignich, the north point of the entrance to Loch Sunart, and is only 0·6 metre high, drying up to a cable on all sides.

Sligneach Beag, half a mile west of Sligneach Mor, dries 3·3 metres, with other drying rocks up to a cable off its north side.

**Approach from west**

The traditional clearing mark is the summit of Risga in line with the north point of Oronsay, 083°, but Risga may be difficult to identify. If you can't make out this line, steer towards Maclean's Nose at the base of Ben Hiant, the highest hill on the north side of the entrance; then towards a waterfall east of Auliston Point, the south point of the entrance (to avoid Sligneach Mor), and when you have identified Sligneach Mor, head for the entrance.

## Drumbuie

56°39′N 5°56′W

This is the popular rendering of Loch na Droma Buidhe, the name of the basin south of the island of Oronsay, two miles east of Auliston Point on the south side of the entrance to Loch Sunart.

The entrance is ¾ cable wide but clean almost to the steep rocky sides of the channel.

North of the entrance drying rocks extend up to a cable off the west point of Oronsay.

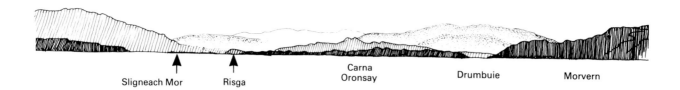

Sligneach Mor    Risga    Carna Oronsay    Drumbuie    Morvern

Loch Sunart approach from the west

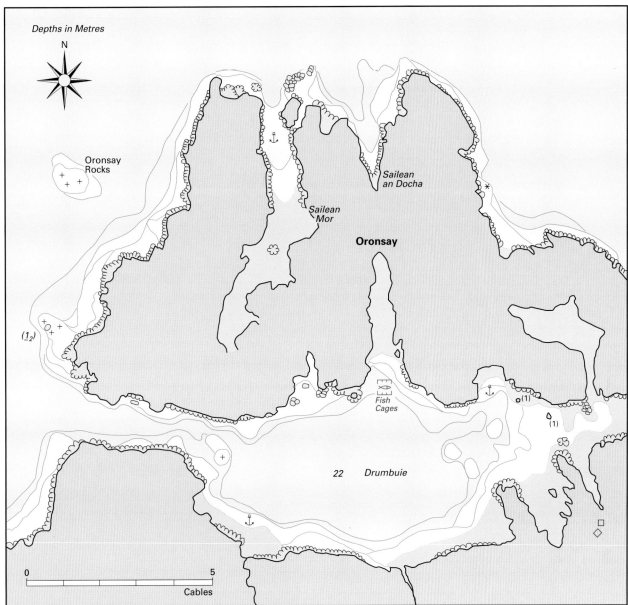

**ORONSAY AND DRUMBUIE**

About a cable inside the entrance a submerged rock, with less than 0·5 metre over it, lies just south of the continuation of the line of the south side of the entrance. The north side of the rock is cleared by keeping the west end of the south side of the entrance in sight.

During or after strong westerly winds some sea runs in through the entrance. While this does not affect the anchorage, going out may be a matter of some anxiety.

In 2006 the fish cages had migrated to the S side of Drumbuie.

## Anchorages

There is shelter somewhere in the loch from any wind, but allow for possible changes in wind direction. Strong southeasterlies tend to be deflected to blow from east. The most popular anchorage is in the southwest corner, but a drying bank lies off the mouth of the burn, and the bottom quickly drops away.

The next bay to the east, halfway between a second burn and a conspicuous promontory, is also a suitable anchorage. Beyond this promontory the loch is mostly shoal and drying.

The view from the highest point of a track on the south side of the loch is well worth the effort of scrambling up the hillside.

The main inlet on the south side of Oronsay mostly dries out. Fish cages lie in the mouth of the inlet.

The next bay to the east, north of the promontory towards the head of the loch on the south side, and west of a 1-metre high rock, is clean.

## Anchorages north of Oronsay

These can be reached without any difficult pilotage, but Oronsay Rocks on which the least depth is 1·5 metres, lying two cables off the middle of the west side of Oronsay, must be avoided.

Drumbuie from south (2003)

*Sailean Mor* 56°40′N 5°56′W a narrow inlet on the
north side of Oronsay, dries more than three
cables at the head but there is depth for anchoring
one cable within the entrance.

Note the drying rocks lying more than ½ cable
north of the east point of the entrance.

*Sailean an Docha*, the next inlet to the east, is
obstructed by fish cages.

The bay on the northeast side of Oronsay provides
reasonable shelter in offshore winds, but there is
fish-farming equipment at both ends of the bay.

*Glenmore Bay* on the north side of Loch Sunart
provides shelter on the east side of Eilean Mor,
which is effectively a peninsula except at HW
springs.

Rocks up to ¾ cable off the east side of Eilean
Mor are normally above water, and a submerged
rock lies more than a cable northeast of them.

There are fish cages as well as permanent
moorings for yachts and workboats.

Pass ½ cable east and northeast of the visible
rocks keeping a good lookout for any which may
be covered at HW, and anchor north of them.

Loch Drumbuie and Loch Sunart from southwest (1985)

Traditional cruising; Loch Fyne skiff *Nighean Donn,* with loose-footed
lug mainsail, in Loch Sunart

West Kyle of Carna — Sgeir More and rocks beyond just showing

# Loch Sunart – central section

56°41′N 5°48′W

A mile east of Oronsay on the south side of Loch Sunart, Carna sits in the mouth of Loch Teacuis, while on the north side between Oronsay and Carna is the small island of Risga.

The main channel south of Risga is obstructed by several rocks in the apparently clear water between these islands.

The passage north of Risga is clear but there are submerged rocks on its north side, as well as rocks both submerged and drying outwith each end on the south side.

A further mile from the east side of Carna the islet of Dun Ghallain off the north shore marks the beginning of a straightforward reach leading northeast to Salen.

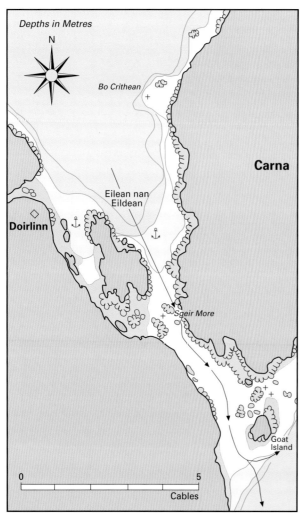

**DOIRLINN AND WEST KYLE OF CARNA**

## Tides

Streams run generally at less than one knot, but north of Carna, and in the entrances to Loch Teacuis, they run at 2½ knots. At Laudale Narrows, four miles from the head of the loch, the streams run at three to 3½ knots.

The in-going stream begins about –0500 Oban (+0200 Dover).

The out-going stream begins about +0130 Oban (–0400 Dover).

At Salen (Loch Sunart) the constant is as Oban.

*Height in metres*

| MHWS | MHWN | MTL | MLWN | MLWS |
|------|------|-----|------|------|
| 4·6 | 3·4 | 2·6 | 1·7 | 0·6 |

## Dangers

Oronsay Rocks with a least depth of 1·5 metres, lie two cables west of Oronsay.

A rock with a least depth of 2·1 metres, lies one cable WNW of Risga.

Ross Rock with a least depth of 0·3 metre, lies one cable south of Risga.

Drying and submerged rocks lie ¾ cable east of Risga.

Broad Rock, with a least depth of 0·3 metre, lies almost exactly halfway between Risga and Carna.

Bo Crithean and other drying rocks lie within ½ cable of the west side of Carna.

South of Dun Ghallain lies a rock drying 2·4 metres, and Dun Ghallain Rock, awash, lies ¾ cable south of the east end of Dun Ghallain.

## Directions

Only Ross Rock and Broad Rock are at all close to the fairway, and for most of us will only be a hazard within 2½ hours of LW.

Ross Rock is avoided by keeping the north point of Oronsay under the third step in the profile of Rubha Aird Shlignich on the north shore bearing 283°.

Broad Rock is best avoided simply by keeping well away from mid-channel, preferably towards Carna so as to avoid also the rocks east of Risga.

The main anchorages are in Loch Teacuis and the passages on either side of Carna, and at Salen, but other occasional anchorages can be found on the chart.

## Carna

The passages either side of Carna are among the trickiest bits of rock-dodging anywhere on the west coast, and there is still some doubt about the position of some of the rocks.

In both passages the tidal streams run at 2½ knots springs.

The channel east of Carna is the easier to follow as there are more rocks above water by which to establish your position.

Oronsay and the passages to Loch Teacuis (1991)

## West Kyle of Carna

56°39′·5N 5°54′W

Named on charts as Caol Achadh Lic, which translates as something like 'the channel of the field of stones', or 'Stonefield Channel'.

The cleanest passage seems to be between Carna and the mid-channel rock, Sgeir More, which dries about 1·7 metres.

The pilotage is easiest before Sgeir More covers; the ideal time would be just before LW neaps.

Keep at least a cable off the west side of Carna to avoid Bo Crithean, and steer for the east side of Eilean nan Eildean.

Near the south end of that island cross to the Carna shore and keep about 20 metres off it as there are also submerged rocks about 10 metres off Carna.

After this keep closer to the mainland to avoid rocks which cover, northwest of Goat Island (Eilean nan Gabhar).

### Anchorages

*Doirlinn*, west of Eilean nan Eildean, has a sandy bottom but limited swinging room. A mooring ring is fixed on the second tidal islet southeast of the white cottage on the mainland.

*The north entrance* to the west kyle is a good anchorage; within the kyle the tide runs more strongly although the shelter is better.

## Caol Charna

56°39′·5N 5°52′W

The passage east of Carna is more straightforward than that to the west.

A ridge of rock, Drochaid Charna ('bridge of Carna') extends over halfway across the passage from the southeast side, and its middle point stands just above MHWS.

Caol Charna approach

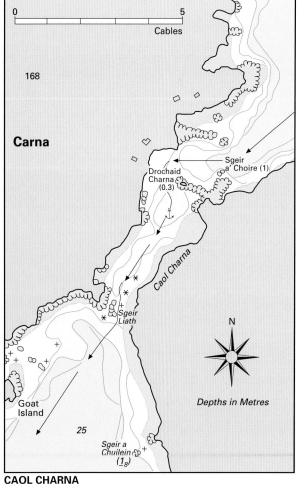

CAOL CHARNA

THE ISLE OF MULL AND ADJACENT COASTS     ***103***

Caol Charna from east with Drochaid Charna in the foreground (2001)

Sgeir a' Choire, on the northeast side of Drochaid Charna, stands about a metre high, and various drying and submerged rocks lie to the north of it, near the Carna shore.

In the channel between Carna and the northwest end of Drochaid Charna the greatest depth is just over two metres.

At the next narrows, 3½ cables southwest of Drochaid Charna, a reef lies along the shore of the southeast point of Carna, and Sgeir Liath, which covers, lies near mid-channel.

Northeast of Sgeir Liath a submerged rock (1·5 metres) lies nearer to the mainland shore than to Sgeir Liath, and two drying rocks lie further northeast. There is no passage west of Sgeir Liath.

### Directions

Identify and steer for Sgeir a' Choire and when about ¼ cable from it, turn to pass between Drochaid Charna and the promontory on Carna close north of it, steering for the south side of the promontory. Pass midway between Carna and the west end of Drochaid Charna.

At the next narrows identify Sgeir Liath and pass southeast of it, closer to the rock than to the mainland.

### Anchorage

The pool southwest of Drochaid Charna is said to provide good shelter even in strong northeast winds, although it is subject to the strong tide.

# Loch Teacuis

56°38′N 5°50′W

The basin south of Carna is entered by either of the passages described above.

Sgeir a' Chuilein, ½ cable off the east side of the basin, dries 1·8 metres with an uncharted submerged rock ¼ cable southwest of it, and the south side of the basin dries off ¼ mile.

A mile southeast of Goat Island the rock-infested narrows of Rahoy (Caolas Rahuaidh) lead to the head of Loch Teacuis. Generally this passage should be taken just northeast of mid-channel. In the narrowest part a rock, drying 1·2 metres, lies south of mid-channel.

The inner basin is more than a mile long with a narrower part about the middle of its length.

Between this narrow part and the head of the loch, about a cable off the southwest side, an uncharted rock awash was found by Hilary King in 1985. On old uncorrected charts, its approximate position is close south of the 4-metre sounding on chart *2394*.

The head of this basin dries off two cables, and the sides about ½ cable. Depths are otherwise moderate throughout the southeast part of the basin, and the bottom is mud.

## Salen

56°43′N 5°46′W

A convenient anchorage on the north side of Loch Sunart 4½ miles beyond Carna, with some provisions and a hotel.

A drying reef west of the middle of the bay is marked on its E side by a port hand buoy. The former beacon has been destroyed.

The jetty on the west side of the bay dries and its side is uneven in places.

The whole bay has been appropriated for permanent moorings, leaving a small area for visitors to anchor on the west side north of the jetty, as well as the area between the reef and the west shore. There are so many moorings here that anchors should be buoyed.

Visitors' moorings. Pay at Jetty Shop.

### Tides

The constant is as Oban.
*Height in metres*

| MHWS | MHWN | MTL | MLWN | MLWS |
|------|------|-----|------|------|
| 4·6  | 3·4  | 2·6 | 1·7  | 0·6  |

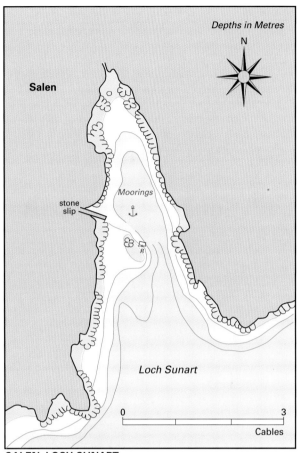

SALEN, LOCH SUNART

Salen Sunart from southwest. Note the reef is now marked by a port-hand buoy

**V. LOCH SUNART**

### Supplies

For all supplies and services it is recommended to phone in advance.

Diesel, shop, post office, phone box, hotel; water at pier. Limited chandlery, showers, launderette. Visitors' moorings (15 tons maximum).

The Jetty Shop can arrange delivery of provisions by 1800 hours on the same day, given reasonable notice, and delivery of Calor Gas the following morning. The Jetty Shop, Salen ☎ 01967 431333; VHF Ch M.

# Loch Sunart – upper part

56°41′N 5°36′W

The loch continues for a further eight miles beyond Salen and it is in this part that the large-scale chart 2394 will be most needed.

For the first two miles beyond Salen, as the loch bends round to the southeast, submerged and drying rocks lie up to two cables off the south shore.

In the next mile, off two islands on the northeast side, several submerged rocks are disposed at random (one of them having been reported in 1979 at a point where the chart shows a depth of 25 metres). To most yachts these are probably only a hazard within two hours of LW springs or one hour of LW neaps.

A cable west of Garbh Eilean, the larger and more southerly of the two islands, a rock dries 3·3 metres. Rubha an Daimh, on the north shore four cables southeast of Eilean Garbh, has drying rocks extending up to two cables southwest of it.

Opposite this point, at the mouth of the Laudale river, a bank of stones dries off two cables, and on both sides of the loch between Rubha an Daimh and Laudale Narrows, a mile further southeast, the foreshore dries up to ¼ mile in the bays on either side of the loch.

Immediately before Laudale Narrows, at Glas Eilean a shoal bank with a least depth of 1·2 metres extends two cables WNW of the island.

From Laudale Narrows to the head of the loch the south shore is generally clean, but on the north side there are drying banks at the mouths of rivers, particularly at Strontian.

Eilean a' Mhuirich, ¾ mile west of Strontian, has a rock drying 1·8 metres ¼ cable off its south side.

The head of the loch dries for half a mile.

### Anchorages

*Camas na h'Airbhe*, on the southwest shore 1½ miles west of Laudale Narrows, has suitable depths for anchoring close to the west side, but quickly becomes very deep away from the shore.

*Garbh Eilean* has reasonable depths off its southeast side.

*Liddesdale*, on the south shore 1½ miles east of Laudale Narrows, has reasonable depths east of the mouth of the valley, but there is probably no space clear of fish cages.

*Strontian* There are reports of sandbanks shoaling both at Strontian and at the head of the loch. Keep a close watch on the chart and the echo sounder in this area.

The mouth of the river at the head of the loch dries out a long way. Anchor beyond a concrete slip with a green shed east of a granite obelisk which stands on a low cliff east of the village. In easterly winds there are violent squalls from the head of the loch.

Visitors' moorings are provided by Kilcamb Lodge Hotel ☎ 01967 402257. Call before arrival to confirm availability.

### Supplies

At Strontian, a shop, hotel, restaurant, post office, phone box, Calor Gas and refuse disposal.

# VI. The west coast of Mull

The areas described in the previous chapters have been for the most part enclosed by hills or at least sheltered behind islands. The west of Mull is predominantly open to the Atlantic and the landscape is more rugged. On the Ross of Mull and Iona the shore is mostly granite, often pink in colour, with brilliant white sand. There are several good anchorages, a few of them excellent, and many attractive occasional ones.

The easiest approach is from the Sound of Mull, but in clear and moderate weather with careful pilotage you can sail direct from the Sound of Islay or from the Firth of Lorn by the south side of Mull, but you have to negotiate the passage between Mull and the Torran Rocks. This is described, together with the approach to the Sound of Iona, in Chapter VII on page 124.

## Charts

*2171* (1:75,000) covers all of the west of Mull included in this chapter.

Chart *2652* (1:25,000) is desirable for Loch na Keal and the off-lying islands, and *2392* (1:25,000) covers the northwest coast of Mull.

## Tides

Off Caliach Point and Rubh' a' Chaoil, the next point to the south, tidal streams run at up to 2½ knots.

The north-going stream begins –0510 Oban (+0145 Dover).

The south-going stream begins +0115 Oban (–0415 Dover).

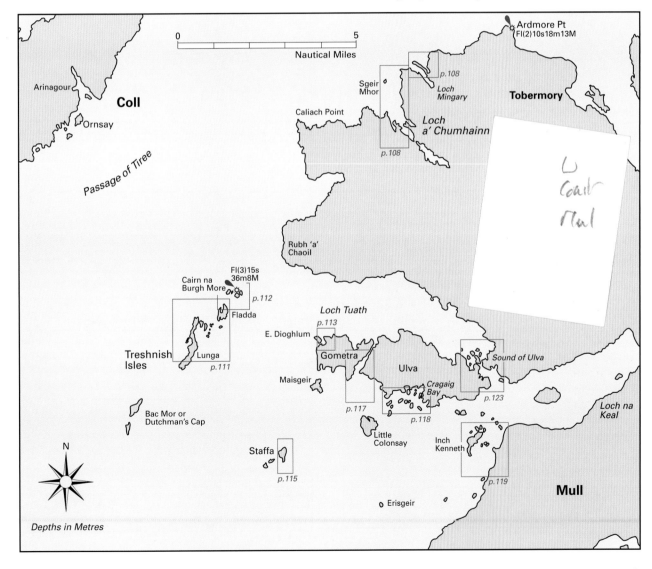

There are strong tidal streams around the Treshnish Isles, but not generally elsewhere. Those in the Sound of Iona are described in the next chapter.

Tidal constants are, on average: at Bunessan on the north side of the Ross of Mull, –0015 Oban (–0545 Dover); at Arinagour, Coll, +0020 Oban (–0510 Dover).

*Height in metres* at Bunessan

| MHWS | MHWN | MTL | MLWN | MLWS |
|------|------|-----|------|------|
| 4·3  | 3·0  | 2·4 | 1·8  | 0·6  |

## Passage notes and dangers

In the passage from the Sound of Mull to Iona there are, with the exceptions described below, no dangers outwith a quarter of a mile from the shore; nor are there any artificial marks – you need to be able to identify various islands, and features on Mull. The dangers beyond ¼ mile from the shore are as follows.

Sgeir Mhor, a reef drying at half tide, three miles ENE of Caliach Point, lies ¾ mile from the shore in the mouth of Loch a' Chumhainn.

East of the Treshnish Isles, many drying rocks lie up to ½ mile outwith the line of the ESE side of the islands.

WSW of Staffa, drying rocks lie up to ½ mile from the island.

The 20-metre contour will generally keep you out of trouble, although sometimes by only a small margin, and a few shallower banks further out may give you a fright, but the echo sounder will be some help in this area in combination with the chart.

The most prominent point of this side of Mull is Caliach Point (56°36′N 6°20′W) and very heavy seas can be met with off it, particularly with wind against tide. It is worth taking care to be there at the most favourable time, particularly at springs or in fresh or strong winds; otherwise stand a couple of miles offshore.

A drying reef extends nearly two cables from Rubh' a' Chaoil, the point 2½ miles south of Caliach Point.

## At night

A light has been established at Cairn na Burgh More, NE of Treshnish Isles, Fl(3)15s36m8M.

There are no other lights on the west coast of Mull except for a sectored light of 6–8 mile range in the approach to Bunessan (next chapter).

A 16-mile light at Scarinish, Tiree, Fl.3s16M, and Dubh Artach lighthouse, Fl(2)30s20M, 13 miles SSW of Iona provide some help in fixing one's position in this area.

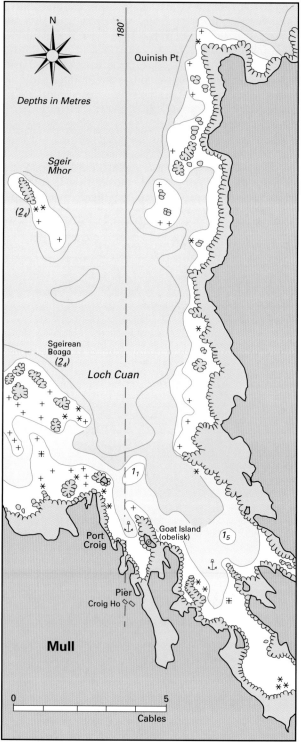

LOCH CUAN

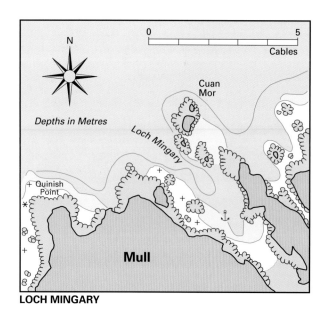

LOCH MINGARY

Port Croig, Loch a'Chumhainn (Loch Cuan), north west Mull. Goat Island is just above the centre of the photo (1987)

Ardnamurchan Lighthouse is obscured by Caliach Point south east of 020°.

## Anchorages – northwest Mull

*Loch Mingary* 56°38′N 6°13′W is an occasional anchorage for a quiet day. The entrance is little more than ½ cable wide between the islets south of Cuan Mor and drying reefs on the southwest side of the entrance. Be prepared to clear out sharpish if the wind or swell start to come onshore.

*Loch Cuan (Loch a' Chumhainn)* 56°37′N 6°14′W This anchorage has more space than Loch Mingary, but it could be almost as much of a trap in an onshore wind, although a shoal-draught boat would find more shelter further in.

It is best to approach before half-flood, when Sgeir Mhor covers, although the swell will usually reveal it after that time.

Sgeirean Beaga covers at the same time, so an approach can be made from northwest, or from north, passing two cables east of Sgeir Mhor.

Croig House which is difficult to identify among the trees, in line with the ill-defined summit of Carn Mor, the highest hill to the south, bearing 180°, leads east of Sgeir Mhor.

Otherwise the only mark is a stone obelisk on Eilean nan Gobhar (Goat Island), on the south side of the loch.

*Anchorages* If near LW springs, take care to avoid the 1-metre patch nearly ¼ mile north of the obelisk. Anchor either east of the promontory southeast of the obelisk, or in Port Croig, the creek northwest of Goat Island, but this has very little swinging room.

*Provisions* Shop, hotel and post office at Dervaig, two miles by dinghy or three miles by road.

*Calgary Bay*, two miles south of Caliach Point, is another temporary anchorage if there is no swell, but perhaps less attractive than the two above, being accessible by road and fairly popular with tourists ashore.

Drying reefs extend ¼ mile southwest from the north point of the entrance, and submerged and drying rocks lie up to 1½ cables from the southeast side of the bay. Restaurant.

# Treshnish Isles

56°30′N 6°25′W

These interesting and attractive islands are a breeding ground for grey seals and for many sea birds. The rocks and islets provide some shelter but they are rarely free from swell.

The approach, particularly from the north, needs careful pilotage, and the tide runs strongly between the islands.

The main islands are, from north to south, Cairn na Burgh More, which has ruins of a chapel and a castle on it, Fladda, which is flat; Lunga, the largest and highest of the group; and Bac Mor, otherwise known as The Dutchman's Cap, whose summit is a pronounced knob.

Aerial photo of rocks at Treshnish Is. (2003)

## Approach and clearing marks

*From north* identify Tighchoie, the northwestern-most rock with a prominent rectangular block eight metres high, and the leading beacons on Lunga which are stone cairns, one close to the shore and one on the summit (see photos).

These beacons in line bearing about 195° lead through the north channel, but they – especially the lower beacon – may be difficult to identify against the sky.

North Rock (Bogha Tuath) and the drying rocks west of Cairn na Burgh More are cleared by keeping the summit of Bac Mor bearing 214° open west of Tighchoie.

Pass between Tighchoie and Sgeir Eirionnaich, the flat-topped island east of it, keeping the beacons in line. About midway along Sgeir Eirionnaich alter course to the east of the line as it leads over rocks east of Sgeir a' Chaisteil and steer for the east point of Lunga.

The east tangent of Lunga just open west of the west side of Sgeir Eirionnaich, bearing 183°, leads clear of rocks on the west side of the passage, but all these lines pass close to drying rocks NNW of Sgeir Eirionnaich.

*From east* approach with Staffa astern: rocks on the east side of the group are cleared by keeping the south point of Lunga well open of the north point

Treshnish Isles from southwest, about half tide. Sgeir Eirionnaich is above the centre of the photo, and Sgeir a'Chaisteil at bottom left. Tighchoie at upper left (1987)

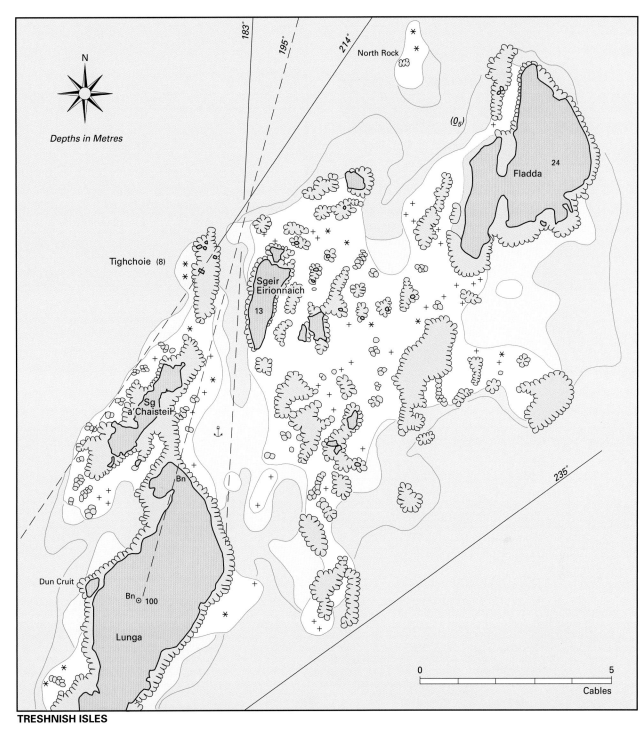

N

Depths in Metres

183°

195°

214°

North Rock

(0₅)

Fladda

24

Tighchoie (8)

Sgeir
Eirionnaich

13

235°

Sg
a'Chaisteil

Bn

Dun Cruit

Bn ⊙ 100

Lunga

0                                    5

Cables

**TRESHNISH ISLES**

Beacon

Bac Mor

Beacon

Tighchoie

Treshnish Isles north entrance. Sgeir Eirionnaich is on the left and Tighchoie
on the right, with the summit of Bac Mor showing beyond (2003)

Bac Mor open east of Lunga 235° clears rocks shown on page 110 (2003)

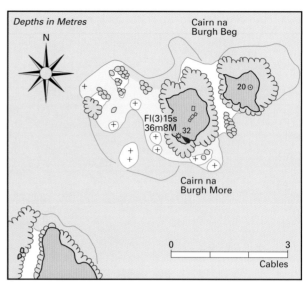

**CAIRN NA BURGH ISLANDS**

of Bac Mor, bearing 235°. The mouth of a prominent cave on the shore below the summit of Lunga kept open bearing 300° leads south of drying rocks east of Lunga.

A submerged rock lies one cable east of Lunga, and a drying rock more than a cable southwest of it.

North of the position of the drying rock keep within a cable of Lunga to clear a very shoal patch (0·4 metre), which lies 1½ cables northeast of Lunga; a 1·8-metre patch lies ½ cable WNW of the 0·4-metre patch.

### Anchorage

Anchor east of the boulder spit at the north end of Lunga. Small boats sometimes also anchor in a pool between Sgeir a' Chaisteil and the reef southeast of it.

### Cairn na Burgh

In very quiet weather the Cairn na Burgh Islands make an interesting visit, but the tides run very strongly here and there is no shelter.

Anchor at either end of the sound between the two islands.

Cairn na Burgh Beg from Cairn na Burgh More. With neither shelter nor good holding, these can only be visited in the quietest weather (1984)

Acarsaid Mor, Gometra from north (2003)

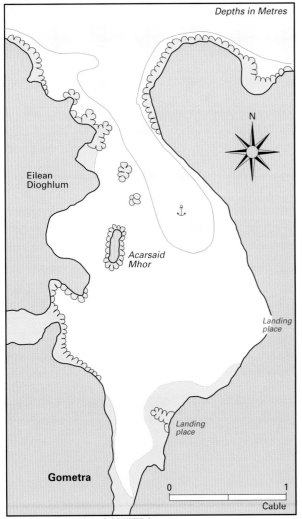

**ACARSAID MHOR, GOMETRA**

## Loch Tuath

56°31′N 6°13′W

Loch Tuath lies between the north west part of Mull and the island of Ulva.

Loch na Keal can be reached from the head of Loch Tuath through the Sound of Ulva but the passage should only be attempted on a rising tide and even then at a very cautious pace. The approach to the Sound of Ulva from the south is easier, and both entrances are described on pages 120 and 121.

### Tides

For the Sound of Ulva the constant is –0010 Oban (–0540 Dover).

*Height in metres*

| MHWS | MHWN | MTL | MLWN | MLWS |
|------|------|-----|------|------|
| 4·4  | 3·2  | 2·5 | 1·8  | 0·6  |

### Dangers towards the head of the loch

Sgeir Dubhail, which dries 2·6 metres lies in the middle of the loch, a mile and a quarter from its head. There are many rocks around the approach to the Sound of Ulva, and the head of the loch should be avoided entirely unless you have the large-scale chart, *2652*.

### Anchorages

*Acarsaid Mhor*, Gometra 56°30′N 6°18′W A popular anchorage on the northwest corner of Gometra at the south point of the entrance to Loch Tuath.

Most of the inner part of the inlet is too shallow for yachts of even moderate draught, and shoal-draught boats have a great advantage here.

Keep towards the east side on entering to avoid drying rocks on the west side outside the entrance, some of which are showing in the photo, but don't overdo it as a drying shelf of rocks and boulders lie on the east side.

Port Rainich from northeast (1987)

Staffa from SSW. The Buachaille stands at the right, with drying rocks showing beyond it (1987)

Anchor near the east side, no further in than abreast the north end of the islet (unless it is neaps or you have a shoal-draught boat).

*Port Rainich* 56°31′N 6°12′W is not named even on the large-scale chart and is difficult to find. It lies behind Eilean Rainich on the north side of Loch Tuath about four miles from the entrance and is best found by identifying Torloisk House, a large house among trees on the hillside, from which Port Rainich is ESE. Swinging room is very limited.

An Carraigean, the rock at the outer end of the reef on the south side of the entrance, does not normally cover. Enter from southwest rather closer to An Carraigean than to Eilean Rainich to avoid drying rocks at the south end of the island, and then turn north towards the head of the inlet, keeping closer to Eilean Rainich. Anchor when the south high-water line of Eilean Rainich is in line with the north point of Eilean Dioghlum at the south side of the entrance to the loch.

*Soriby Bay* 56°29′N 6°11′W at the southeast of Loch Tuath has a good reputation for shelter although it seems open to northwest. Drying and submerged rocks lie more than a cable WNW of Eilean Liath which is about the middle of the south shore of the bay. Anchor at the south end of the west side of the bay, or in the mouth of the inlet in the southeast corner of the bay, but not far in as there are submerged and drying rocks.

# Staffa

56°26′N 6°20′W

With its basalt columns and several sea caves, of which Fingal's Cave is the best known, Staffa is one of the most spectacular natural features anywhere.

The island has no adequate anchorage and yachts have to take their chances outside some drying rocks off the landing place on the east shore. The island itself provides little shelter and the slightest sea will make a visit a matter of anxiety for the skipper. The wind and sea can get up quickly and an eye should be kept on the boat at all times.

### Dangers and anchorages

The plan shows the approximate location of rocks on the east side of the island.

Frequent visits by tourist launches should be taken into account.

The usual anchorage is off the landing place at the north end of the Buachaille, but there are no marks for avoiding any of the rocks; the bottom is rocky and falls away sharply.

A gap in the rocks two cables NNE of the landing place, with moderate depths, might be less affected by seas from the west but the bottom is covered with weed.

At the northeast end of the island is a small beach sheltered from south and southwest suitable for landing a dinghy, but a yacht would have to stand off.

At anchor off Fingal's Cave, Staffa

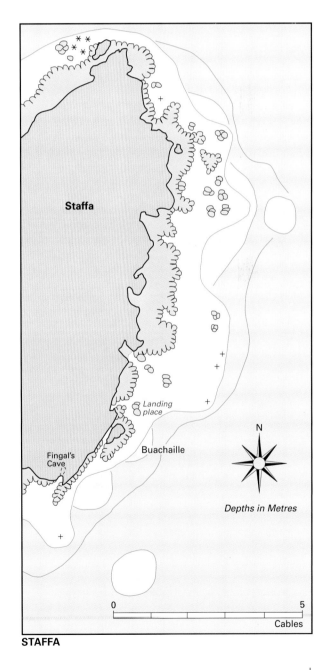

Staffa

Landing place

Buachaille

Fingal's Cave

N

Depths in Metres

0                    5

Cables

**STAFFA**

# Loch na Keal

56°23′N 6°04′W

This is the principal inlet on the west coast of Mull but there are so many rocks that it would be unwise to enter without chart *2652* or, at the least, *2171*. There are no villages around this loch and the main interest is in the pilotage and the anchorages themselves. Climbers will want to have a go at Ben More, which is the only island mountain more than 915 metres (3000 feet) apart from the Cuillins of Skye.

### Tides

Ulva Ferry constant –0010 Oban (–0540 Dover).
*Height in metres*

| MHWS | MHWN | MTL | MLWN | MLWS |
|------|------|-----|------|------|
| 4·4  | 3·2  | 2·5 | 1·8  | 0·6  |

Tidal streams are not significant.

### Dangers

A mass of rocks off the south side of Ulva and Gometra will be described in greater detail in relation to each anchorage.

Maisgeir, a reef mostly above water, extends six cables south of the west end of Gometra; however it is black and low-lying and difficult to see at dusk or in hazy weather.

The passage four cables wide northeast of Little Colonsay is clear except for drying rocks which lie more than a cable north of its north west end, as well as a 2·1-metre patch two cables off its north side, and a rock 1-metre high 1½ cables north of its east end.

Erisgeir, about the middle of the entrance to the loch, 2¼ miles south of Little Colonsay, is a conspicuous islet 22-metres high with drying rocks more than ½ cable off its north and west sides, and a detached rock drying 4·4 metres more than a cable south of it.

On the southeast side of the loch, up to two miles SSW of Inch Kenneth, there are several submerged and drying rocks, all of which are avoided by keeping the east point of Ulva (which may not be easy to identify) open of the northwest side of Inch Kenneth bearing 027°.

Rocks above water and drying extend four cables north of Inch Kenneth. The light beacon at the entrance to Loch na Lathaich on the Ross of Mull bearing 208°, open of the northwest side of Inch Kenneth leads close west of these.

Geasgill Islands between Ulva and Inch Kenneth have rocks drying up to ½ cable all round, except south of Geasgill Mor, the larger island, and a drying reef extends one cable east of the southeast point of Geasgill Mor.

MacQuarrie's Rock which dries 0·8 metre, ½ mile south of the east point of Ulva, is the most dangerous rock in the loch. Various transits using the Geasgill Islands and other islands lead clear of the rock.

The traditional clearing mark is the south extremity of Garbh Eilean, northeast of Little Colonsay, touching the north extremity of Geasgill Beag bearing 266°; an easier line to identify is the south side of Geasgill Mor in line with the south side of Little Colonsay bearing 259°.

To pass north of MacQuarrie's Rock, keep the south side of Little Colonsay open north of Geasgill Beag bearing 255°. Once east of the point half a mile northeast of Geasgill Mor, alter course so that Little Colonsay is almost hidden behind it 252°.

MacQuarrie's Rock is safely passed when the west side of the Sound of Ulva begins to show north of the east extremity of Ulva, bearing 348°.

In the inner part of Loch na Keal, Eorsa has drying rocks up to a cable off its east end, and Scarisdale Rocks extend east from a point 1¼ miles east of Eorsa.

### Directions

The straightforward approach is south of Little Colonsay and north of Erisgeir; pass a cable south of Geasgill Mor and choose a suitable clearing mark to avoid MacQuarrie's Rock.

If continuing to the head of the loch pass either side of Eorsa but then keep to the north side of the loch which is clean outside a cable from the shore. Alternative passages should be tried only with chart *2652*.

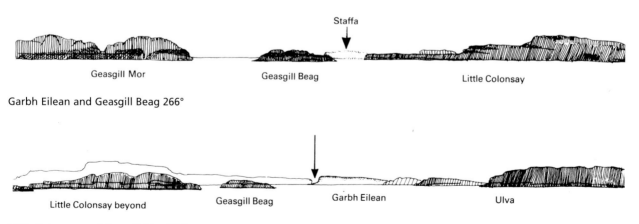

Staffa

Geasgill Mor  Geasgill Beag  Little Colonsay

Garbh Eilean and Geasgill Beag 266°

Little Colonsay beyond  Geasgill Beag  Garbh Eilean  Ulva

Little Colonsay and Geasgill Mor 255°

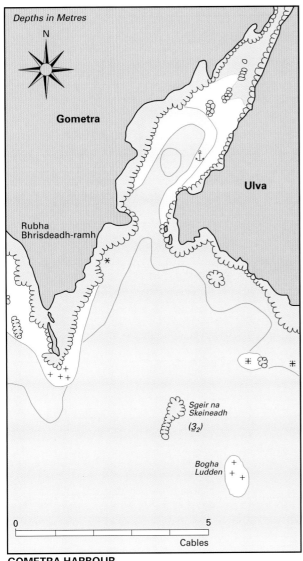

Depths in Metres

N

Gometra

Ulva

Rubha
Bhrisdeadh-ramh

Sgeir na
Skeineadh

$(3_2)$

Bogha
Ludden

0                                              5

Cables

**GOMETRA HARBOUR**

## Anchorages

### Gometra Harbour

56°29′N 6°16′W

The inlet between Ulva and Gometra continues NNE as a drying channel separating the two islands, across which lies a bridge.

Drying rocks lie up to a cable off the east side of Rubha Bhrisdeadh-ramh (Broken Oar Point), the promontory on the west side of the entrance.

Sgeir na Skeineadh, a detached rock three cables east of the promontory, dries 3·2 metres, and there are submerged rocks two cables further southeast.

Care should be taken not to mistake the next bay to the west for Gometra Harbour.

Approach with the Sound of Iona astern between Staffa and Little Colonsay and pass one to two cables east of Broken Oar Point.

A dark bluff on the northwest side of the basin in line with the middle of the entrance leads clear.

Anchor in the basin beyond the narrow entrance,

Cragaig Bay from Ulva (2003)

Gometra Harbour. Note that Bogha Ludden and Sgeir na Skeineadh are out of the photo (2003)

**VI. THE WEST COAST OF MULL**

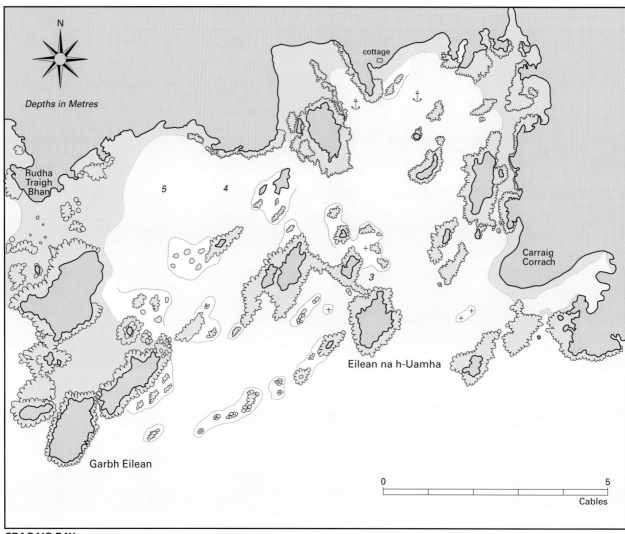

**N**

Depths in Metres

Rudha
Traigh
Bhan

5        4

Carraig
Corrach

cottage

3

Eilean na h-Uamha

Garbh Eilean

0        5
Cables

**CRAGAIG BAY**

near the east shore, which is the cleanest; drying rocks lie up to a cable from the west side and ¼ mile from the head of the inlet. Substantial seas come in with strong southerly winds.

### Cragaig Bay

56°28′N 6°13′W

Northeast of Little Colonsay, Cragaig Bay is filled with islets, one or two of which have sandy beaches attached to them.

There is only one straightforward inlet, the entrance to which lies east of Eilean na h-Uamha which is grass-topped, 1¼ miles ENE of Little Colonsay.

As you sail past the islets the entrance opens up, leading to an inconspicuous stone cottage under the more easterly of the twin peaks of Ulva.

Anchor towards the head of this inlet, southwest or southeast of the promontory south of the cottage.

Some sea comes in with strong southerly winds.

An abandoned village on the northeast side of the

bay with the ruins of a water mill in the northeast corner, is best seen early in the summer before the bracken takes over.

Many other pools can be found, particularly with a dinghy or shoal-draught yacht. There is no simple way of reaching the large basin in the northwest of the bay, but a determined rock-dodger may be able, on a rising tide, to find a way in at the northeast corner.

### Inch Kenneth

56°27′N 6°09′W

The usual anchorage is east of the island, approached from the north.

Rocks extend four cables north of Inch Kenneth; Sunday Rock (Maol an Domhnaich), the broad rock three cables from the island, rarely covers (dries 4·4 metres) but other drying and submerged rocks lie up to a cable further northwest.

Clearing marks depend on identifying one of several white buildings on the Mull shore; the

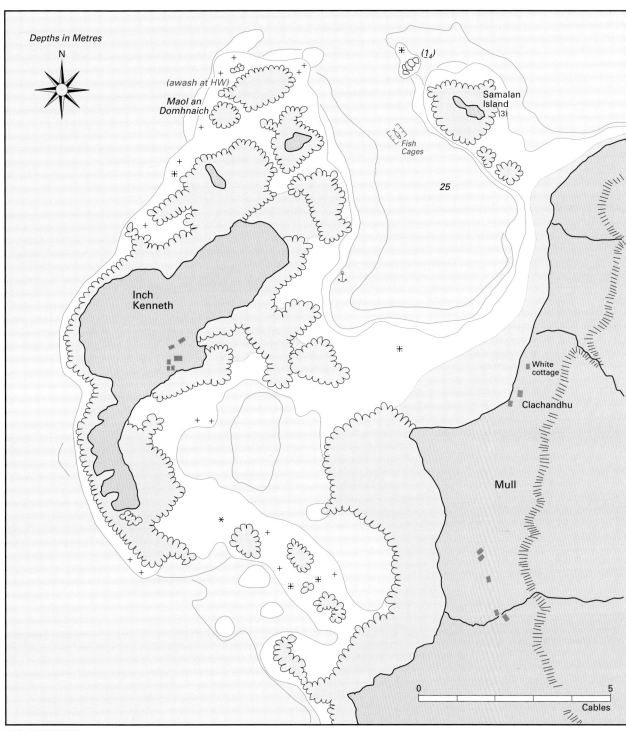

Depths in Metres

N

(awash at HW)

Maol an Domhnaich

$(1_4)$

Samalan Island (3)

Fish Cages

25

Inch Kenneth

White cottage

Clachandhu

Mull

0    Cables    5

**INCH KENNETH**

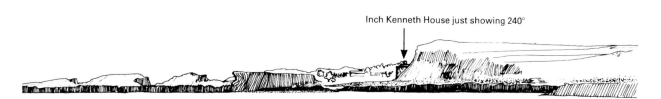

Inch Kenneth House just showing 240°

Inch Kenneth House just showing beyond cliffs 240°

problem is compounded by a note 'White Cottage' beside one of the buildings on the chart, but compass bearings should identify which building is referred to.

On the east side of the entrance rocks drying and awash two cables northwest of Samalan Island are cleared by keeping a white shed bearing 130° open west of rocks on the west side of the island.

Approach from NNW keeping one of two white cottages on the southeast shore bearing 150° midway between visible rocks.

When Inch Kenneth House is open south of the cliffs on the south side of the northeast part of the island, bearing 240°, turn towards the island and anchor in about five metres; the bottom shoals abruptly further in. Holding is said to be poor.

The anchorage east of the south point of the island has been used and may be suitable in quiet weather. The outermost of rocks southeast of the point rarely cover. Approach from south – cautiously.

Either of these anchorages is subject to violent squalls from the cliffs of Mull in southeast winds.

Inch Kenneth from northeast (2003)

## Sound of Ulva

56°28'·5N 6°08'W

An attractive anchorage between Ulva and Mull, but parts of it are shallow, and even though the cliffs on the south side of Loch na Keal are two miles away it is subject to fierce squalls in southerly winds.

The intricate passage through from Loch Tuath should only be taken on a rising tide and at a cautious pace. It is far from certain that all the rocks in this passage have been charted.

### Tides

Constant –0010 Oban (–0540 Dover).
*Height in metres*

| MHWS | MHWN | MTL | MLWN | MLWS |
|------|------|-----|------|------|
| 4·4  | 3·2  | 2·5 | 1·8  | 0·6  |

The flood runs northwestwards but tidal streams are not significant.

### Dangers and marks

*The south entrance* For MacQuarrie's Rock see page 116. In the mouth of the sound, where it narrows to two cables north of the east point of Ulva, Sgeir Beul a' Chaolais (which means 'the rock at the mouth of the sound') dries 4·4 metres with a low concrete beacon on it. Northeast of it drying rocks extend a cable south of the north point of the entrance.

Ulva Sound from southeast (2003)

*The northwest entrance* lies between Eilean a' Bhuic and a rock 0·9 metre high off Torr Ardalum on Ulva.

Sgeir Dubhail, ½ mile NNW of the northwest entrance, dries 2·6 metres.

South of Eilean a' Bhuic drying rocks lie on the south side of the channel.

Two cables southeast of Eilean a' Bhuic is an unnamed 5-metre islet with a larger, but lower, islet (Sgeir Feoir) close to its east side.

Half a mile southeast of the 5-metre islet a passage about a third of a cable wide leads to the Ulva Ferry passage.

Many submerged and drying rocks as well as moorings lie in the basin between the 5-metre islet and the narrows.

### Directions – through passage

*From south*, pass close northeast of Sgeir Beul a' Chaolais and head for the ferry house on Ulva. Pass southwest of moorings and keep south of the middle of the narrow passage north of the cable beacon on Ulva.

Head initially south of the south point of the northwest entrance and come round gradually towards the point. An electricity transformer on a pole astern, at the car park at the northeast side of the ferry in line with a prominent notch in the hills beyond, bearing approximately 100° astern, leads south of rocks in the next section of the passage. A pink plastic buoy apparently marks the north side

Ben More

Eilean a' Bhuic

Ulva

Rock, 0·9m

Sound of Ulva, northwest entrance

**VI. THE WEST COAST OF MULL**

Ulva Sound narrows, from south. A broad rock lies south of the fairway, marked by a small plastic buoy (1991)

*From northwest*, identify Eilean a' Bhuic and keep the summit of Ben More south of it bearing 126°.

Pass north of the 0·9-metre high rock and 20 metres south of Eilean a' Bhuic, then east of the 5-metre islet and come round gradually to head for the narrows ½ mile southeast.

Identify the transformer pole referred to above, and steer with it in line with the notch in the hills beyond bearing about 100°.

Keep south of the middle of the narrows towards the south east end of Eilean a' Chaolais, pass southwest of the moorings and come round gradually to pass north of Sgeir Beul a' Chaolais.

## Anchorages

*WNW of Sgeir Beul a' Chaolais*, clear of Sgeir Lach and rocks on the north side, as well as cables crossing the sound.

*In settled weather only*, east of the drying rocks off the point of Mull northeast of Sgeir Beul a' Chaolais.

Note Do not anchor among moorings, or pick up any of them unless invited by a local boat owner to do so.

*The pool northeast of the ferry house* is taken up with moorings for local boats, and underwater cables cross the sound north and south of the ferry.

Restaurant, water, and pay phone at the Visitor Centre on the south side of Ulva Ferry.

of a broad submerged rock south of the fairway (see upper photo).

Pass east of the 5-metre islet off Ulva and then within 20 metres of Eilean a' Bhuic to avoid rocks on the south side of the channel, and pass north of the 0·9-metre rock.

Continue on the same course for a mile to be sure of avoiding Sgeir Dubhail.

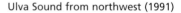

Ulva Sound from northwest (1991)

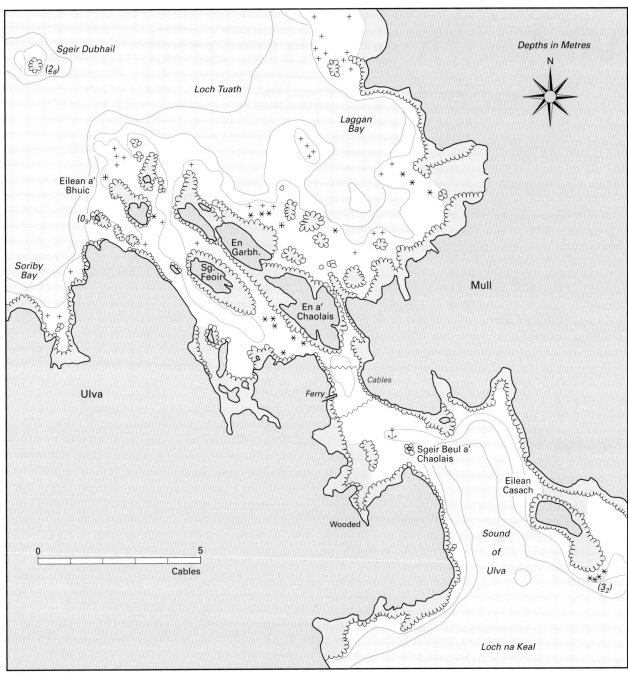

Depths in Metres

N

Sgeir Dubhail
(2₆)

Loch Tuath

Laggan
Bay

Eilean a'
Bhuic

(0₉)

Soriby
Bay

En
Garbh.

Sg.
Feoir

En a'
Chaolais

Mull

Cables

Ferry

Ulva

Sgeir Beul a'
Chaolais

Eilean
Casach

Wooded

Sound
of
Ulva

(3₂)

0          5
Cables

Loch na Keal

**ULVA FERRY**

## Anchorages – upper Loch na Keal

*Eorsa*, ENE of the island on the 5-metre line. Keep at least a cable off the southeast and east sides of the island to avoid drying rocks.

*Dhiseig*, SSE of Eorsa. Temporary anchorage southeast of Eorsa to land a party to climb Ben More. A stony bank lies off the mouth of the two burns, outside which the bottom falls away steeply.

*Scarisdale* provides better anchorage if you can find your way in south of the main group of rocks. A' Chrannag, the 116-metre hill at the south east end of Ulva over the north edge of Eorsa bearing 270° astern leads to a pool with moderate depth south of Scarisdale Rocks. Note carefully position of rocky shoal patches on either side of the entrance.

# VII. South of Mull and Loch Scridain

The south coast of the Ross of Mull and the Torran Rocks are described from east to west.

Distances to the Steamer Passage southwest of Erraid are as follows: from a point south of Frank Lockwood's Island (⊕56°17′N 5°50′W) at the northwest side of the entrance to the Firth of Lorn is 20 miles.

From Corryvreckan, and from the North end of the Sound of Islay it is about 25 miles.

From the west end of Cuan Sound is 27 miles.

### Charts

Admiralty chart *2169* covers the south coast of Mull and approach from south at 1:75,000.

*2617* is essential for the Sound of Iona and the Ross of Mull, and the plan on page 129 should be treated as diagrammatic only, to illustrate the transits described.

## Passage notes

A direct passage can be made from the Firth of Lorn to the Sound of Iona by the south side of Mull, but it is a lee shore to the prevailing southwest wind and there is no good sheltered anchorage on the way.

An approach may also be made from Islay passing east and north of Colonsay.

The usual passage is between Mull and the Torran Rocks which extend over an area four miles by four miles, southwest of Mull.

The nearest of the Torran Rocks to Mull, the unpronounceable Bogha nan Ramfhear, dries 1·4 metres and lies seven cables south of the east end of Eilean a' Chalmain.

The only (visual) way to establish your position is by reference to various natural features together with a stone beacon on one of the Torran Rocks; good visibility is needed to identify these features at a range of several miles.

### Tides

Tides are weak between Frank Lockwood's Island and the Garvellachs, reaching one knot at springs.

The northeast-going stream begins +0430 Oban (–0100 Dover).

The southwest-going stream begins –0155 Oban (+0335 Dover).

### East of the Torran Rocks

The north-going stream begins +0415 Oban (–0115 Dover).

The south-going stream begins –0210 Oban (–0350 Dover).

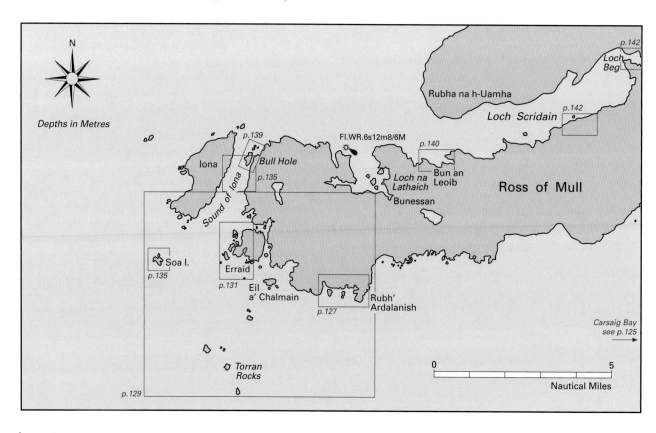

## Anchorage

### Loch Buie

Loch Buie has no shelter from seaward and only very occasional anchorage at the head, east of Eilean Mor.

Drying rocks lie one cable east of the islet on the east side of Eilean Mor; there are several moorings used by small working boats.

### Carsaig

56°19′N 5°59′W

An occasional anchorage on the south coast of Mull a couple of miles west of Loch Buie, providing some shelter at the north side of Gamhnach Mhor, a low islet off the southeast of the bay.

A fine masonry quay stands on the northeast side of the bay, but there appears to be less than 1·5 metres depth alongside it at half-tide. Two iron perches mark reefs on the northeast side of the approach to the pier. A phone box stands ¾ mile along the road.

In quiet weather an alternative temporary anchorage is off the beach in the northwest corner of the bay.

### Tides

Constant −0010 Oban (−0540 Dover).

Height in metres

| MHWS | MHWN | MTL | MLWN | MLWS |
|------|------|-----|------|------|
| 4·1 | 3·1 | 2·4 | 1·8 | 0·6 |

## Landmarks – from east to west

Rubh' Ardalanish, the most southerly point of the Ross of Mull with, to the north, Beinn a' Chaolachaidh, the highest hill in the west part of the Ross. To the east of Ardalanish the rocks are grey; to the west they are mostly pink.

## Anchorage

### Rubh' Ardalanish

56°16′N 6°17′W

The inlet on the west side of Rubh' Ardalanish is particularly attractive in settled conditions. It has been spoken of as safe in a gale, but I haven't put this to the test, and it would not be safe to enter or leave if there were much sea running.

Do not cross the 20-metre contour until you have identified Sgeir an Fheidh which at most states of the tide appears to be two separate rocks; approach with the northeast rock in line with a deep valley 350°, and then pass midway between the rock and the west side of Rubh' Ardalanish. It may be easier to find your way in ESE of Eilean Mor and north of Sgeir an Fheidh.

There are two inlets at the north end of the west side of the promontory, the more southerly of which provides more swinging room but may be more subject to swell.

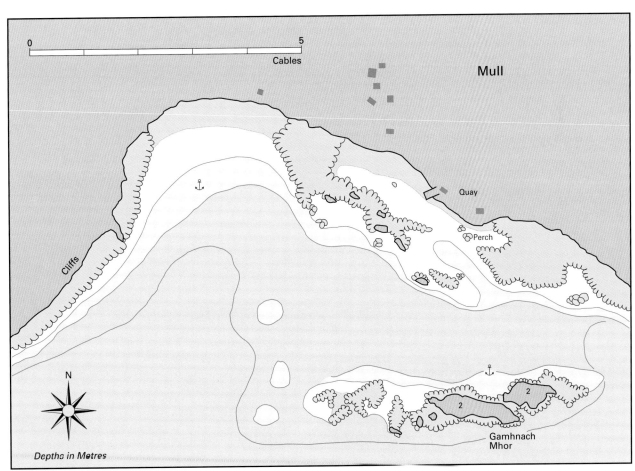

**CARSAIG BAY**

Carsaig from southeast. The stone pier lies beyond the islands (1991)

Ardalanish (1984)

Ardalanish anchorage, with Torran Rocks beyond; note the rock breaking well beyond Sgeir an Fheidh in the middle of the bay (1991)

## Passage notes west of Ardalanish

### Dangers and marks

A submerged rock has been reported and is charted lying six cables southwest of Ardalanish.

Eilean a' Chalmain three miles west of Ardalanish, has a drying rock nearly a cable southwest of its south point.

The unnamed islet two cables southwest of Eilean a' Chalmain is a useful reference point.

Sgeir na Caillich is an islet six cables west of Eilean a' Chalmain.

Na Torrain is a group of three above-water rocks in the middle of the Torran Rocks and provide the key to pilotage within the area. From the south these are 23, 15 and 19 metres high, and Torr an t-Saothaid, ½ mile east of Na Torrain, is about 18 metres high. These are sometimes mistaken at a distance from the east for Soa Island, several miles further north west.

Ruadh Sgeir, the most easterly of the Torran Rocks, on which there is the stump of a stone beacon, must be clearly identified in approaching from the east.

Bogha na Ramfhear, which dries 1·4 metres, lies seven cables NNE of Ruadh Sgeir.

Dubh Sgeir, two cables southwest of Eilean nam Muc, is the most southwesterly island off Erraid.

Soa Island, 34 metres, stands 1½ miles SSW of Iona.

Dubh Artach lighthouse, 10 miles southwest of the Torran Rocks, has a broad red band round it.

### Directions

*From the Sound of Islay* pass east of Colonsay and steer 330° for Beinn a' Chaol-achaidh, the highest hill of the west part of the Ross of Mull, and continue as below. Yachtsmen familiar with the area take other passages through the Torran Rocks.

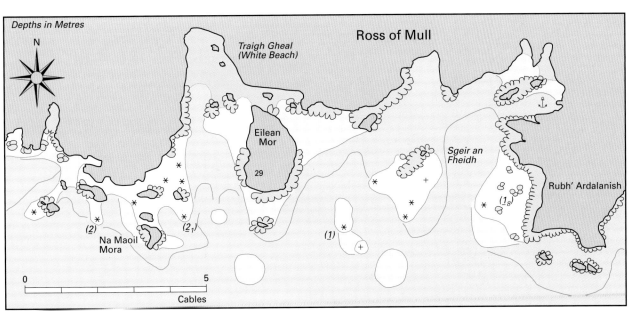

ARDALANISH

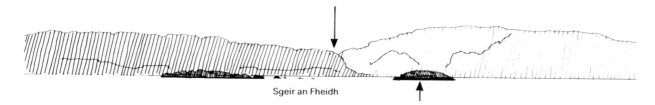

Sgeir an Fheidh

Ardalanish – the right hand part of Sgeir an Fheidh in line with the left hand side of the valley leads clear of rocks in the approach

*From the east* steer to pass outside Ardalanish. Identify Ruadh Sgeir and Na Torrain. These two in line will provide a preliminary position line.

Steer along the Mull shore and, if you can identify Soa Island, bring it not more than its own width open of the islet southwest of Eilean a' Chalmain, the islet bearing 295°.

A further useful position line is a back bearing (from this direction) of Na Maoil Mhora in line with the rocks south of Rubh' Ardalanish 094° (see drawing on following page).

If tacking, it is essential to know your position relative to the Torran Rocks in general and Bogha nan Ramfhear in particular. Bogha nam Ramfhear is now marked on its north side by a N car light buoy Q.

Bogha nan Ramfhear is safely passed when Dearg Sgeir, which is ¾ mile WNW of Ruadh Sgeir, is in line with Na Torrain.

A large rock drying 3·6 metres lies two cables north of Dearg Sgeir.

The passage eastward is generally easier than westward as the clearing marks are more easily identified before the dangers become critical.

Pass south of Sgeir na Caillich and Dubh Sgeir, southwest of Eilean nam Muc, and alter course for the Sound of Iona; keep more than ¼ mile west of the islands on the east side of the sound to avoid rocks at a depth of 1·9 metres.

The east end of the former Free Church (now a house but identified by the belfry at its east end, shown on the left side of the aerial photo on page 136) in line with the cathedral tower, bearing about 012° leads west of these rocks.

Bogha hun a Chuhoil, about six cables southwest of Dubh Sgeir, lies in a depth of 1·6 metres. The line described above leads close east of it. Bogha hun a Chuhoil is now marked on its SW side by a S car light buoy Q(6)+L.Fl.15s one cable SW of Bogha hun a Chuhoil.

Traigh Gheal; the more easterly bay of the same name, this is less than a mile west of Ardalanish (2003)

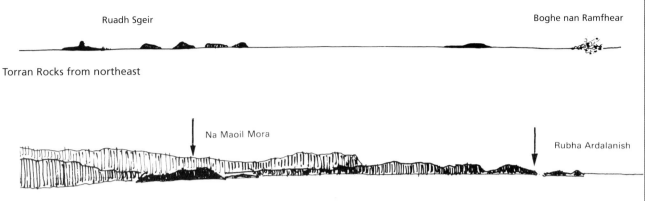

Ruadh Sgeir

Boghe nan Ramfhear

Torran Rocks from northeast

Na Maoil Mora

Rubha Ardalanish

Na Maoil Mora in line with Rubh'Ardalanish bearing 094° leads inside Bogha nam Ramfhear

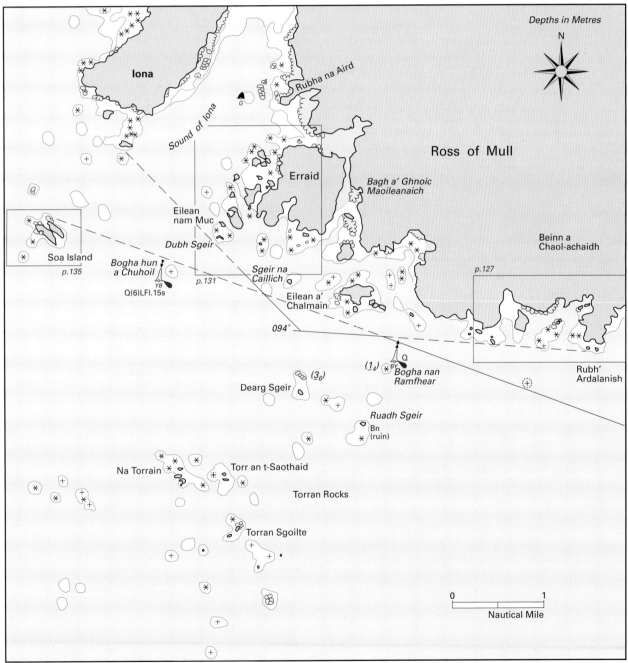

**PASSAGE INSIDE THE TORRAN ROCKS**

Bagh a'Ghnoic Mhaoileanaich between Erraid and Mull, from the south (1973)

The 'Steamer Passage' north of Eilean nam Muc is the route traditionally taken by MacBraynes' steamers when they used to operate a day trip round Mull.

Rankin's Rocks, in the approach to this passage from southeast, are one and two metres high, with drying rocks around them. Take care not to confuse Sgeir na Caillich with Rankin's Rocks.

In the narrow passage a rock drying 2·3 metres lies in the middle of the entrance to Tinker's Hole, but it is not in the way of a yacht passing directly to or from the Sound of Iona. At the north west end of the passage a rock drying or just submerged lies outside the line of the first and second islets from the northwest end.

When approaching the passage from northwest there are so many rocks and islets that the main difficulty is to find the entrance in the first place. The key is to identify Eilean nam Muc and look for the clear passage inside it as you approach; note the rock drying 4·2 metres on the south side of the entrance, which is not normally covered.

### Anchorage

*Bagh a' Ghnoic Mhaoileanaich*, between Erraid and Mull, provides an occasional anchorage in settled weather, with the use of chart *2617*.

## Tinker's Hole

56°17'·5N 6°23'W

One of the most popular anchorages on the west coast, although one visitor likened it to a half-flooded quarry, Tinker's Hole lies between Eilean Dubh and the west side of Erraid at the south end of the Sound of Iona. In places it is less than ½ cable wide and on the east side the shore consists of walls of pink granite. R L Stevenson visited Erraid when his uncle was building Dubh Artach lighthouse. He knew this as Fiddler's Hole, and used it as the location for several of his writings.

The cottages on the north side of Erraid, built for the shore station for Dubh Artach lighthouse, are now occupied by members of the Findhorn Community.

### Tides

At Iona the constant is –0005 Oban (–0535 Dover).
*Height in metres*

| MHWS | MHWN | MTL | MLWN | MLWS |
|------|------|-----|------|------|
| 4·0 | 3·0 | 2·2 | 1·5 | 0·5 |

### In Tinker's Hole

The north-going stream begins about +0445 Oban (–0045 Dover).
The south-going stream begins about –0130 Oban (+0530 Dover).

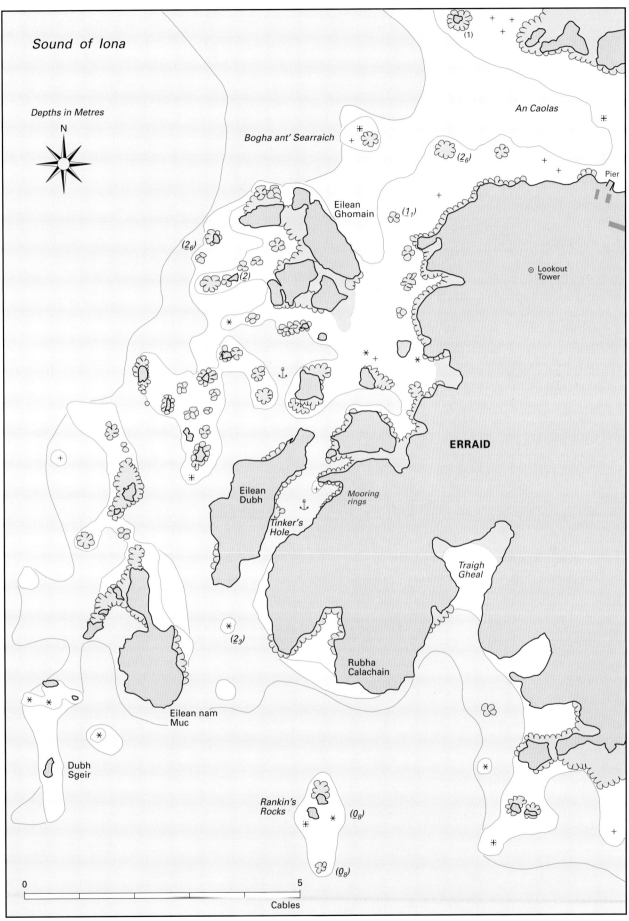

Sound of Iona

Depths in Metres

N

An Caolas

Bogha ant' Searraich

(2₆)

Eilean
Ghomain

(1₁)

Pier

Lookout
Tower

(2₆)

(2)

ERRAID

Eilean
Dubh

Mooring
rings

Tinker's
Hole

Traigh
Gheal

(2₃)

Rubha
Calachain

Eilean nam
Muc

Dubh
Sgeir

Rankin's
Rocks

(0₈)

(0₈)

0                                                    5

Cables

**TINKER'S HOLE AND ERRAID**

Tinker's Hole and the passage inside Eilean nam Muc from south. Rankin's Rocks on the right (1991)

## Dangers

Tinker's Hole is usually approached from the passage between Eilean Dubh and Eilean nam Muc. In the middle of this entrance lies a rock drying 2·3 metres.

## Anchorages

*Between Eilean Dubh and Erraid,* wherever convenient. At times the tidal stream runs strongly here. Mooring rings at the head of the bight on the Erraid side are maintained by CCC members.

Tinker's Hole and skerries from northeast (1991)

A submerged reef extends 20 metres south from the northwest point of this bight, which point defines the edge of the tidal stream. Lobster keepboxes are sometimes moored in the fairway.

*Traigh Gheal* on the south side of Erraid, known as David Balfour's Bay after the hero of *Kidnapped*, is a delightful daytime anchorage, but a trap if the wind strengthens from between south and southwest.

## Passages north and west of Tinker's Hole

The approach to Tinker's Hole from the north is not difficult above half-tide. Keep within ½ cable northeast of Eilean Ghomain to avoid drying rocks further off.

If your charts have not been corrected, note there is no longer a beacon on Bogha ant'searraich, 1½ cable NNE of Eilean Ghomain.

The main hazard is a drying rock a cable SSE of Eilean Ghomain; steer to bring the east side of Eilean Dubh in line with the west side of Erraid bearing 198° – if you can see the east end of Eilean nam Muc you will probably run over the rock.

There is slightly deeper water inshore close to Erraid and here there is no alternative to feeling your way, but the bottom is clear white sand – see also the air photos on pages 132 and 134.

Some yachts have used the passage from the west but there is at least one uncharted rock, on the north side of the entrance, and no clear leading line.

North entrance to Tinker's Hole, looking northeast, too shallow for most boats within two hours of low water. En Ghomain can be seen in the bottom left of the photo (1991)

Tinker's Hole from northeast. The mooring rings are at the head of the bay right of centre; note the submerged reef off the north west point of the bay (1991)

Skerries west of Tinker's Hole, from southwest (2003)

## Anchorage

The pool immediately north of Tinker's Hole is an alternative anchorage; others may be found among the skerries north and northwest of Eilean Dubh, particularly by shoal-draught boats, or others at neaps; also close northeast of Eilean Ghomain or towards the pier on the north side of Erraid.

Erraid Pier (2003)

# Soa

An attractive island to visit on a quiet day. The inlet is apparently free from hazards, but a previously uncharted drying rock lies about half a cable off the northern point of the entrance (see photo). The tide floods to the northwest.

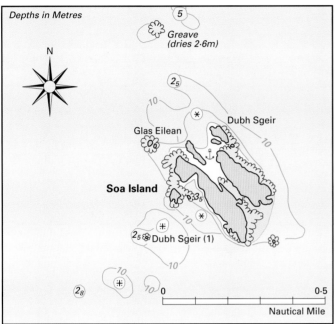

**SOA ISLAND**

Soa. An uncharted rock is breaking off the north point of the inlet (2003)

# Sound of Iona

56°20′N 6°23′W

The west end of the Ross of Mull consists mainly of pink granite with brilliant white sands and the sea shading from jade green at the edges to indigo further out; add a blue sky overhead, the white sails of yachts and the occasional paddle steamer, and you have all that the Tourist Board could ask for – quite apart from a fine, although heavily restored, cathedral.

Iona has a heavy traffic in day visitors, and it is well worth arranging to go ashore there early in the day, or after most of the visitors have left.

Most of the width of the sound is blocked by a shoal which, the chart indicates, consists of sand, black shingle and coral, and below half-tide this needs careful pilotage.

Apart from any swell from the open sea, the tide over the shallows generates its own sea.

The anchorage off the village at Iona is usually unsettled except very close inshore.

The passage between the Firth of Lorn and the Sound of Iona is described on pages 124–129.

**Chart**

*2617* (1:25,000) is essential.

**Tides**

At Iona the constant is –0005 Oban (–0535 Dover).
Height in metres

| MHWS | MHWN | MTL | MLWN | MLWS |
|------|------|-----|------|------|
| 4·0  | 3·0  | 2·2 | 1·5  | 0·5  |

Tidal streams in the sound run at up to 2½ knots.

There is some uncertainty about the times at which the tides turn, but the following is a guide:

The north-going stream begins +0515 Oban (–0015 Dover);
the south-going stream begins –0015 Oban (–0545 Dover).

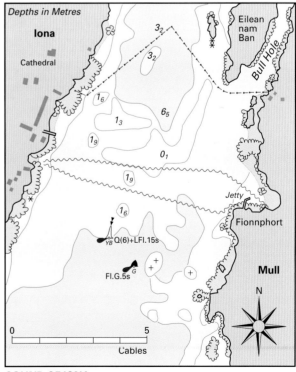

**SOUND OF IONA**

Anchorage off the village at Iona. Martyrs' Bay on the left and the ferry slip to the right. The cathedral is out of the photo to the right. The old Free Church is on the extreme left (page 128) (1991)

Anchorage off the ruined pier at the south entrance to Bull Hole. Despite its sheltered and peaceful appearance this anchorage is subject to an uncomfortable tidal swell (1984)

The retreat from Iona; day visitors boarding the ferry

## Dangers and marks

The most conspicuous reference marks are the cathedral on Iona north of the village, and the hill Dun I, 99 metres, ½ mile NNW of the cathedral.

In the south part of the sound many rocks lie up to three cables off the Mull shore, and two cables off Iona.

A green conical buoy near the east shore marks a 3-metre rock and lies two cables west of the nearest drying rocks.

The principal hazard is the shoal bank which stretches across the middle of the sound from Iona village to Eilean nam Ban, ½ mile north of Fionnphort, on which the depth is only 0·1 metre in places.

South of the bank are an unlit south cardinal buoy, and a green conical buoy on the west side of a submerged rock ¼ mile off the Mull shore.

North of the bank rocks dry up to a cable off either shore.

Breug, an isolated rock 1½ cables west of the north end of Eilean nam Ban, covers at HW.

## Directions

*From south* pass west of both green conical buoys.

The course you take at the mid-sound bank will depend on your draught and the state of the tide; if over 2-metres draught and near LW springs turn to head obliquely towards the Mull shore to keep Bull Hole just open, until Eilean Annraidh at the north end of Iona is touching Eilean Liath, west of Eilean nam Ban.

Then pass ½ cable southwest of Eilean nam Ban and continue towards the middle of the sound.

Otherwise pass west of the south cardinal buoy and a cable from Iona until past the cathedral.

*From north* keep two cables off either shore unless you are carefully following the large-scale chart. Yachts over 2-metres draught, if it is near LW springs, should pass no more than ½ cable southwest of the south end of Eilean nam Ban, then parallel to the west shore of Mull for half a mile keeping Bull Hole just open astern, before altering course to pass between the green conical buoy and the south cardinal. The shallowest part of the bank lies close west of this course.

Yachts of moderate draught, and deep-draught yachts within four hours of HW springs, can pass about a cable off the Iona shore between a point abreast of the cathedral and the south end of the village. A short steep sea is raised here when the tide turns against the wind.

Towards the south end of the sound keep west of a line joining the two green conical buoys.

For the passage along the south coast of Mull see pages 124–129.

## Anchorages

Two underwater telephone cables cross the sound from Fionnphort to Martyrs' Bay, south of the ferry slip on Iona, and a water pipeline takes an irregular course from the south end of Eilean nam Ban to a point north of the ferry slip on Iona.

Yachts usually anchor south of the slip – often, probably, over the telephone cables – but take care to avoid both the cables and the ferry's line of approach to the slip. Permanent moorings for tourist launches are laid here.

A more peaceful anchorage with less tide may be found ENE of the cathedral. Further north again the landing place of an underwater electricity cable is marked by a cable beacon.

*Fionnphort* Temporary anchorage WNW of the ferry jetty, avoiding both the cables and the approach to the jetty.

## Supplies

Shops and phone box at both Iona and Fionnphort. Hotels and post office on Iona. Water tap on the end wall of public toilet at the jetty on Iona. Other supplies at Bunessan.

The south entrance to the Bull Hole, from the west (1991)

The shallow pool at the north end of the Bull Hole (1991)

# Bull Hole

56°20′N 6°22′W

Between Eilean nam Ban and Mull, near the north end of the sound. Much of the basin at the north end is only deep enough for shoal-draught yachts except at neaps, and most of the deeper water is taken up with moorings.

Inside the west side of the entrance the Little Bull rock which dries 0·5 metre south of the Bull rock, which stands above water, is marked by a perch with a triangular topmark.

An underwater pipeline to Iona crosses the entrance, and the bottom is sand and weed.

If space can be found the best anchorage is close to the Mull shore east of the north end of Eilean nam Ban, taking care to avoid the Limpet rock.

The anchorage on the west side of the south entrance north west of the ruined pier is often subject to tidal swell, and space must be left for the ferry to approach and leave by the east side of the channel her mooring which lies north of The Bull. If she does not have enough space clear of shoals on the east side, everyone will hear about it.

Fionnphort is ½ mile by footpath from the pier.

Dedicated rock-dodgers will find it possible to leave Bull Hole on a rising tide by one of several passages, used by tourist boats and shown in the aerial photo opposite.

### Occasional anchorage

*Camas Tuath* is an occasional anchorage ¼ mile west of Loch na Lathaich. The granite quarry there supplied the stone for building Skerryvore and Ardnamurchan lighthouses. The head of the bay is foul and drying and a detached drying reef lies ½ cable off the east shore.

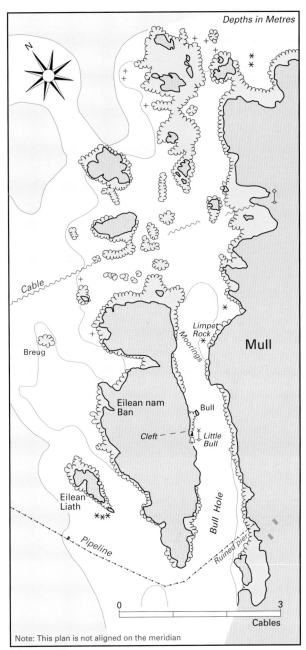

Depths in Metres

Cable

Breug

Limpet Rock

Moorings

Mull

Eilean nam Ban

Bull

Cleft

Little Bull

Eilean Liath

Bull Hole

Pipeline

Ruined pier

0     3

Cables

Note: This plan is not aligned on the meridian

**BULL HOLE**

Camas Tuath (2003)

Bunessan from east (1991)

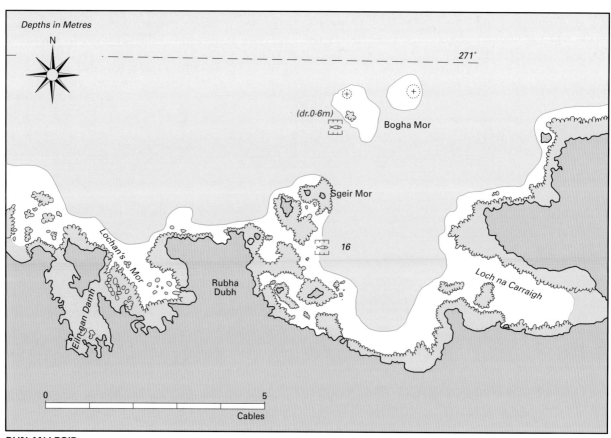

**BUN AN LEOIB**

# Loch na Lathaich (Bunessan)

56°20′N 6°16′W

A well sheltered inlet on the north side of the Ross of Mull, halfway between Loch Scridain and the Sound of Iona. It has a straightforward entrance, with light beacon; a shop and hotel, and a bus service to the Oban ferry at Craignure.

## Tides

Constant –0015 Oban (–0545 Dover).

*Height in metres*

| MHWS | MHWN | MTL | MLWN | MLWS |
|------|------|-----|------|------|
| 4·3 | 3·0 | 2·4 | 1·8 | 0·6 |

## Dangers and marks

Eileanan na Liathanaich is a group of islands and rocks off the west side of the entrance of the loch. The largest and most easterly island has a light beacon on its south side.

Rocks above water and drying extend a cable WNW of the west island, and a detached drying rock lies ½ cable northeast of the east island.

Ionain Rock, drying 3·4 metres, extends 1½ cables from the east side of the loch. Towards the southeast corner of the loch are two islets, Eilean nam Meann and Eilean Ban, which is the larger and further southeast. Eilean nam Meann in line with a prominent hill on the south side of the loch, Cnoc an t-Suidhe 173°, leads west of Ionain Rock.

Eilean nam Meann in line with Cnoc an-t-Suidhe bearing 173°, to clear Ionain Rock

Approach either side of Eileanan na Liathanaich, but look out for lobster pot floats around the islands.

## Light

Eileanan na Liathanaich, Fl.WR.6s12m8/6M, shows red to the west between 088° and 108° and white elsewhere.

## Anchorages

*Southwest corner* in three to four metres clear of moorings and fish cages. This part of the loch is now well used for mooring and anchoring.

*Southeast corner* south of Eilean Ban. Anchor clear of the approach to the pier, and no further east than a line between the pier and the east side of Eilean Ban as it is shoal and drying beyond this. The bottom is mud with increasing weed. Show an anchor light at night. The pier has at times had a lot of fishing traffic in the evening and at night, but its ramp is a good place to land a dinghy, ¼ mile from the village.

## Services and supplies

Petrol, shops and hotel at Bunessan in the southeast corner of the loch. Diesel at filling station 2½ miles along road to Fionnphort.

Bus service to Oban ferry and Iona ferry.

*Communications* Post office and phone box at Bunessan.

# Loch Scridain

56°22′N 6°05′W

Loch Scridain, running five miles ENE on the north side of the Ross of Mull, has no really good anchorages. The north side is fairly clean but on the south side several groups of drying rocks extend half a mile from the shore; of these the most significant are described below.

## Chart

*2771* (1:25,000) is hardly necessary except for exploring close inshore. Chart *2617* extends as far east as Bogha Mor.

## Dangers and clearing marks

Bogha Mor, three cables off the entrance to a bay on the south side of the entrance to the loch, dries 0·6 metre, with a submerged rock two cables ENE of it. Meall nan Carn, a conspicuous conical hill, 64 metres in height on the south shore of the loch, over the extremity of Ardtun, the nearest point to the west, bearing 271°, leads close north of Bogha Mor.

An Carraigean, three miles further east, three cables offshore, ¾ mile ENE of the promontory Ard Fada, dries 0·6 metre.

Bogh' an Rubha ¾ mile ENE of An Carraigean, two cables offshore, dries 2·1 metres. Ardchrishnish House open of Ard Fada bearing 249°, leads close north of both An Carraigean and Bogh' an Rubha.

Sgeir Alltach, a reef drying three metres, extends four cables from the shore, with other drying rocks east of it, four miles from the entrance, opposite Kilfinichen Bay. Dun I, the highest hill on Iona, over the high-water line of the north point of the entrance of the loch bearing 263° leads close north of Sgeir Alltach.

## Anchorages

*Bun an Leoib* (which appears on chart *2617*), on the south side of the entrance to Loch Scridain, provides shelter from the west behind the above-water rocks Sgeir Leathen and Sgeir Mor, but little shelter from northwest and north.

Pass ½ to one cable north of Sgeir Mor to pass inside Bogha Mor, and anchor either on the south side of the bay or NNE of a tidal islet ¾ cable off the southwest side of the bay.

A drying reef extends a cable east of the islet, with other drying rocks between the reef and the south shore.

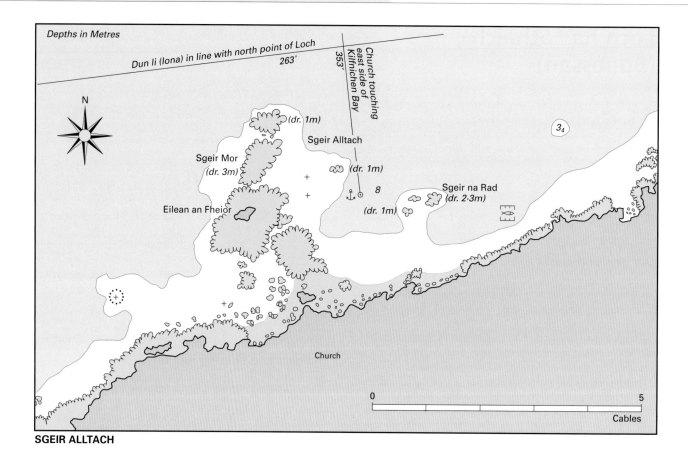

**SGEIR ALLTACH**

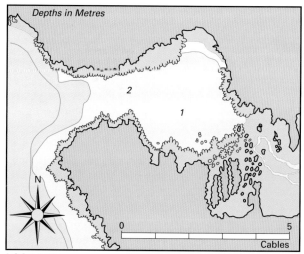

**LOCH BEG**

*Eilean an Fheoir*, five miles from the mouth of Loch Scridain, provides some shelter on its east side. The outermost rock, Sgeir Alltach, dries three metres; nearly two cables northwest of Eilean an Fheoir which stands on the reef.

Sgeir Chailleach, more than a cable ENE of Eilean an Fheoir, dries one metre.

*Sgeir na Rad*, 3½ cables east of Eilean an Fheoir, dries 2·1 metres, with lesser drying rocks within ½ cable WSW of it.

This anchorage should only be approached within 2½ hours of LW, when Sgeir na Rad shows, to give some guide to the position of the other rocks.

*Kilfinichen Bay*, on the north side of the loch, is a suitable anchorage for quiet settled weather. Keep a cable off the west point of the entrance to the bay to avoid Sgeir Mhor, which dries 2·1 metres there.

*Loch Beg*, at the north side of the head of the loch, is the most satisfactory anchorage in Loch Scridain.

Most of the basin dries out and there is only depth to anchor within a couple of cables of the entrance. It is subject to any sea running up Loch Scridain, and violent squalls in easterly winds. Hotel at Pennyghael, 1½M.

# VIII. Coll and Tiree

These two islands are mostly low-lying and exposed, and neither of them has an anchorage which is secure, let alone comfortable in winds from all directions. There is more of an edge-of-the-world feeling about these islands than about any other area covered by this book. Loch Eatharna (Arinagour) on Coll is only seven miles from Caliach Point on the west side of Mull and has a clean sandy bottom and a welcoming hotel, but if the wind is from anywhere between ENE and SSW, you will pitch and roll more or less uncomfortably, depending on its strength.

Similarly, Gott Bay which is the main anchorage on Tiree, is uncomfortable in any wind between ENE and south. Either can be dangerous in strong winds from these directions.

Both islands may be visited from the Sound of Mull or from Iona, or from anchorages in between, the distance from Tobermory to Arinagour, or from Iona to Gott Bay being about 20 miles.

### Chart

Large-scale plans are referred to at individual anchorages and passages. *2171* (1:75,000) shows all of Coll and the northern part of Tiree. *1778* (1:100,000) shows all of Tiree. Ordnance Survey map *46* or Explorer map *372* may be found helpful.

### Tides

In the Passage of Tiree, the channel between Coll and Tiree and Mull, tidal streams run at up to 1½ knots at springs — enough to cause an unpleasant sea with wind against tide. Off Caliach Point and around the Treshnish Isles tidal streams increase to 2½ knots.

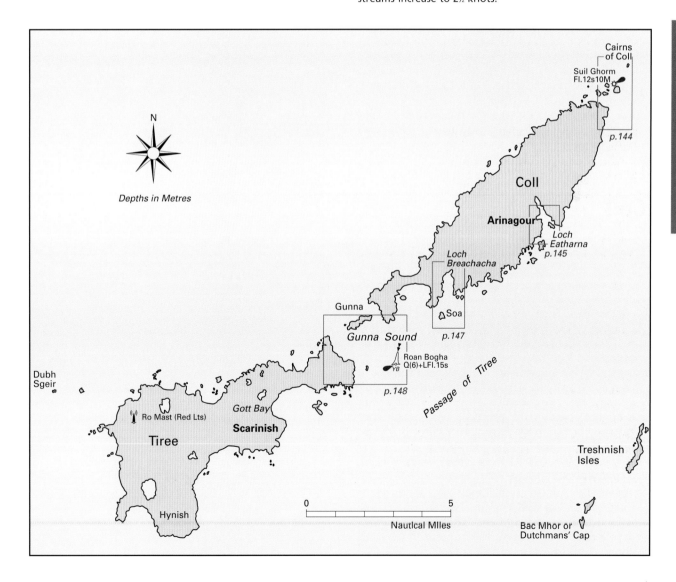

Off the middle of the southeast side of Coll, the northeast-going stream begins –0430 Oban (+0230 Dover); the southwest-going stream begins +0200 Oban (–0330 Dover). Towards the south end of Tiree, the northeast-going stream begins +0600 Oban (+0030 Dover); the southwest-going stream begins at HW Oban (–0530 Dover).

### Passage notes

Between the Sound of Mull and Arinagour there are no particular hazards apart from drying rocks within the line of headlands on the northwest coast of Mull. There is no way of identifying Arinagour until you are fairly close to it, when houses will begin to appear. Bearing in mind that you will be approaching the coast of Coll obliquely, make for a point about a quarter of its apparent length from the south end of the island.

*Approaching Tiree from southeast* The most conspicuous features on the island are Beinn Hough on the west side of the island (119m) with a radar installation near its summit, and Ben Hynish (138m) at the south point of the island.

A small latticed communications tower stands at Scarinish, ½ mile southwest of the south point of Gott Bay and about five miles northeast of Ben Hynish.

Crossing from the north end of the Sound of Iona there are no particular hazards.

A direct passage can be made from the Sound of Islay. Dubh Artach may be passed on either side but if you go north of it keep well south of the Torran Rocks, as there are submerged rocks south of those which are visible.

For ten miles west of Iona the bottom is very uneven, causing overfalls which are dangerous with any wind or swell.

For Gunna Sound see page 148.

# Coll

### Occasional Anchorages

*Eilean Mor* At the north end of Coll, a pool among the skerries on the south west side of Eilean Mor provides some shelter to anchor and watch birds and seals on a quiet day.

Note the Cairns of Coll, an unmarked reef ½ mile north east of Suil Ghorm light beacon, and rocks, submerged and drying lying east and south of Eilean Mor.

Identify An Glas Eilean and approach from east; pass north of it and head NNW towards a sandbar joining the two skerries west of Eilean Mor, keeping a cleft in the profile of An Glas Eilean astern. Look out for drying rocks noted on the plan on either hand.

The tide sets through between the skerries at up to two knots.

*Sorisdale Bay,* an occasional anchorage southeast of the north end of Coll. An underwater power cable is landed at the head of the bay, and a detached drying rock lies off the northeast point. Anchor off concrete blocks on northeast shore.

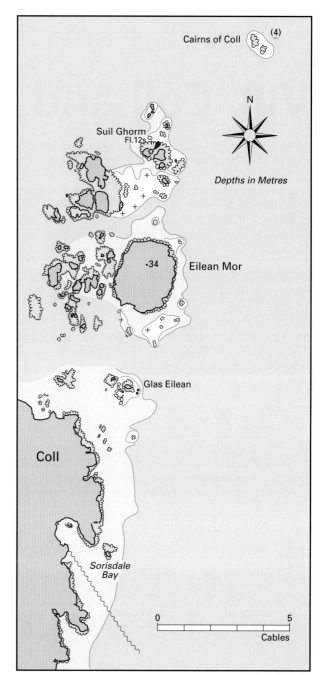

**EILEAN MOR, COLL**

Eilean Mor, Coll at upper left, from northwest, Glas Eilean at upper right (2003)

## Loch Eatharna (Arinagour)

56°37′N 6°31′W

A popular anchorage in the middle of the southeast side of Coll with a clean sandy bottom, but exposed to any sea running, even along the coast, which is aggravated by the shallowness of the loch.

### Chart

Plan (1:10,000) on chart *2474*.

### Tides

Constant is +0017 Oban (−0513 Dover).
*Height in metres*

| MHWS | MHWN |
|------|------|
| 4·4 | 3·2 |

### Approach and anchorages

The main anchorage is west of Eilean Eatharna and there are visitors' moorings north of the concrete pier near the west side of Eilean Eatharna.

If approaching from southwest keep more than a cable off Ornsay at the southwest point of the entrance, to avoid a submerged rock there.

From any direction identify Bogha Mor green conical buoy and leave it to starboard. Steer to pass close east of the head of the concrete pier to avoid McQuarry's Rock, unmarked, drying 2·9 metres, a cable east of the pier. Keep the right side of the hotel in line above the root of the stone pier at Arinagour village.

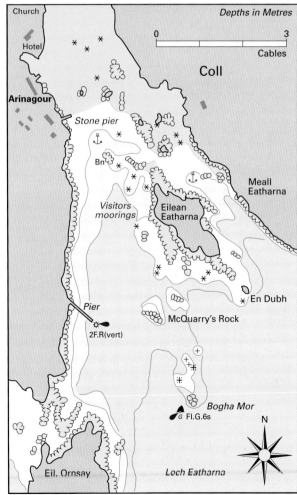

**LOCH EATHARNA**

Arinagour, Loch Eatharna, Coll from southeast, with Eilean Eatharna on the left (1984)

The head of Loch Eatharna from north with the passage north of Eilean Eatharna at upper left (1987)

The most northwesterly of drying rocks off Eilean Eatharna has a stone beacon on it. Anchor between the beacon and the stone pier. The deepest water is towards the beacon; at neaps a medium-draught yacht can lie fairly close to the pier. There is limited space to the northeast of the beacon.

East of Eilean Eatharna keep closer to the northeast shore until near the most northeasterly point of Eilean Eatharna. Keep the hotel in line above the left-hand edge of the low islet ahead 309° to clear a rock which dries 1·2 metres, ½ cable off the northeast shore.

At neaps the best shelter is north of Eilean Eatharna; otherwise anchor further southeast, clear of the rocks shown.

A half-tide passage north of Eilean Eatharna can be used – with great caution – in quiet weather. See also photo on previous page.

### Lights

At night Bogha Mor buoy is lit Fl.G.6s and the head of the concrete pier has lights 2F.R(vert), so that the approach as far as the visitors' moorings is fairly simple.

### Supplies

Shop, hotel, launderette, showers, *Calor Gas*. Diesel and petrol (not always available). Post office; phone box at stone pier. Water tap at the back of toilets on the stone pier. Bicycle hire from Coll Hotel.

## Loch Breachacha

56°35′N 6°37′W

An occasional anchorage towards the southwest end of Coll, identifiable initially by Soa Island, 15m high, and nearer at hand by the old and new castles, of which the 'new' one is a grey castellated 19th-century building with symmetrical wings and small corner turrets. The inlet is sandy and open to any southerly swell. There are many rocks on both sides of the entrance and inside the loch.

### Chart

Plan on new edition of *2474*.

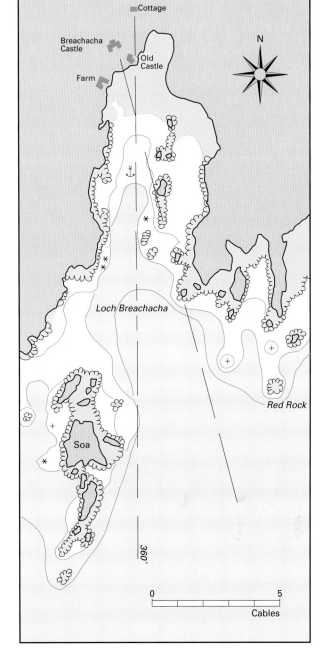

LOCH BREACHACHA

VIII. COLL AND TIREE

Loch Breachacha from seaward showing, from left to right, the farm, the 'new' castle, the 'old' castle, and the cottage referred to in the text          *Jean Lawrence*

### Approach and Anchorage

The 20-metre contour clears all dangers. Steer with the highest point of the sand dunes to the west of the loch bearing 330°. When the 'new' castle appears clear west of above-water rocks at the east point of the entrance, all rocks to the south of that point are cleared.

A line to clear rocks within the loch is to keep the middle window of a cottage which stands behind the 'old' castle just open of the right-hand side of that castle 360°; this line leads rather close to drying rocks in the middle of the loch.

The loch shoals very gradually but evenly; anchor as far in as depth allows.

### Crossapoll Bay

It is unwise to enter this bay without the large-scale chart *2474*. Do not use the old chart *2475* without the Block Correction to NM 2749/07, which identifies substantial variations on the previous chart.

## Gunna Sound

56°33′N 6°43′W

The passage between Coll and Tiree is used by boats on passage to the Outer Hebrides from south of Mull. There are several dangerous rocks but the two most hazardous are marked by light buoys.

### Chart

*2474* includes a plan of Gunna Sound at 1:25,000.

### Tides

Tidal streams run at up to three knots causing heavy overfalls at the windward end with an opposing tide.

The northwest-going stream begins +0535 Oban (+0005 Dover); the southeast-going stream begins –0120 Oban (+0540 Dover).

### Directions

*From south and east* identify Roan Bogha south cardinal buoy and pass either south or ¼ mile north of it. Identify Placaid Bogha green conical buoy and pass south of it.

*From southward*, an alternative course is to pass a cable west of Creachasdal Mor heading 360°. Do not alter course northwest until Placaid Bogha appears about the middle of the northwest entrance so as to clear Bogha Hoshmish, a rock drying 2·3 metres two cables off the northeast point of Tiree.

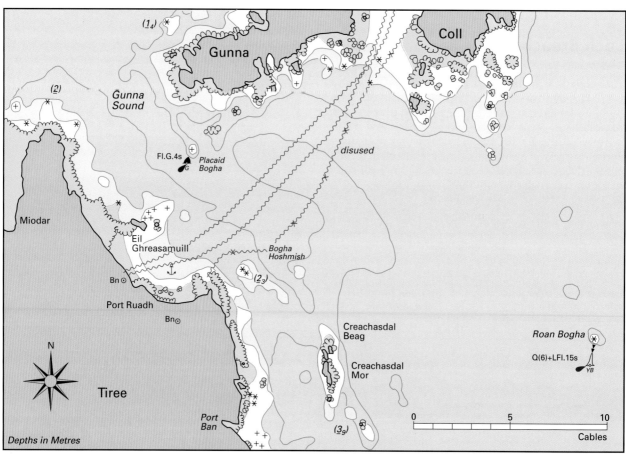

GUNNA SOUND

Port Ruadh (previously Clach Chuirr), Gunna Sound (2003)

*From north and west* make for the centre of the channel to avoid rocks on either hand, but especially drying rocks up to two cables all round the north point of Tiree. Identify and pass south of Placaid Bogha buoy and follow the reverse of the directions above.

### Lights

**Roan Bogha** light buoy Q(6)+LFl.15s5M.
**Placaid Bogha** light buoy Fl.G.4s.

### Anchorage

*Port Ruadh (previously Clach Chuirr)* on the southwest side of the sound gives some shelter from south and west. Underwater power cables marked by a beacon on the southwest side of the bay runs ENE towards Coll, but there is space to anchor on either side of them in three metres, sand. Another cable beacon inshore from the south side of the bay may mark a disused cable which crosses the sound from the southeast point of the bay.

# Tiree

## Gott Bay

56°31′N 6°47′W

A broad sandy bay towards the northeast end of the southeast side of Tiree exposed over a wide area and only suitable for anchoring overnight in settled westerly or calm weather. It is initially identified by the latticed communications tower ¼ mile south of Scarinish.

Submerged and drying rocks lie ¼ mile southwest of Soa at the northeast side of the entrance.

Anchor northwest of the pier on the southwest side of the bay, as close inshore as depth permits.

Gott Bay, Tiree, with the ferry terminal (2003)

A RoRo terminal stands at the east end of the head of the pier. There is nowhere for a yacht to lie alongside, but a stone slip on the west side of the pier is convenient for landing from a dinghy.

### Chart

Plan (1:15,000) on chart 2474.

### Tides

The constant is +0007 Oban (–0523 Dover).

*Height in metres*

| MHWS | MHWN | MTL | MLWN | MLWS |
|------|------|-----|------|------|
| 4·1 | 3·0 | 2·3 | 1·7 | 0·6 |

### Lights

**Scarinish LtHo** Fl.3s11m16M.
**Gott Bay** pier Ldg Lts 286·5°F.R.

### Services and Supplies

Diesel, petrol, Calor Gas; garage near pier, Maclennan Motors ☎ 01879 220 555. No water at pier. Restaurant at Glassary ☎ 01879 220 684 will collect and return yacht's crew by car.

## Scarinish

This is the main village on Tiree but the creek and its drying harbour can only occasionally be used by yachts if there is no sea coming in. Towards HW or at neaps there might be a temporary berth at the old pier, or anchored in the middle of the creek, but avoid obstructing access to the drying harbour.

Cul Bo, nearly a cable SSE of the east point of the entrance, dries 1·8 metres. The east end of a white

Scarinish, Tiree (2003)

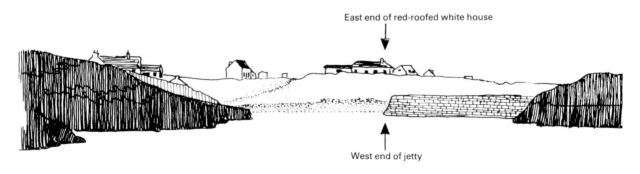

East end of red-roofed white house

West end of jetty

Scarinish Harbour leading line

house with a red roof at the head of the creek bearing 330°, over the west end of the jetty at the harbour, leads clear WSW of this rock.

### Supplies

Shops, post office, phone box, hotel.

## Milton Harbour

Lights F.G (front) and Oc.G.5s (rear) on a bearing 349° lead west of detached drying rocks to a quay at the east side of a rocky creek east of Soa in Gott Bay. This tiny harbour, which is shown on chart 2474, is quite insufficient even for the fishermen who use it, and should not be approached by a yacht except in an emergency.

## Hynish

56°27′N 6°53′W

On the northeast side of the south point of Tiree, east of Ben Hynish, is a masonry pier and dock built by Alan Stevenson in 1825 as a shore station for Skerryvore lighthouse, and the buildings are now used as a lighthouse museum.

Hynish has been visited by yachts on rare occasions in very settled weather; some shelter from southward is given by the point Am Barradhu and drying rocks lie up to ¼ mile south of this point.

The pier dries alongside and the dock fills with sand, but a reservoir built to retain water to flush out the sand awaits restoration.

### Skerryvore lighthouse

56°19′N 7°06′W

On a group of drying rocks ten miles SSW of Tiree, Skerryvore lighthouse is only likely to be of interest to yachts on a direct passage from Islay to the Outer Hebrides.

Drying rocks lie three miles southwest and one mile northeast of the lighthouse, and the bottom between the lighthouse and Tiree is very uneven with rocks both submerged and awash.

Strong tides run round Skerryvore with overfalls, and yachts should pass at least five miles southwest of the lighthouse in a depth of not less than 15 metres.

Hynish, Tiree, the original shore station for Skerryvore lighthouse (1987)

Skerryvore, from a Northern Lighthouse Board helicopter. The weather curtailed operations on this day (2007)
*Peter Mackay*

VIII. COLL AND TIREE

# Appendix

## I. CHARTS AND OTHER PUBLICATIONS

The Imray chart *C65* at a scale of 1:150,000 covers all of this volume. It is available at most chandlers and from the Clyde Cruising Club (see page 154), folded and printed on water-resistant material, but for any boat which has a large enough chart table it is better to order a flat copy.

The Imray chart pack *2800 The West Coast of Scotland* is designed to be used with this volume. The small format charts are as follows:

| Chart | Title | Scale |
|---|---|---|
| 2800.1 | Crinan to Tobermory and Fort William | 160 000 |
| 2800.2 | Loch Crinan to Garbh Eileach | 1:50 000 |
| | *Plans* Craobh Haven, Crinan Basin | |
| | *Inset* Continuation of Loch Melfort | |
| 2800.3 | Cuan Sound to Loch Spelve and Kerrera Sound | 1:50 000 |
| | *Plans* Oban, Loch Feochan Entrance, Cuan Sound | |
| | *Inset* Continuation of Loch Spelve | |
| 2800.4 | Oban to Loch Aline and Port Appin | 1:50 000 |
| | *Plans* Dunstaffnage Bay, Oban | |
| 2800.5 | Loch Aline to Tobermory and Loch Sunart | 1:50 000 |
| | *Plan* Tobermory | |
| 2800.6 | Loch Linnhe South and Loch Creran | 1:50 000 |
| | *Inset* Continuations of Loch Etive | |
| 2800.7 | Loch Linnhe and Loch Leven | 1:50 000 |
| | *Plans* Corpach Sea Lock, Corran Narrows, Loch Leven Narrows | |

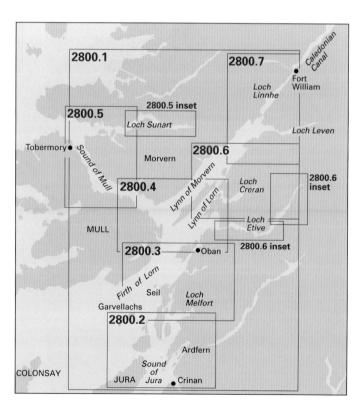

A useful general chart for the whole west coast of Scotland is Admiralty chart *2635* at a scale of 1:500,000

The following Admiralty charts and OS maps relate to the waters covered by this volume. Some of these are essential, and the more you have, the less your pilotage will be fraught with anxiety. The relevant Ordnance Survey maps are also listed.

| Chart | Title | Scale |
|---|---|---|
| **Chapter I** | | |
| 2169 | Approaches to the Firth of Lorn | 75,000 |
| 2326 | Loch Crinan to the Firth of Lorn | 25,000 |
| | Loch Crinan | 7,500 |
| OS55 | Lochgilphead | 50,000 |
| **Chapter II** | | |
| 2169 | Approaches to the Firth of Lorn | 75,000 |
| 2386 | Firth of Lorn – southern part | 25,000 |
| 2387 | Firth of Lorn – northern part | 25,000 |
| 1790 | Oban and approaches | 10,000 |
| 2171 | Sound of Mull and approaches | 75,000 |
| OS49 | Oban & East Mull | 50,000 |
| **Chapter III** | | |
| 2389 | Loch Linnhe – southern part | 25,000 |
| 2379 | Loch Linnhe – central part | 25,000 |
| 2380 | Loch Linnhe – northern part | 25,000 |
| 2388 | Loch Etive and Approaches | 25,000 |
| 2372 | Corran Narrows | 10,000 |
| | Approaches to Corpach | 6,250 |
| OS41 | Ben Nevis | 50,000 |
| **Chapter IV** | | |
| 2171 | Sound of Mull and approaches | 75,000 |
| 2390 | Sound of Mull | 25,000 |
| 2474 | Tobermory Harbour | 10,000 |
| 2392 | Sound of Mull – western entrance | 25,000 |
| **Chapter V** | | |
| 2394 | Loch Sunart | 25,000 |
| OS49 | Oban & East Mull | 50,000 |
| OS47 | Tobermory | 50,000 |
| **Chapter VI** | | |
| 2171 | Sound of Mull and approaches | 75,000 |
| 2392 | Sound of Mull – western entrance | 25,000 |
| 2652 | Loch na Keal and Loch Tuath | 25,000 |
| OS47 | Tobermory | 50,000 |
| OS48 | Iona & Ben More | 50,000 |
| **Chapter VII** | | |
| 2169 | Approaches to the Firth of Lorn | 75,000 |
| 2617 | Sound of Iona | 25,000 |
| 2771 | Loch Scridain | 25,000 |
| OS48 | Iona & Ben More | 50,000 |
| **Chapter VIII** | | |
| 2171 | Sound of Mull and approaches | 75,000 |
| 2474 | Loch Eatharna (Arinagour) | 10,000 |
| | Gott Bay and Scarinish Harbour | 15,000 |
| 2475 | Gunna Sound | 25,000 |
| OS46 | Coll and Tiree | 50,000 |

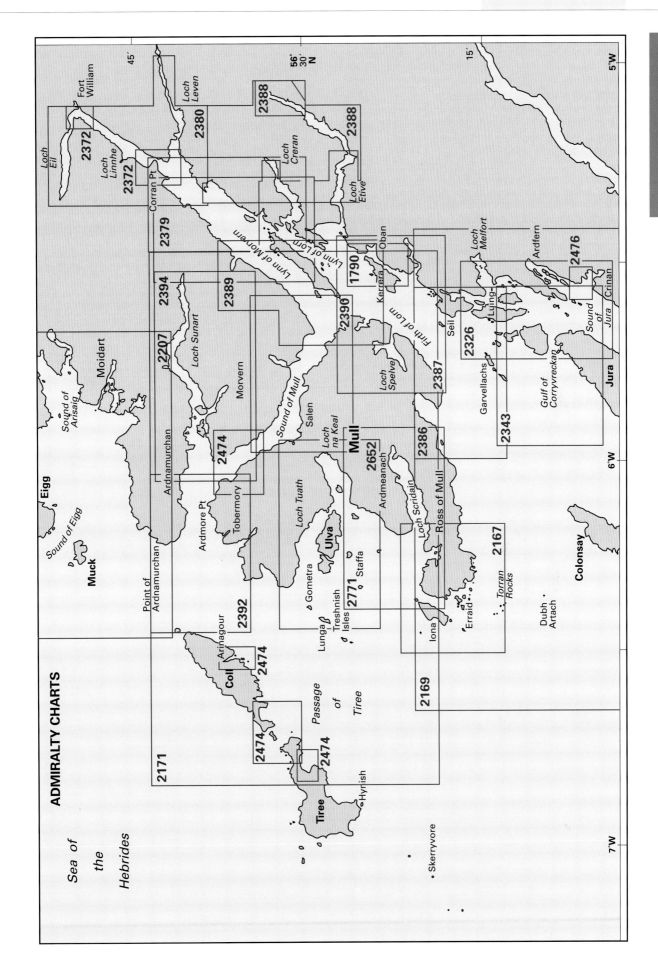

ADMIRALTY CHARTS

Sea of

the

Hebrides

Charts should be obtained early so that you have time to inspect them and order more, if it looks as though your first choice was not enough. There are Admiralty chart agents throughout Britain, and in most other countries.

Chart agents on the West Coast are:
Crinan Boats, Crinan ☎ 01546 830232
Nancy Black, Oban ☎ 01631 562550
Seafare, Tobermory ☎ 01688 302277
Kelvin Hughes, Glasgow ☎ 0141 221 5452

Don't rely on buying charts locally without ordering in advance – they may not be in stock. Some other chandlers stock Admiralty charts, although sometimes at a higher cost.

Imray, Laurie, Norie & Wilson Ltd are Admiralty chart agents and will supply charts by post; Wych House, The Broadway, St Ives, Cambridgeshire PE27 5BT, ☎ 01480 462114, *Fax* 01480 496109, *Email* ilnw@imray.com www.imray.com

Some charts which have long been discontinued provide much more detail, at a larger scale, than any now published for the same area. Two large-scale plans are *3608* (Loch Aline and Loch Corrie), and *3015* (Loch na Keal, Mull).

All older charts, particularly the fine Victorian engravings, show more detail inshore and on land than the current publications, although they may be less accurate.

Old charts should only be used to supplement current ones, not as a substitute for them.

Photocopies of old charts – of editions not less than 50 years old, for copyright reasons – may be obtained from the National Library of Scotland Map Room Annexe, 33 Salisbury Place, Edinburgh ☎ 0131 226 4531. Photocopies can be supplied on a single sheet up to A0 size.

Current charts show much less detail ashore than older charts, and Ordnance Survey maps at a scale of 1:50,000 and 1:25,000 help to fill in the picture.

Coll and Tiree are shown on Imray chart *C65*, and Coll with part of Tiree on Admiralty chart *2171*, but for the whole of both islands at a larger scale OS Explorer map *372* will be found helpful.

Loch Linnhe is very well covered, but for a brief visit you may find OS maps *41* and *49* sufficient, in combination with *C65*. Imray's folio 2800 at 1:50,000 covers this well.

Small Craft editions of the following Admiralty Charts of the west coast are currently published: *2169*, *2171*, *2326* and *2390*. These editions are printed on thinner paper, folded, and not kept corrected, are somewhat cheaper than standard charts.

(For the information of continental yachtsmen) small-scale charts of the west coast are also published by the German Hydrographic Office.

The Clyde Cruising Club *Sailing Directions and Anchorages* is also available from the CCC, Suite 101, The Pentagon Centre, 36 Washington Street, Glasgow, G3 8AZ ☎ 0141 221 2774, as well as from chandlers.

The Admiralty *West Coast of Scotland Pilot (NP 66)*, new edition 2008, and The Admiralty *Tidal Stream Atlas for the North Coast of Ireland and West Coast of Scotland (NP 218)*, 1995 are very useful.

*The Mariner's Handbook (NP100)*, is available on the internet, in a version edited for yachtsmen, but the whole publication is 87 pages. It is also available on paper, and many yachtsmen would benefit from studying it.

Tide tables are essential, preferably for Oban and giving heights of each high and low water. These can be had as a separate publication from local chandlers, yacht centres and boatyards, as well as chandlers in Glasgow.

# II. GLOSSARY OF GAELIC WORDS COMMON IN PLACE NAMES

Many varieties of spelling are found, so it is as well to search for possible alternatives; variations of the same word are listed together but usually at least have the same initial letter. Many words beginning with a consonant take an 'h' after the initial letter in certain cases; notably nouns of the feminine gender and their adjectives, and the genitive cases of many nouns, so that most of the words below could have an 'h' as the second letter.

There is no possibility of guiding the reader on pronunciation except to say that consonants followed by an 'h' are often not pronounced, and that 'mh' and 'bh' at the beginning of a word are pronounced as (and of course in anglicised versions often spelt with) a 'v'. *Mhor* is pronounced – approximately – *vore*; *claidheamh* is something like *clayeh*, and *bogha* is *bo'a*.

Some names, particularly those of islands ending in 'a' or 'ay', are of Norse origin. Anyone at all familiar with French and Latin will see correspondences there, for example Caisteil – also Eaglais and Teampuill.

Many words are compounds made up of several often quite common parts, frequently linked by *na/nam/nan*. The following are the most usual forms of words which commonly occur in Gaelic place names. They often set out to describe the physical features and so give some clues to identification. Some of them occur almost everywhere; most lochs have a Sgeir Mhor and an Eilean Dubh, or vice versa.

| *Gaelic* | *English* |
|---|---|
| a, an, an t, -a' | the |
| abhainn (avon) | river |
| acarsaid | harbour (acair = anchor) |
| achadh (ach, auch) | field |
| allt | stream, burn |
| aird (ard) | promontory |
| aros | house |
| ba | cattle |
| bairneach | limpet |
| bagh ('bay') | bay |
| ban | white, pale; as a prefix = female (ban-righ = queen) |
| bealach | narrow path, pass |
| beag, beaga (beg) | small |
| beinn (ben) | mountain |
| beul (bel) | mouth of (belnahua = mouth of the cave) |
| bodach | old man |
| bogha (bo') | a detached rock, usually one which uncovers |
| breac | speckled (as noun: trout) |
| buachaille | shepherd |
| buidhe (buie) | yellow (also: pleasing) |
| bun | mouth of a river |
| cailleach | old woman |
| caisteil | castle |
| camas | wide bay |
| caol, caolas, (a' chaolais) | narrow passage (kyle) |
| caorach | sheep |
| ceall, cille (keills, kells, kil) | monastic cell, church |
| ceann (kin...) | head |
| clachan | usually a group of houses (clach = stone) |
| claidheamh | sword (hence 'claymore' = great sword) |
| cnoc (knock) | rounded hill |
| coire (corrie) | cauldron, hollow among hills, whirlpool |
| craobh | tree |
| creag | cliff, rock (crag) |
| darroch | oak tree |
| dearg ('jerrig') | red |
| deas | south |
| dobhran | otter |
| donn | brown (dun) |
| druim | ridge |
| dubh (dhu) | black, dark, (disastrous) |
| dun, duin | fortified place, usually prehistoric |
| each | horse |
| ear | east |
| eilean (or eileach) | island |
| fada | long |
| fir, fear | man |
| fraoch, fraoich | heather |
| garbh | rough |
| geal | white |
| gille | boy |
| glas | grey (sometimes green) |
| gobhar (gour) | goat (gabhar = she-goat) |
| gorm | blue |
| gamhna | stirk, year-old calf |
| iar | west (easily confused with Ear) |
| iolair | eagle |
| keills, kells | church |
| kin... (ceann) | head of |
| liath | grey |
| mara | sea |
| meadhonach | middle-sized |
| meall | lump, knob |
| mor (more, mhor, vore) | large, great (often only relative) |
| muc, muck | pig (often a sea-pig = porpoise or a whale) |
| na, na h-, nam, nan | of |
| (the)naomh (nave, neave) | holy, saint |
| ...nish (ness) | point of land |
| poll, puill | pool |
| righ ('ree') | king |
| ron, roin | seal |
| ruadh, rudha | red, reddish |
| rubha (rhu) | point of land, promontory |
| sailean | creek |
| sgeir, sgeirean (skerry) | rock, above water or covering |
| sron | nose (as a headland) |
| sruth | stream, current |
| tigh | house |
| tober | well |
| traigh | beach |
| tuath (or tuadh) | north |
| uamh | cave |

## III. SUBMARINE EXERCISE AREAS

Scottish submarine exercise areas including SUBFACTS. SUBFACTS may also be obtained from COMCLYDE using the 'Fishermens' Hotline', ☎ 0410 321704 (Mobile)

Transmissions of:

| | | | |
|---|---|---|---|
| 0060 | Anglesey | 32. | Linnhe X5624 |
| 0121 | Belfast CG | 33. | Jura Sound X5623 |
| 0085 | Buchan | 34. | Fyne X5603 |
| 0059 | Cardigan Bay | 35. | Minard X5602 |
| 0088 | Cullercoats (GCC) | 36. | Tarbert X5517 |
| 0070 | Clyde | 37. | Skipness X5516 |
| 0072 | Clyde CG | 38. | West Kyle X5518 |
| 0077 | Hebrides (GHD) | 39. | Striven X5520 |
| 0073 | Islay | 40. | East Kyle X5519 |
| 0078 | Lewis | 41. | Goll X5604 |
| 0062 | Morecambe Bay | 42. | Long X5606 |
| 0074 | Oban | 43. | Cove M5605 |
| 0075 | Oban CG | 44. | Gareloch X5620 |
| 0065 | Portpatrick (GPK) | 45. | Rosneath X5506 |
| 0076 | Skye | 46. | Cumbrae X5507 |
| 0086 | Stonehaven (GND) | 47. | Garroch X5508 |
| 0079 | Stornoway CG | 48. | Laggan X5509 |
| 0080 | Wick (GKR) | 49. | Blackstone X5542 |
| | | 50. | Place X5541 |
| 1. | Tiumpan X5816 | 51. | Colonsay X5543 |
| 2. | Minch North X5817 | 52. | Boyle X5540 |
| 3. | Stoer X5818 | 53. | Orsay X5539 |
| 4. | Shiant X5815 | 54. | Islay X5538 |
| 5. | Minch South X5814 | 55. | Otter X5535 |
| 6. | Ewe X5813 | 56. | Gigha X5534 |
| 7. | Trodday X5715 | 57. | Earadale X5533 |
| 8. | Rona West X5716 | 58. | Lochranza X5515 |
| 9. | Rona North X5717 | 59. | Davaar X5514 |
| 10. | Lochmaddy X5713 | 60. | Brodick X5510 |
| 11. | Dunvegan X5714 | 61. | Irvine X5511 |
| 12. | Portree X5720 | 62. | Lamlash X5513 |
| 13. | Rona South X5718 | 63. | Ayr X5512 |
| 14. | Raasay X5719 | 64. | Skerries X5537 |
| 15. | Neist X5711 | 65. | Rathlin X5536 |
| 16. | Bracadale X5709 | 66. | Kintyre X5531 |
| 17. | Ushenish X5712 | 67. | Sanda X5530 |
| 18. | Hebrides North X5710 | 68. | Stafnish X5523 |
| 19. | Canna X5708 | 69. | Pladda X5522 |
| 20. | Rhum X5707 | 70. | Turnberry X5521 |
| 21. | Sleat X5706 | 71. | Torr X5528 |
| 22. | Barra X5633 | 72. | Mermaid X5529 |
| 23. | Hebrides Central X5632 | 73. | Ailsa X5524 |
| 24. | Hawes X5635 | 74. | Maiden X5529 |
| 25. | Eigg X5636 | 75. | Corsewall X5526 |
| 26. | Hebrides South X5631 | 76. | Ballantrae X5525 |
| 27. | Ford X5630 | 77. | Magee X5407 |
| 28. | Tiree X5634 | 78. | Londonderry X5401 |
| 29. | Staffa X5627 | 79. | Beaufort X5408 |
| 30. | Mackenzie X5626 | 80. | Ardglass X5402 |
| 31. | Mull X5628 | 81. | Peel X5403 |

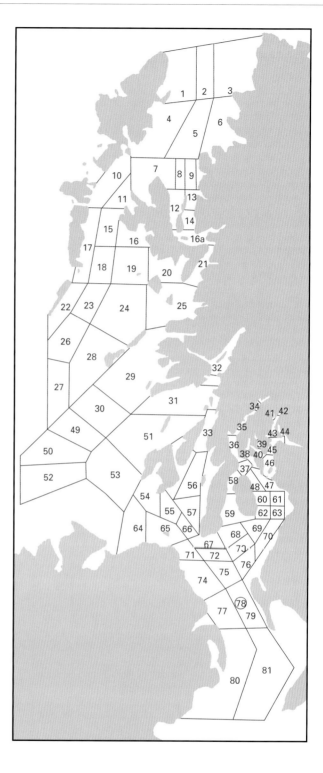

# IV. QUICK REFERENCE TABLE OF PROVISIONS, SERVICES AND SUPPLIES

**1 Water**
A  supply by hose alongside
T  tap on quay or pontoon
N  tap nearby

**2 Provisions**
S  several, or supermarket
L  local, village shop
B  basic stores

**3 Fuel, bottled gas**
A  supply by hose alongside
G  garage (may be some distance)
P  petrol (may be some distance)
C  Calor Gas

**4 Repairs**
H  Hull
M  Engine and machinery
E  Electronic (engineer may have to come from a distance)

**5 Chandlery**
Y  yacht chandlery

**6 Moorings**
P  pontoon
V  visitors' moorings (expect to pay, but may be provided free of charge for customers of local hotel

**7 Catering**
R  Restaurant (may be within hotel)
B  Bar
S  Showers

**8 Medical**
Dc  Doctor
Dt  Dentist
H  Hospital

**9 Bank/ATM**
£  ATM may be within a shop or ferry terminal

**10 Refuse Disposal**
D  dedicated skip or container near landing place

| Page | Location | 1 | 2 | 3 | 4 | 5 | 6 | 7 | 8 | 9 | 10 |
|------|----------|---|---|---|---|---|---|---|---|---|----|
| 18 | Crinan | A | L2 | AC | HME | Y | PV | RBS | Dc | | D |
| 20 | Ardfern | A | L | AC | HME | Y | PV | RBS | | | D |
| 23 | Craobh | A | B | APC | HME | Y | P | RBS | | | D |
| 24 | Melfort Pier | A | | | | | | RBS | | | D |
| 24 | Kilmelford | A | L1 | APC | HME | Y | V | RBS | | | D |
| 26 | Balvicar/Seil Sound | T | L½ | APC | HME | | V | | Dc | | D |
| 33 | Cullipool | N | B½ | C | | | | | | | |
| 39 | Easdale | N | L | | | | | | | | D |
| 45 | Loch Feochan | A | L2 | AC | HME | | V | RB2 | | | D |
| 47 | Gallanach | A | B | AP | M | | | | | | |
| 48 | Oban | A | S | APC | ME | Y | V | RB | DcDtH | £ | D |
| 51 | Ardentrive | A | | AC | HME | Y | PV | RBS | | | D |
| 57 | Dunstaffnage | A | L | APC | HME | Y | P | RBS | Dc | | D |
| 57 | Connel | | L | GP | | | | RB | | | |
| 63 | Bonawe | T | S½ | GP½ | | | | RB | | | |
| 66 | Port Appin | T | L | GP | | | V | RB | Dc | | D |
| 67 | Barcaldine | A | L½ | GPC½ | HME | | V | | | | D |
| 73 | Ballachulish/Glencoe | A | L½ | GP½ | | | P | RBS | DcDt | | D |
| 76 | Kinlochleven | | L½ | GP½ | | | | B | Dc | | |
| 74 | Onich | | | GP1 | | | | B | | | |
| 76 | Corran | | L1 | GP1 | | | | | | | |
| 79 | Fort William | T | S½ | GPC1 | | Y | | RB | DcDtH | £ | D |
| 79 | Corpach | A | S | GPC | | | P | RBS | | | D |
| 82 | Craignure | T | L | GPC | | | V | RB | | | D |
| 84 | Loch Aline | T | L | GP | | | | RB | Dc | | D |
| 87 | Salen (Mull)/Aros | | L | GPC | | | | | Dc | | |
| 98 | Tobermory | A/T | S | APC | | Y | V | RBS | DcDt | £ | D |
| 90 | Kilchoan | T | L | GP | | | V | RB | | | |
| 99 | Salen (Sunart) | A | L | APC | | | V | RBS | | | D |
| 100 | Strontian | | L | C | | | | RB | Dc | | |
| 103 | Port Croig | | L3 | GP3 | | | | | | | |
| 116 | Ulva Ferry | T | | | | | | R | | | |
| 131 | Iona | N | S | C | | | | R | Dc | | D |
| 131 | Fionnphort | | L | GP | | | | RB | | | |
| 133 | Bunessan | T | S | GP2 | | | | RB | Dc | | D |
| 140 | Arinagour | T | L | GPC | | | V | RBS | | | D |
| 142 | Scarinish/Gott Bay | T | L | GPC | | | | RB | Dc | | D |

*Note*
Figures following codes in any column indicate approximate distance in miles from landing place.
Sailmaker: Owen Sails, Tralee Bay, Benderloch PA37 1QR ☎ 01631 720485 collect and return from marinas and yacht centres.

# Index